MANAGEMENT AND ENTREPRENEURSHIP

MANAGEMENT
AND
ENTREPRENEURSHIP

N.V.R. Naidu

B.Tech., M.Tech(Indl.Engg)., PhD (Indl.Engg)
Professor and Head
Dept. of Industrial Engineering and Management
M.S. Ramaiah Institute of Technology, Bangalore

T. Krishna Rao

B.E, M.S (Mech) (IIT-M), PhD, M.B.A
Principal
Siddharth Institute of Engineering & Technology
Puttur, Dist. Chittoor, A.P.

TECHSAR™

NEW DELHI

Published and Printed by
Techsar Pvt. Ltd.
4435–36/7, Ansari Road, Daryaganj
New Delhi-110002 (India)
E-mail: tech_info@techsarworld.com
Website: www.techsarworld.com

ISBN: 978-81-906757-8-9

Reprint 2025

Dedicated to our parents

Shri N. Naraiah Naidu		*Shri T. Sree Rama Murthy*
	and	
Smt. N. Padmavathi		*Smt. T. Atchuthamba*
N.V.R. Naidu		***T. Krishna Rao***

PREFACE

This book presents a various topics like management, entrepreneurship, small scale industry, institutional support, preparation of project at one place.

This book is organized in two parts. Part one deals with management and its functions like planning, organising, staffing, directing and controlling, marketing management, product development, sales management and cost accounting. Part two deals with entrepreneurship, small scale industry, institutional support, preparation of report and industrial ownership.

Entrepreneurship is a new emerging subject, the details available on it are limited and scattered. The details of small scale industry, institutional support and preparation of report help and provide insight and guidelines to the young and promising entrepreneurs to start an enterprise.

The contents are planned in a systematic and a logical sequence to understand the subject with ease. It is presented in simple and self learning style; no previous knowledge of management is required to understand the subject.

This book is meant for engineering and management students of various universities.

The authors will be very grateful for any suggestions and corrections for the improvement of this book.

N.V.R. Naidu
nvrnaidu@gmail.com

T. Krishna Rao
krishnaraot@rediffmail.com

ACKNOWLEDGEMENTS

We express our sincere thanks to the Management and Directors of Gokula Education Foundation, Bangalore for their support. We extend our hearty thanks to Dr. K. Rajanikanth, Principal, M.S. Ramaiah Institute of Technology, Bangalore for his encouragement.

Special thanks to Smt. Devika for DTP work.

Our thanks are also due to our family members for their help and support without which this book would not have taken this shape.

We thank all those who have directly or indirectly contributed in preparing this book.

N.V.R. Naidu
T. Krishna Rao

CONTENTS

MANAGEMENT

ENTREPRENEURSHIP

CHAPTER 1

INTRODUCTION

Management is a function of guidance and leadership control of efforts of a group or individuals in order to achieve goals/objectives of an organization.

Before the industrial revolution, there were no manufacturing industries. There were few individuals who were carrying out the production of the commodities. This was mostly family oriented and head of the family was managing the business. During the later half of 18th century, industrial revolution had started and factory systems had evolved. Then on, management became necessary.

1.1 ELEMENTS OF MANAGEMENT

The management process is conceived, evolved and implemented based on the following elements.

(i) A well defined ambiance within which management must perform.

(ii) A good organization that gives shape of management.

(iii) A need for planning, implementation and monitoring.

(iv) Self content.

(v) Need for leadership and direction.

(vi) A good and effective communication network.

(vii) Effective co-ordination.

(viii) Constant evaluation, monitoring and control.

(ix) Innovation of new ideas and techniques.

The management has gained importance in present days life. By bringing together the 4 Ms (Money, Men, Material and Machines) the fifth 'M' management enables the country to reach a substantial level of economic development. Without management, a country's resources for production remain as resources and never become products. Principles of management are now universally used not just for managing business organizations, but are extended and practiced by service organizations like educational, social, government etc. Management is generally the same process in all forms of organizations, but may vary in its complexity with size and nature of organization. Management is a dynamic and life-giving element in every organization. It resolves disputes, provides leadership and adopts the organization to its changing environment. It plans the activities, sets individual and over all goals, engage right and suitable people, provide necessary training to carry out the work more effectively and efficiently, leads, monitors, controls and helps in overall functioning of any organization.

A business develops in course of time with complexities. With increase of complexities, managing the business concern becomes a difficult task. As a result, the need for management arose. All the organization have objectives and goals. Coordinated efforts of all the concerned people are essential to achieve these goals. The process of management ensures the proper coordination of concerned people to lead them to achieve the objectives. As rightly told by a management author, the management is not a matter of pressing a button, pulling a lever, issuing orders, preparing and studying profit and loss statements or including rules and regulators, but it is the process to determine what happens to the people and their happiness and shape the further of the nation. Thus management is a group of activities that plans, prepares policies arranges resources like men, money, machines and material that are required to achieve the set objectives. Management is the activity of a person who strives for better living in the complex and competitive world. In addition to this, the management gives satisfaction and rewards to its employees and ensures better performance.

Thus management is a must for every enterprise. The existence of management ensures proper functioning and running of the enterprise. Management can plan the activities to achieve the objectives and to utilize the available resources at minimum cost. Every business needs planning and direction. Management provides necessary direction. The resources of production are converted into production. The conversion process is performed through the coordination of management. The resources will remain resources if management does not exist.

Management is a creative process which integrates and utilizes various available resources effectively and efficiently to accomplish the goals of an organization. To carry out this, an individual is responsible to develop ideas to plan and to get the things done through the workers. This concerned individual is designated as "Manager". Thus any person who performs the function of Management for the accomplishment of predetermined objectives or goals is called a manager. Manager does not by himself carry out work but guides the others to carry out the work. The growing tendency in business requires professionally qualified persons. There is an urgent need for professional management in India because of the reasons like major portion of our economy is unorganized, poor infrastructure, less utilization of modern technology and techniques leading to low productive efficiency, and wide spread poverty and unemployment.

CHAPTER 2

MANAGEMENT

INTRODUCTION

2.1 MEANING

Managing is one of the most important activities of human life. To accomplish aims that could not be achieved individually, people started forming groups. Managing has become essential to ensure the coordination of individual efforts. Management applies to all kinds of organizations and to managers at all organizational levels. Principles of management are now used not only for managing business but in all walks of life viz., government, military, social and educational institutions. Essentially, management is same process in all forms of organization. But it may vary widely in its complexity with size and level of organization. Management is the life giving element of any organization.

Definitions suggested by some of the management experts are presented below:

Henri Fayol: "Management is conduct of affairs of business, moving towards its objective through a continuous process of improvement and optimization of resources".

Koontz: "Management is the process of designing and maintaining an environment in which individuals, working together in groups, efficiently accomplish selected aims".

Mary Parker Follett: "Management is the art of getting things done through people".

George R. Terry: "Management is a process consisting of planning, organizing, actuating and controlling, performed to determine and accomplish the objectives by use of people and resources".

ILO: "Management is the complex of continuously coordinated activity by means of which any undertaking administration/public or private service conducts its business".

Lawrence A. Appley: "Management is guiding human and physical resources into a dynamic, hard hitting organization until that attains its objectives to the satisfaction of those served and with a high degree of morale and sense of attainment on the part of those rendering the service".

2.2 NATURE AND CHARACTERISTICS OF MANAGEMENT

As seen above, the production process involves land, labour, capital, organization and entrepreneurship. So long as these factors remain separated, there is no possibility for production. Production is the result of their combined efforts. Thus success of production depends on their effective combination and cooperation. In today's complex business organization, it has become a difficult and challenging task to strike an effective balance of and harmony of various factors of production. This calls for a special skill, knowledge and characteristics to seek their fullest cooperation to achieve the objectives set by an enterprise. Such skills and knowledge is the management.

Based on vast experience it has been found that the analysis of management is facilitated by a useful and clear organization of knowledge.

The following are some of the important characteristics of management.

1. It should be stable.
2. It should be applicable to all kinds of organizations.
3. It is transparent.
4. Its approaches are to be clear and goal oriented.
5. It should be simple yet effective.
6. It should be responsive to many external elements like economic, technological, social, political and ethical factors that affect the areas of operation.
7. It should have well defined goals, and effective means to accomplish the goals.
8. It should have good planning, organizing, staffing, directing and controlling functions.
9. It should provide conducive atmosphere of work.

2.3 SCOPE

The management is a must for every organization. The existence of management ensures proper functioning and running of an enterprise. Management plans the activities, coordinates and utilizes the available resources effectively and efficiently at minimum cost. Every business needs direction. This direction is given by the management. The resources of production are converted into production or services. The scope of management is not limited only to business organization, but it is extended to business establishments, hospitals, educational institutions, government officers, service organizations, security organization, financial organizations, stores management etc. The nature of functions of management may differ from one type of organization to another, but all these form the essence of management.

As discussed earlier, the management is not limited to only industries, but its scope can be extended to the following important areas of life.

- Developing management
- Distribution management
- Financial management
- Marketing management
- Personnel management
- Production management
- Office management
- Transport management
- Purchase management
- Sales management
- Supply chain management
- Business management (Like Hospital management, Hotel management, Educational institute management, Stores management etc.)

Management can be applied in any area of business and life. Its scope starts from self management to home management and to the management of big office, industry, organization of a government etc.

2.4 FUNCTIONAL AREAS OF MANAGEMENT

Though many authors have defined several functions of management, there are five essential and well accepted functions of management. They are:

- Planning.
- Organising.
- Staffing.
- Directing (leading) and
- Controlling.

Planning: Planning is an executive function that is referred to as decision making. It involves missions and objectives and the actions to achieve them. This requires decision making, that is, choosing future courses of action from available alternatives. This involves the following:

- Setting short and long term goals for organization.
- Selecting objectives, strategies and policies for accomplishing the planned goals.

- Deciding in advance what to do, how to do, who has to do, when to do and where to do.
- Planning bridges the gap from where we are now to where we want be in future.

Organising: Organising is a part of management that involves in establishing an intentional structure of roles for people to fill in an organization. To organize a business well, it is required to provide all the useful things for its proper functioning. They are raw materials, tools, capital and personnel. The purpose of an organization structure is to help in creating an environment for human performance. This involves in:

- Determination of activities required to achieve goals.
- Grouping these activities into department.
- Assigning such groups of activities to managers.
- Forming deligation of authority.
- Making provisions for coordination of activities.

Staffing: Staffing is considered as an important function which makes provision for man power to fill different positions. It involves in building the human organization by filling, and keep filling the staff. This is done by identifying work-force requirements, taking inventory of people available, recruiting new staff, selecting, placing, promoting, apprising, planning their career, training the staff to accomplish their tasks effectively and efficiently. This involves in:

- Finding the right person for right job.
- Selecting the personnel.
- Placement, training and developing new skills required for present and future jobs.
- Creating new positions.
- Apprising the staff and planning their growth and promotions etc.

Directing: After planning, organizing and staffing, the next important function of management is directing or leading the people towards the defined objectives. Directing involves three sub-functions namely communication, leadership and motivation. Communication is the process of passing information and understanding from one person to another. Leadership is the process by which a manager guides and influences the work of his subordinates. Motivation means arousing desire in the minds of employees of an organization to perform their best. If properly motivated, the employees will put their best efforts with dedication, loyalty and carry out the assigned task effectively. There are two types of motivations viz., financial and non-financial. Financial motivations are in the form of salary, bonus, profit-sharing, rewards etc. The common non-financial motivations are job security, promotions, recognition, praise, felicitation etc.

Controlling: Controlling is measuring and correcting of activities of subordinates to make sure that the work is going on as per the plans. It measures performance against goals and plans, shows where short falls or deviations exist and takes necessary corrective actions to achieve the goals. Controlling generally relates to the measurement of achievement. This involves three elements.

- Establishing standards of performance.
- Measuring performance and comparing with established standards.
- Taking necessary corrective action to meet the set standards.

With accomplishment of this function, the "Management Cycle" is said to be complete.

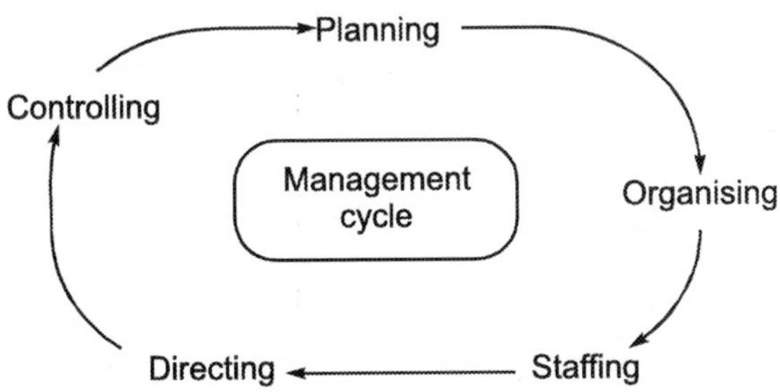

Management Cycle

2.5 MANAGEMENT AS A SCIENCE, ART OR PROFESSION

Managing, like any other practice – whether medicine, music composition, engineering, accounting or even cricket – is an art. It is a know-how. It is doing things in the light of the realities of a situation. Under 'art' one normally learns the "how" of a phenomenon. It is the art of getting things done through others in dynamic and mostly non-repetitive situations.

Science is an organized knowledge. A discipline can be called scientific if its methods of inquiry are systematic and empirical, information can be accumulated and analysed and results are commutative and communicable. The essential feature of any science is the application of scientific methods to the development of knowledge. Being systematic means being orderly and unbiased. All the scientific information collected first as raw data is finally arranged in order and analysed with the help of statistical tools. Science is also cumulative in that what is discovered is added to that which has been found before. We learn from past mistakes and go in right direction in future. On the basis of the above discussions of science, it can be accepted that management is also a science.

It is seen that management is partly an art and partly a science. Management does not possess the characteristics of a profession. A profession is expected to have organized and systematic knowledge, formalized methods of acquiring training and experience, ethical code to regulate the behaviour of the members of the profession, charging of fees based on service etc. Unlike medicine and law, the management does no have any fixed norms of managerial behaviour. There is no uniform code of conduct or licensing of managers. Lawyers and doctors take up profession after obtaining a valid academic qualification where as a manager job is not restricted to individuals with a special academic degree only. Based on this, it can be concluded that management is not a profession. However, the present trend is towards the professionalisation of management.

Nowadays, it has become essential to acquire management degrees or training in management to be called as good manager. There is increased demand for qualified managers with M.B.A degree after graduation. This gave scope for establishment of large number of business schools in India. Managing a business is no longer just a matter of a family or institution. In this contest, one should remember Peter Drucker's opinion on management. "A degree in management does not by itself make an individual a professional manager any more than does a degree in philosophy make an individual a philosopher". By insisting on holding a degree, we are over emphasizing knowledge and completely over looking skill. This leads to loosing of good and skilled managers who do not have required degree. There have been good examples of efficient managers without any professional managerial degree. Some of them are, Ford of Ford Motors, Bill Gates of Microsoft, Jemshedji Tata, Birla, Dhiru Bhai Ambani of Reliance group etc.

But nowadays, management has become a profession than art or science.

2.6 MANAGEMENT AND ADMINISTRATION

There is lack of concurrence among management writers over the meaning and use of the words management and administration.

One group of management writers feels that administration involves "thinking". It is a top level function that centers around the preparation of plans, rules, policies and objectives of an organization. Where as management involves "doing" and is a lower level function, concerning with execution and direction of policies and operations. Hence, administration is more important at lower levels.

Another group of management writers feels management as comprehensive generic term that includes administration. Management is regarded as comprehensive generic function covering entire process of planning, organizing, directing and controlling. Administration is regarded as a branch of management that comprises of two functions – planning and controlling. According to them, the function of management is divided into two categories – the upper level management usually called as administrative management and the lower level management which is termed as operative management.

According to Peter Drucker, the basic difference between management and administration lies in use of these terms in different fields. According to him, managing of business enterprises is called management and managing non-business organizations is called administration. Hence financial performance plays key role in management. But in managing non business organizations like educational institutions, government offices, military etc., administration is more priority than financial decisions.

Administration is the function in industry concerned with determination of the corporate policy, the coordination of finance, production and distribution, the settlement of compass of the organization under the ultimate control of the executives".

"Management is the function in industry concerned with the execution of polity within the limits setup by the administration and the employment of the organization for the particular objects set before it". (Oliver Sheldon)

"Administration is primarily the process and the agency used to establish the object or purpose which an undertaking and its staff are to achieve, secondarily, administration has to plan and stabilize the broad lines of principles which will govern action. These broad lines are in turn called policies. Management is the process and the agency through which the execution of policy is planned and supervised". (G.E. Milward)

"Administration is that phase of business enterprise that concerns with overall determination of institutional objectives and the policies necessary to be followed in achieving those objectives. Administration predetermines the specific goals and lays down the broad areas within which those goals are to be attained. Administration is a determinative function, management on the other hand is an executive function – which is primarily concerned with the carrying out of the broad policies laid down by the administration. (William R. Spriegal)

Thus administration is a "thinking" function and management is a "doing" function. According this concept, managers get salary and administration staff get dividends.

Administration determines the policies upon which the enterprise is to be conducted while the function of management is to carry out the policies that are laid down by the administrative group.

The differences between administration and management are listed below:

	Characteristic	Administration	Management
1.	Main functions	Planning, Organising and Staffing	Leading, motivating and controlling.
2.	Status	Acts as owner	Acts as an agency
3.	Skills	Requires good administrative skills	Requires more technical skills.
4.	Level in the organization	Top level	Lower level
5.	Position	Managing Director, Owner, CEO, etc.,	Managers, Supervisors, Foremen etc.,
6.	Objectives	Makes the policies, objectives and goals to be achieved.	Implements the plans and policies
7.	Involvement	No direct involvement in production or services	Directly involves in the execution of plans and achieving goals.

2.7 ROLES OF MANAGEMENT

Manager in any organization plays variety of roles responding to a particular situation. The three important roles played by a manager are Interpersonal roles, Decision roles and Informational roles.

(i) Interpersonal roles: These includes figurehead, leader and liaison roles:

In figurehead role, the manager will perform some duties that are casual and informal ones like, receiving and greeting visiting dignitaries, attending to social functions of employees, entertaining customers by offering parties and lunches etc.

As a leader, managers motivate, direct and encourage his subordinates. He also reconciles the needs with the goals of the organization.

In the role of liaison, the manager works like a liaison officer between top management and the subordinate staff. He also develops contacts with outside people and collects useful information for the well being of the organization.

(ii) Decision roles: There are four decision roles played by a manager. They are resource provider, arbitrator, entrepreneur and negotiator.

As a resource allocator, the manager divides the work, provides required resources and facilities to carryout the allocated work and delegates required authority among his subordinates. He decides who has to do what and who gets what.

As a arbitrator, a manager works like a problem solver. He finds solutions of various un-anticipated problems both within and outside the organization.

As an entrepreneur, a manager continuously looks for new ideas and tries to improve the organization by going along with changing work environment.

He also acts as a negotiator negotiates with the employees and tries to resolve any internal problems like trade agreements, strikes and grievances of employees.

(iii) Information roles: A manager plays as monitor, spokesman and disseminator.

A manager monitors his environment and collects information through his personal contacts with colleagues and subordinates.

As a spokesman, he communicates the information/goals of organization to his staff, and the progress of work to his superiors. He also communicates the performance of company to shareholders and the rules and responsibilities to his subordinates.

As a disseminator, the manager passes some of the information directly to his subordinates and to his bosses.

2.8 LEVELS OF MANAGEMENT

Although all managers perform almost the same functions of management –planning, organizing, directing and controlling, there are levels among them. These are top management, middle management and first line or supervisors. The top management consists of Chairman, Directors, Company Presidents, Vice-Presidents, CEO's. These are the people who make policies for the company, set goals and targets. They should possess conceptual and design skills.

Middle management is essentially a vast and diverse group that include finance manager, sales manager, marketing manager, personnel manager, departmental heads etc.

The lower level managers are the supervisors and foremen. They are basically one step above the workers.

The various levels and skilled required at different management levels are shown below.

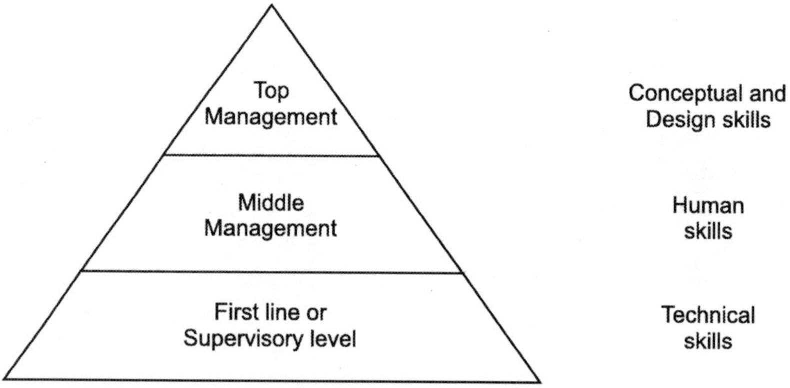

Skills at different Management level

2.9 DEVELOPMENT OF MANAGEMENT THOUGHT

Management has emerged as a powerful and innovative force on which the today's society depends for material support from a unrecognized situation in the past one or two centuries. Seventeen and Eighteen centuries had seen Industrial Revolution. Lots of inventions and new technologies had emerged. The importance of management was focused. Division of labour concept was evolved. Importance of planning was identified. But management as a separate field of study had emerged only during early 20th century when new industrial era began. Business organizations had a stage shift from ownership towards joint stock companies. As an answer to the problems like insufficient systems, inefficiency of labour and discrepancy in wage payment, "management" has been recognized as a separate and important field of study. Subsequently, management has evolved as a scientific discipline of study and practice.

The evolution of management can be divided into two parts – Early management approach and Modern management approach.

2.10 EARLY MANAGEMENT APPROACHES

History of the management is as old as a man. Evidence of well organized principle of management can be seen in ancient Greece and India. Those Kings used the concepts of management like planning, organizing, leading and controlling the various activities.

The process of early management approaches are:

- Psychological development

- Scientific management
- Administrative management and
- Human relations movement.

2.10.1 Psychological development: (Before 17th century)

In olden days when there was no experience and knowledge of business, they had to depend upon their inborn abilities. This gave rise to management that was totally based on Psychological process. As a result, people were having universal belief that managers are born and cannot be made such as artists, directors, poets, kings etc.

2.10.2 Scientific management: (18th – 19th century)

During this time the development was brought about by the following two important factors.

- The effort of scientists to demonstrate the application of science and scientific methods.
- The effort of establishing standard practices.

Thus during this development, management was adopted with scientific approach. The work made use of scientific methods for achieving standard practice and higher efficiency. Thus, scientific management came into existence. Many pioneers have contributed for this development.

Frederik Winslow Taylor (1856 – 1915) has been considered to be father of scientific management. He had conducted series of experiments and promoted the development of management thought through his experiments and writings. Some of the contributions of F.W. Taylor for the scientific management are explained here.

(i) Work study

Work-study includes time and motion study. Taylor observed that the workers were not producing their full capacity for the fear that their piece rate would be cut with rise in production. Hence he started time and motion study. He recorded the time required for each motion of a job with the help of stop-watch. Shorter and fewer motions were developed. Unwanted motions were eliminated. The best way of doing a particular job was arrived at. With this, the time required to complete one job was calculated called standard time.

(ii) Differential payment

Motion and time study and establishment of standard time further helped in arriving at the production rate of a particular piece or job. Taylor also introduced payment plan called "differential piece work". He linked the incentives with production. As per this, a worker gets a minimum guaranteed wage if he produces a standard number of pieces and if he produces more than this standard number, he is paid incentive. It was thought that this would motivate workers to produce more.

(iii) Reorganization of supervision

In his tenure Taylor observed that the worker himself had to plan his work and do the job. The supervisor's work was just to allocate the work to be done. But Taylor advocated that, the planning of work and selection of tools and sequence of doing the work are to be done by the foreman and the worker had to simply carry out the work without wasting his time as to how to do that. He also suggested that there should be separate foreman for each function of job.

(iv) Scientific requirement and training

Taylor also suggested the need for scientific training and development of a worker to carry out a specific task in a more productive way. He also believed that a good cooperation between the management and workers would lead to increased production and profits to both.

Taylor's concepts of scientific management were well accepted and practiced by almost all industries. Gantt and Gilbert had modified and improved the Taylor's concepts further.

Gantt had felt that Taylor's incentive scheme was not really motivating the worker. He proposed a new idea in Taylor's incentive schema. If a worker completes his day's target, he gets some incentive. Also, the foremen gets some incentive for each worker who works under him completes his day's target. This would motivate the foreman to involve in work, train the worker to do the job better. He also developed bar chart to record the day-wise performance of each worker for better monitoring purpose. He further extended this concept of bar chart for production control and monitoring of projects. These are still in wide use.

Gilberth conducted motion study with the help of motion pictures. He had identified the motions of work and classified them into 18 basic types. These are called Therbligs (named after him by reversing his name). Each motion is identified by a symbol.

He started his career in a brick industry and had gone through various levels as tradesman, foreman and manager and eventually he had realized all his dreams. His contributions are listed below.

(i) He had developed motion study with a main idea to minimize waste movements and developed SIMO charts.

(ii) He evolved principles of motion economy.

(iii) He established Therbligs that are the fundamental motions involved in doing any activity.

(iv) He had carried out study on fatigue due to repetitive work by conducting experiments.

Objectives of Scientific Management

The objectives of scientific management are:

(i) To assess industrial and market tendencies and to regularize continuous operation.

(ii) To earn a larger profit from a given expenditure on man and materials by minimizing waste work and waste movements.

(iii) To provide healthy and safe working environment.

(iv) To build character through proper work.

(v) To develop self realization and self satisfaction among workers there by improving their morale.

(vi) To give better opportunity for individual through scientific methods of working.

(vii) To ensure happier and social life to workers.

(viii) To promote justice among the workers by treating them equal.

(ix) To perform planned and balanced operations.

The time and motion study of scientific management had created awareness of using right tools and minimizing waste movements while performing a work. Further the scientific management also insisted the scientific selection of workers and made the management to realize the training needs to do a job. The scientific management suggested the work design, that is, one best way of doing a job. The scientific management had developed a rational approach to solve the problems of an organization and contributed to the professionalisation of management.

But Taylor's concept of monitory benefits to motivate workers did not fetch expected results. Taylor's time and motion study was not accepted as entirely scientific because there is no "one best way" of doing a job. Separation of 'planning' and 'doing' functions coupled with greater specialization led to greater monotony of work.

2.10.3 Administrative Management

Henri Fayol (1841-1925) is considered as father of administrative management. His theory was focused on the development of administrative principles applicable to middle and top level managers. He used the word 'administration' which is otherwise known as management nowadays. He wrote a book titled "General and Industrial Administration", in which he explained the process of administration. His thinking is beyond the worker and shop level production but of a wider perspective, covering the common administrative and managerial functions and processes of the managers. He suggested that activity of any business organization could be divided into six groups viz., financial, technical, accounting, commercial, managerial and security. His main focus was on managerial or administrative activity. He divided the management function into five functions:- Planning, organizing, commanding, coordinating and controlling. These functions are very similar to what are being practical in today's management. He also told that these activities are same at all levels of any organization and are same for all organizations. Fayol had suggested 14 principles of management as a guideline to the process of management practice. They are given below:

Principles of Management:

(i) Division of work
(ii) Authority and responsibility
(iii) Discipline
(iv) Unity of command
(v) Unity of direction
(vi) Subordination of individual interest to general interest
(vii) Union is strength
(viii) Initiative
(ix) Equity
(x) Scalar chain
(xi) Order
(xii) Stability of tenure of personnel
(xiii) Remuneration and
(xiv) Centralisation.

2.10.4 Human Relations Movement

Taylor and Fayol's management techniques did not completely achieve the efficient production and harmony at work place. The unpredicted and irrational pattern of behaviour of workers made the task of managers more difficult. These two theories did not consider or focus on human side of the organization. Hence there was a need to focus on human side. Elton Mayo conducted series of experiments at Western Electric Company, which are commonly known as Hawthorne experiments. They are broadly classified as:

- Illumination experiments
- Relay assembly test room
- Interviewing programme
- Bank wiring test room

The outcomes of the above movement are as follows.

The business organization is not merely a technical and economical unit where only production and profits are anticipated but it is also socialistic human system. In addition to financial incentives, it is also important to create human relation to workers for better productivity. A worker does not merely work for money, but he expects social respect and belongingness by his co-workers and supervisors.

Worker-centered and participative type of supervisor ship works better and more effective than task-centred leadership.

2.11 MODERN MANAGEMENT APPROACHES

There are 4 important modern management approaches:

- Behavioural approach
- Systems approach
- Quantitative approach and
- Contingency approach.

2.11.1 Behavioural Approach

The Behavioural approach to management is concerned with the applications of methods and findings psychology and sociology for the purpose of understanding the organizational behaviour. This is an improved and extended version of the human relations approach to management. Maslow, McGregor, Herzberg, Warren Bennis are some of the well known behavioural scientists who made significant contributions to the behavioural approach to the management. Motivation theory, leadership, communication and employee motivation and development are some of the important behavioural theories of management.

Behavioural scientists regarded the classical approach as highly mechanical and routine and resulting in demoralizing human aspect. They insisted for a more flexible structure of organization rather than a traditional or hierarchical type of authority. They had given more importance for participative management. This was expected to resolve problems in a better way and result in better human satisfaction since the decisions are taken in consultation with workers.

2.11.2 Quantitative Approach

Quantitative approach is also known as management science approach which was developed during Second World War to find solutions to some complex new problems in warfare. As a result the quantitative approach called Operations Research (OR) was developed by a team of interdisciplinary members. This deals with formulating a mathematical model to simulate a given problem that includes the feasibilities, constraints, costs of events etc. An optimum mix of these critical variables is arrived at, either for minimizing time or cost, or maximizing profit or production or service etc., enabling the management to take up a logical decision.

OR techniques are widely used in project planning and control where better benefits have been obtained with its use.

2.11.3 Systems Approach

The classical approach emphasizes on the structure and task, the behavioural approach emphasizes on people and the quantitative approach on mathematical modeling and decision-making based on the model. But systems approach provides the management the integrated approach of problem solving.

A system is defined as a set of independent parts together form a unitary whole that performs a defined task. Organisation is a system that consists of people, task, structure and technology. Each part of the system has an independent relation with other part. The systems approach tries to emphasize to regard the organizations as a whole, rather than dealing the parts separately. A system can be either an open system or closed system. A system that interacts with outside environment is called open system and a system that works with in closed boundary is called closed systems.

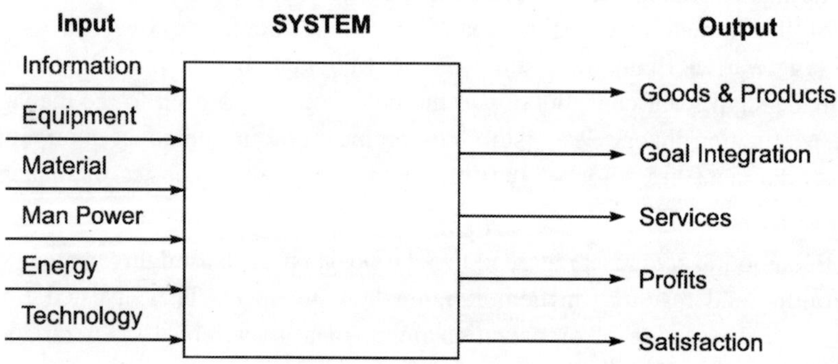

Systems Approach

2.11.4 Contingency Approach

The contingency approach is the most recent development in the field of management. This attempts to integrate all the management approaches. There is no one best way of doing things under all conditions in all organizations. The techniques and method that are highly effective in one particular situation may be failure in similar situation in other area. Hence the contingency approach suggests that the task of managers is to identify the correct techniques that will suit a particular situation and apply them to solve a problem. This approach is very much applicable in preparing organizational structure, in deciding degree of decentralization, motivational and leadership approaches, establishing the communication systems, resolving conflicts, training the employees etc.

REVIEW QUESTIONS

1. Define Management. List and explain the functions of Management?
2. What are nature and characteristics of Management?
3. Explain the scope of Management?
4. Differentiate between administration and management?
5. Write about roles of management?
6. What are different levels of management? Explain them?
7. Is management a science, art or profession? Explain.
8. Explain top Management. What are its roles and functions?
9. Discuss in brief the nature of management.
10. Explain early management approaches.
11. Explain the modern management approaches.
12. Explain briefly the contingency approach of management.
13. What are the objectives of scientific management?

CHAPTER 3

PLANNING

3.1 NATURE OF PLANNING

Planning is the most basic function of management. It is referred to as "deciding in advance" as to what to do, how to do, when to do and who has to do it etc. It is an intellectual process, which requires a manager to think before acting. It is nothing but thinking in advance. As regarded by Koontz and O'Donnell, planning is a continuous process. A manager should continuously watch the progress of the plans like a navigator who constantly checks where his ship is going in the vast ocean. Planning involves selection of objectives and goals and determines the ways and means of achieving them. Thus planning bridges the gap from where we are to where we want to be. A plan is to be rigid in the sense that it should not be modified or altered under the influence of local disturbances. A plan should be flexible to change to adapt to the changing situating without undue cost. This calls for flexibility in the areas like technology, market, finance, personnel and organization. Planning is vital at all levels of an organization. Top level managers are concerned with long range planning involving 2 to 5 years, middle level managers are concerned with medium range planning involving few months to one year and lower level managers are concerned with planning the activities of daily or week or upto a month, where as a worker plans his day's work.

Nature of planning indicates essential quality or general characteristics of planning. Any planning involves four essential qualities:

(i) It must contribute to accomplish purpose and objectives.

(ii) It must be considered as parent exercise in all processes.

(iii) It must spread through all management functions and

(iv) It must be efficient in such a manner so as to achieve the designed goals at the least cost.

Planning is non-static and is basically a discrete exercise. It is dynamic in nature. It is a blue print to which the accomplishment must confirm.

3.2 IMPORTANCE OF PLANNING

Without planning, business decisions would become difficult. Planning is the beginning of all other functions of management. Planning is important because:

(i) It overcomes uncertainty and change and minimizes risk.

(ii) It facilitates effective control.

(iii) It focuses attention and concentration only on the objectives of enterprise.

(iv) It makes economic operation and leads to success.

(v) It forms the bridge between the present and the future.

(i) Uncertainity and minimize risk

In the today's complex organizations, decision making cannot be relied only upon intuition, planning plays a vital role in decision making in such complex situations. Planning provides logical facts and procedure to managers for making decisions. This logical decision making based on plans to organization minimizes uncertainty and risk. In a developing country like India, with rapidly changing social and economic conditions, planning helps the managers to cope up with uncertainty and risk.

(ii) Effective Control

Planning sets goals, targets and means to accomplish these goals. These goals and plans become standards or bench marks against which performance can be measured. Thus good plans help effective control on the activities.

(iii) Focuses attention and concentration on the objectives of the enterprise

Planning helps the manager to focus their attention on the goals and activities of organization. This makes the entire organization to walk towards the goals and create coordination in accomplishing the goals.

(iv) Economic operation and leads to success

Mere planning does not ensure success, but planning leads to success. This is because if the work is planned in advance, there will be no confusions arising and things will happen as per plan and achieve goals. This results in economical operation and reduces uncoated expenditure.

(v) Bridge between present and future

Plans bridge gap between present and future. There is a vast gap between what we are today and what we want to be in future. A proper and systematic plan forms the bridge between these two. Without plans, it is very difficult to accomplish goals. Hence planning is very important for success of any organization.

3.3 PURPOSE OF PLANNING

As discussed earlier, planning is the beginning of all other functions of the management. The purposes of the planning are listed below.

(i) To select from many available alternatives so as to achieve the objectives of the enterprise, economically, effectively and efficiently.

(ii) To direct all other functions of management.

(iii) To set up the goals of an enterprise in perspective, within the environment.

(iv) To help planned goals of an enterprise to break-up into more easily handlable additive-segmented goals.

(v) To form the basis for budget.

(vi) To forecast the future to avoid uncertainty and change.

(vii) To provide effective control.

(viii) To search for alternatives and adopt the best way of accomplishing the work and

(ix) To focus the vision on the objectives and goals.

3.4 OBJECTIVES

Objectives are the goals or targets which one wishes to achieve. These are the goals towards which all the business activities are directed. Only after specifying the objectives or goals, the managers can decide the type of organization, kind and nature of personnel with right skills, type of technology, supervision and control etc.

As indicated by Peter Drucker in his textbook "The practice of management", there are eight important areas in which objectives of performance are to be set. They are market-standing, innovation, productivity, physical and financial resources, profitability, manager performance and development, worker performance and attitude and public responsibility.

These objectives may be either tangible or intangible. They have a priority and are generally arranged in hierarchy. The following are some of the requirements of a good objective:

(i) Objectives must be clear and must be acceptable.

(ii) The objectives must support one another.

(iii) The objectives must be precise.

(iv) The objectives must be measurable.

(v) The objectives must be realistic and valid ones.

Although the basic process of planning is the same for every manager. Planning can be of different types depending on nature and type of organization and the level of the management.

A plan may be very elaborative or comprehensive. Some plans are very detailed in nature that cover even the last details. Others may be very simple and only the targets are shown. Planning may begin at the top with top management deciding the targets and is communicated down below for the implementation. Some plans may begin at bottom and are communicated up, to top management for approval. Some other plans may be done jointly with the participation of members from top management and lower level. Thus there are many types of plans. One useful and accepted way of classification of plans is to distinguish between strategic and tactical plans.

3.5 TYPES OF PLANS

Based on nature of planning, the planning is classified as strategic planning (long range planning) and tactical planning (short range planning). The strategic plans are done at top level of management and are generally long term plans, where as tactical plans and done at lower levels and are of short term in nature.

The differences between strategic and tactical planning are given below.

Strategic planning	Tactical planning
1. It is long term.	1. It is short term.
2. Done at top management.	2. Done at lower levels of management.
3. It consists of major goals and policies of an organization and resources and facilities to accomplish the goals.	3. It consists of use of facilities and resources.
4. It is less detailed, focuses only on long tern goals.	4. It is more detailed since it caters to day-to-day operations and activities of the organization.
5. It is based on long term goals and is more uncertain.	5. It is based on performance and is less uncertain.

For example, Tatas idea of marketing a car at a price of Rs. 1 lakh is a strategic plan. How to make that, what resources are required, how and where to manufacture, how to assemble, etc., are tactical plans.

Based on their use, plans are classified as single use plans and standing plans. Single use plans are developed to achieve a specific end. After reaching that target, that plan becomes useless. On the other hand, standing plans are designed for situations that often repeat. These plans can be used again and again.

3.5.1 Standing plans:

These are the policies, procedures, rules and methods of any organization.

(i) Policies:

As defined by Terry, "Policy is a verbal, written or implied overall guide, setting up boundaries that supply the general limits and direction in which managerial action will take place". Thus a policy is a general guideline for decision-making. They deal with "how to do" the work. They only provide a framework within which decisions must be made by the management in different areas of organization. There are several policies in different functions of any organization like personal policy, promotion policy, marketing policy, purchase policy, pricing policy, training policy, recruitment policy, distribution policy, payment policy, wages and incentives policy etc.

The policies are classified on the basis of sources like original policies, appealed policies, implied policies and externally imposed policies, or are classified on the basis of functions like personnel policy, promotion policy, pricing policy, distribution policy, investment policy etc., or may be on the basis of level of organization like: top level policy, departmental policy, shop level policy etc.

(ii) Procedures:

Procedures are the detailed guidelines that are used to carry out the policies. A procedure provides a detailed set of instructions for performing a sequence of actions involved in doing a certain piece of work. Procedures are to be followed every time when that activity is performed. Procedures may also exist for conducting meetings of board of directors, shareholders, issuing raw materials from stores, packaging of finished goods, inspection etc.

The difference between policy and procedures are given below:

Policy	Procedure
1. General guidelines of the organization.	1. General guidelines at the action level.
2. Top level activity.	2. Departmental activity.
3. Policies fulfill the objectives of an organization.	3. Procedures guide the way to implement the policies.
4. Policies are often made without any study or analysis.	4. Procedures are always made after thorough study and analysis of work.

(iii) Rules:

Rules are detailed and recorded instructions that a specific action must or must not be done under the given instructions. Reporting time to office, lunch time, availing of leaves, use of LTC facility etc., are some of the examples that follow rules. A rule is different from a policy or procedure. Since it does not give a guide to thinking, it is not a policy. Since it is not a sequential procedure hence it is not a procedure.

(iv) Methods:

A method is a prescribed way in which one step of a procedure is to be carried out. Thus a method is a part of procedure. A procedure has a number of steps, each step may have number of methods to do it. Methods help in increasing the effectiveness of a procedure.

3.6 DECISION MAKING

Planning is an intellectual process, which requires a manager to think before acting. Through planning, managers of any organization decide what to do, when to do, how to do and who has to do. Hence decision-making is an integral part of planning. It is defined as "the process of choosing among alternatives". Decision-making occurs at many stages of planning process. Decision-making and choosing the best alternative is probably the most important activity of the planning process.

Decision-making is part of all the functions of the management. In planning, through decision-making, objectives and goals are prepared. In organizing, the managers decide upon the choice of structure, type of organization, work allocation, delegation of authority and responsibility etc. In directing, managers decide the course of action, the instructions to be given, providing directions etc. In controlling the managers decide on fixing the standards, how to control, what to control etc.

Types of decisions

Decisions are classified as follows:

(i) Pragmatic and non-pragmatic decisions
(ii) Individual and collective decisions
(iii) Minor and major decisions
(iv) Strategic and routine decisions
(v) Simple and complex decisions
(vi) Temporary (Adhoc) and permanent decisions etc.

(i) **Pragmatic decisions** are those decisions taken within the purview of the policies, rules or procedures. These are also called programmed or routine decisions or structured decisions. These types of decisions are taken frequently and are repetitive in nature. Sanctioning an hour's permission, placing purchase order etc., are some examples of pragmatic decisions.

Non-pragmatic decisions are otherwise called as strategic decisions or non programmed decisions or policy decisions. These decisions involve heavy expenditure and are generally taken by top management.

(ii) **Individual and collective decisions:** Decisions may be taken by an individual or a group of individuals. If the decisions are taken by a single person, they are called individual decisions and if taken by a committee or group of people, than they are called collective decisions. Individual decisions are taken where the problem is of routine nature, and definite rules and procedures exist. Inter departmental decisions and important strategic decisions are generally taken by a group. Group decision-making has advantages like increased acceptance, better communication and better co-ordination. It has some disadvantages also like, delay in arriving at decision, groups may be indecisive, groups may compromise or dominate. To utilize the advantages of group decisions and avoid its disadvantages, two new techniques are proposed known as 'Nominal group techniques' and Delphi Techniques.

In nominal group technique, the members independently generate their idea and give in writing. The ideas are summarised and discussed for clarity and evaluation. Finally each member silently gives his rating and opinion about each idea through voting system. The one with maximum vote is selected as the group's decision.

In Delphi technique, persons who are physically dispersed and anonymous to one another are asked to send their opinion on a topic through mail. A carefully designed questionnaire is circulated for this purpose. The responses are summarized into a feed back report and sent back to them with a second questionnaire. A final summary is developed on the basis of replies received second time.

(iii) **Minor and major decisions:** Minor decisions are those decisions related to day-to-day and periodical occurrences. Purchase of stationary, granting leave and permissions etc., are some examples of minor decisions. Major decisions are those decisions generally taken by top management. Some of them are purchasing new machinery, employing new technology, hiring new people etc., are some of the major decisions.

(iv) **Strategic and routine decisions:** Strategic decisions are similar to major decisions and are generally taken by top management. Some examples are price increase/discount, change in product range etc. Routine decisions are decisions related to day-to-day operations of an organization that are routine in nature.

(v) Simple and complex decisions: A simple decision is one that is related to a problem with few number of variables. When there are many variables, the decisions making will be complex.

(vi) Temporary and permanent decisions: Some decisions are to be taken depending on situation till the solution is found. A decision is taken to meet an unexpected solutions are temporary in nature. These are generally taken by shop managers. Permanent decisions are taken on a permanent basis.

Steps in Decision Making:

Steps in a decision-making are shown in following block diagram.

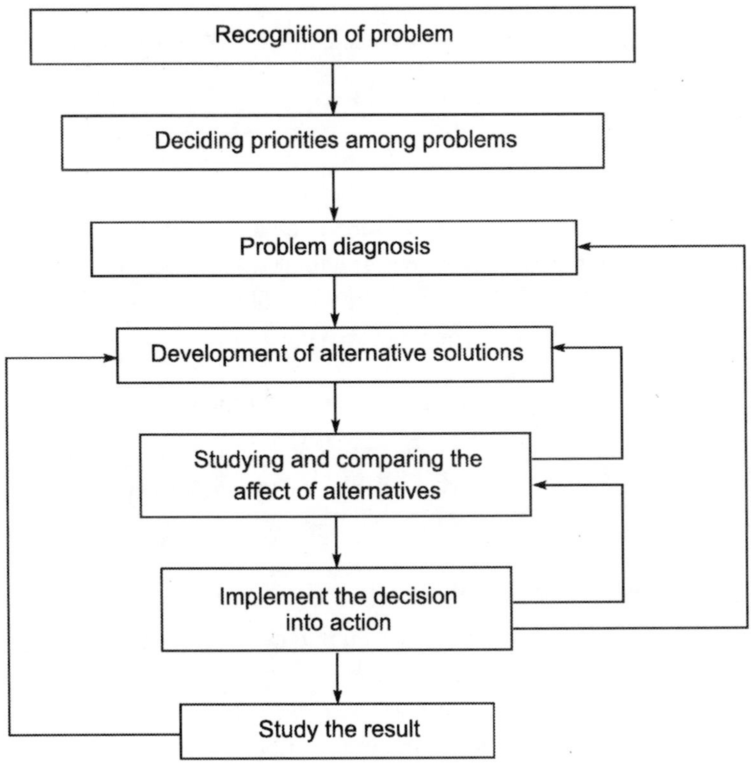

Steps in decision making

(i) Recognition of problem:

The first step in decision-making is the problem recognition. A problem may exist either due to a deviation from the past experience, a deviation from the plan, people bringing problems to the manager or problems arising from competition.

(ii) Deciding priorities among problem:

The manager should identify the problems which he can solve, the problems which he feels that his subordinates can solve and the problems which are to be referred to the higher officers. With this decision, the manager is left with very few problems to solve.

(iii) Problem diagnosis:

Correct diagnosis of the problem is very important for any manager. Managers should follow systems approach in diagnosing a problem. He should make a thorough study of all the sides of a problem coupled with organization before arriving at solution. If the diagnosis is made correctly, then finding solution becomes easy.

(iv) Development of alternate solutions:

After having diagnosed the problem, the next step is to find alternate solutions. For every problem there will be some alternate solutions. It is very rare that there is a problem with only unique solution. Alternatives do exist. Sometimes, in the absence of past history of alternate solutions, the manager has to depend only on his own ability in finding alternatives.

(v) Studying and comparing the affect of alternatives:

The alternative solutions are measured and compared for their consequences. This involves a comparison of the quality and acceptability of these alternatives.

(vi) Implementation of the decision into action:

The next step is to convert the decision into action. This requires the communications of the decisions to the concerned employees in clear and simple terms. If there is any opposition or non-acceptance from the employees, steps should be taken to convince them to accept the same.

(vii) Study of result:

After having implementing the decision, the manager has to carry out the follow up action. If the result is not satisfactory, the manager has to take necessary corrective action or modify his decision.

During the process of decision-making, the managers face many difficulties. Some of them are:

1. Incomplete information
2. Non-conducive environment
3. Opposition by subordinates
4. Improper communication
5. Wrong timing
6. Statutory regulations
7. Government policies
8. External influence
9. Lack of support.

3.7 STEPS IN PLANNING AND PLANNING PREMISES

The main steps involved in planning are as follows:

1. **Being aware of opportunities:** This is very first step and starting point for planning. Once we are aware of opportunities, we can think of setting realistic objectives.

2. **Establishing objectives:** It is very important to establish objectives for the entire enterprise and the objectives for each subordinate work units. That is, the major objectives are broken down into departmental and individual objectives. It is a very crucial step in planning.

3. **Developing planning premises:** The third step in planning is to establish planning premises. It is the process of creating assumptions about the future on the basis of which the plan will be ultimately formulated. Planning premises are important for the success of planning as they reveal facts and information relating to the future such as economic conditions, production costs competition, availability of material, resources and capital, government policies, population trends etc. This tells about which plan is to be carried out. There three types of planning premises:

   (i) ***Internal and external premises:*** Internal premises are premises within the organization. Some of the examples are: policies, forecasts, investment, availability of equipment, capability of work force, funds flow etc. External premises are premises outside the organization. They include: Government policies, technological

changes, business environment, economic conditions, population, buying power, political stability, socialogical factors, demand etc.

(ii) ***Tangible and intangible premises:*** Tangible premises are the measurable premises. For example, population, investment, demand etc., are tangible premises. Intangible premises are those which cannot be quantitatively measurable. Examples of this are: business environment, economic conditions, technological change etc.

(iii) ***Controllable and uncontrollable premises:*** Some of the premises are controllable like, technical man power, input technology, machinery, financial investment etc. Some other premises like, strikes, non-availability of raw material, change in government policies, socio-economic changes, phase-shift in technology, wars etc., are uncontrollable by the organization.

4. **Determination of alternative course:** Next step is to search and identify some alternative courses of action. It is very rare that for a plan there will be no alternatives. In this step alternatives are listed.

5. **Evaluating the alternatives and selecting the best course of action:** Once the alternatives are found, then the next step is to evaluate them with respect to the premises and goals. A desired and best suitable alternative is selected by comparative analysis with reference to cost, risk, and gain etc., keeping in mind the goals and objectives.

6. **Formulating derivative plan:** In order to complete the task, the selected plan must be translated into programs, working plans and financial requirements in the sub-units. These sub-derived plans from main plan are termed as derivative plans.

7. **Monitoring and controlling the plan:** This is the last step in planning. Each activity of plan is monitored on a continuous basis and if any deviation or shortfall is noticed, then the manager will initiate suitable corrective action.

3.8 HIERARCHY OF PLANS

The plans are generally arranged in a hierarchy within any organization. It starts at the top with objectives and goals of an organization. The second level is strategies. As discussed earlier, there are two types of strategies namely single use plans and standing plans. The third level is action plans. The hierarchy of plans is shown below:

Hierarchy of plans

The top management sets the goals and objectives. These occupy the top priority. The goals or objectives include long-term plans and strategies of an organization. For example, a company aims to improve their production by 20% during next 2 years. Such objectives are very broad ideas and are achieved by strategies. Strategies are carried out by means of two types of plans known as single-use-plans and standing plans. Single use plans are developed to achieve a specific goal after reaching the goal, the plan is dissolved. Examples of single use plans are budgets, construction of a bridge, dam or a shopping complex etc. Whereas standing plans are developed for projects that happen again and again. Admission procedure in a college, overhauling procedure of an aircraft, recruitment procedure of an organization etc., are some of the examples of standing plans. Action plans are the plans executed by the lower level organization. These are routine plans executed by the foreman and supervisors of the shop.

REVIEW QUESTIONS

1. What is planning? Explain the steps involved in planning.
2. State and explain importance and purpose of planning process.
3. What are the objectives of planning? Explain.
4. Briefly explain the types of planning.
5. What is nature and purpose of planning?

6. Differentiate between strategic and tactical planning.
7. Explain process of decision-making.
8. State and explain the steps in decision-making.
9. Explain the difficulties faced by manager in decision-making process.
10. What are planning premises?
11. Explain hierarchy of plans.
12. What are different decisions taken by a manager?

CHAPTER 4

ORGANIZING

4.1 NATURE OF ORGANIZATION

Organizing is the grouping of activities necessary to attain objectives, the assignment of each grouping to a manager with authority necessary to supervise it, its provision for coordination horizontally and vertically in the enterprise structure. An organization should be designed to clarify who is to do what and who is responsible for what results, to remove obstacles to the performance caused by confusion and uncertainty of assignment and to furnish decision making and communication network reflecting and supporting enterprise objectives.

Organization can be used to denote an enterprise, company or a firm. But for most practising managers, organization can be defined as :

"Organization provides the structure, the frame on which the management of the enterprise is based."

It can also be defined as "a vehicle moving the management efforts through the management team, with the help of the enterprise resources, to the accomplishment of the goals or plans."

The term organization is used in two different senses. In the first sense it is used to denote the process of organizing and the second is used to denote the result of that process called organization structure. The process of organization is defining and grouping the activities of the enterprise and establishing the authority relationship among them. In the second step is to prepare an organization structure. There are two types of organizations – formal and informal.

4.1.1 Formal Organization

There is nothing inherently inflexible or unduly confining about it. If the manager is to organize well, the structure must furnish an environment, in which individual performance, both present and future contribute most effectively to group goals. Formal organization must be flexible and there should be room for discretion, for taking advantage of creative talents.

4.1.2 Informal Organization

Informal organization is any joint personal activity without conscious joint purpose, even though possibly contributing to joint results. Managers must be aware of the informal Organization & avoid antagonizing it, they will find it advantageous to use it as they manage subordinates.

4.2 PURPOSE OF AN ORGANIZATION

The basic purpose of having organization is to formulate a frame or structure of an enterprise with a view to fulfil the enterprise tasks. The purpose includes the following logical components:

(i) Establishes the pattern of relationship by giving duties and responsibilities to an individual or group.

(ii) Demarcates the authority, responsibility and duties of each individual or group.

(iii) It tells each manager where his accountability lies and, who (below him) are in his sphere of command.

(iv) Provides adequate communication.

(v) Coordinates or integrates (through organization charts) and controls the activities of individuals or groups to achieve common objectives or objectives of the enterprise.

4.3 PRINCIPLES OF ORGANIZATION

The success of a business organization can be ensured if the following basic principles are used. In order to develop a sound and efficient organization structure, there is need to follow certain principles. In the words of E.F.L. Brech, "If there is to be a systematic approach to the formulation of organization structure, there ought to be a body of accepted principles". They are as follows:

(1) **Objectives :** The objectives of the enterprise influence the organization structure and hence the objectives of the enterprise should first be clearly defined. Then every part of the organization should be geared to the achievement of these objectives.

(2) **Specialisation :** Effective organization must promote specialisation. The activities of the enterprise should be divided according to functions and assigned to persons according to their specialisation.

(3) **Span of Control:** As there is a limit to the number of persons that can be supervised effectively by one boss, the span of control should be minimum as far as possible, the minimum, that means an executive should be asked to supervise a reasonable number of subordinates only, say six.

(4) **Exception:** As the executives at the higher level have limited time, only exceptionally complex problems should be referred to them and routine

matters should be dealt with by the lower levels. This will enable the executives at higher level to devote time to more important and crucial issues.

(5) Scalar principle : This principle is some times known as the "chain of command". The line of authority from the chief executive at the top to the front - line supervisor at the bottom, must be clearly defined.

(6) Unity of Command: Each subordinate should have only one supervisor whose command he has to obey. Dual subordination must be avoided, for it causes uneasiness, disorder, indiscipline and undermining of authority.

(7) Delegation: Proper authority should be delegated at the lower level of organization also to carryout the work effectively.

(8) Responsibility: The superior should be responsible for the acts of his subordinates.

(9) Authority: Authority is a tool by which a manager accomplishes the desired objectives, which should be clearly defined.

(10) Efficiency: The organization structure should help enterprise to function efficiently to accomplish the objectives at lowest cost.

(11) Simplicity: The organization structure should be simple and the levels should be as minimum as possible.

(12) Flexibility: Should be flexible, adaptable to changing circumstances, permit expansion, replacement, without dislocation and disruption of the basic design.

(13) Balance: There should be a reasonable balance in the size of various departments, between centralization and decentralization, between the principle of span of control and short chain of command and among all types of factors such as human, technical and financial.

(14) Unity of direction : Should be one objective and one plan for a group of activities having same objectives. Unity of direction facilities unification and coordination of activities at various levels.

(15) Personal Ability: As people constitute an organization, there is need for proper selection, placement and training of staff. Organisation structure must ensure optimum use of human resources and encourage management development programme.

4.4 TYPES OF ORGANISATION

Since organization structure (or organization chart) is not a routine or academic sketch, there can be no standard format which can fit any industrial enterprise. The organization chart has to evolve out of the present possible facilities available to the enterprise. Thus, we may identify five patterns of arrangement which commonly (with adjustments) describe the situation in most enterprises. They are:

(1) Line organization.

(2) Functional or staff organization.

(3) Line and staff organization.

(4) Committee organization.

(5) Matrix organization.

4.4.1 Line Organisation

It is also called as military or scalar organization. It is the simplest form of organization structure. Under this system, authority flows from man at the top to the lowest man vertically. In other words, directions issued by the man in-charge of the whole organization are directly conveyed to the person responsible for the execution of work. This makes the line of authority 'straight and vertical'. It is this authority which channels and directs the response of others and require them to conform to decisions, plans, policies and procedure and goals.

Line authority is thus that relationship in which a superior exercises direct supervision over a subordinate. There are three important principles in this system. They are

(i) Command should be given to subordinate through the immediate superior. There should be no skipping of levels in the chain of command.

(ii) There should be only one chain i.e., command should be received from only one immediate superior.

(iii) The number of subordinates whose work is directly commanded by the superior should be limited.

Any enterprise that starts small organization, probably starts with a line type organization.

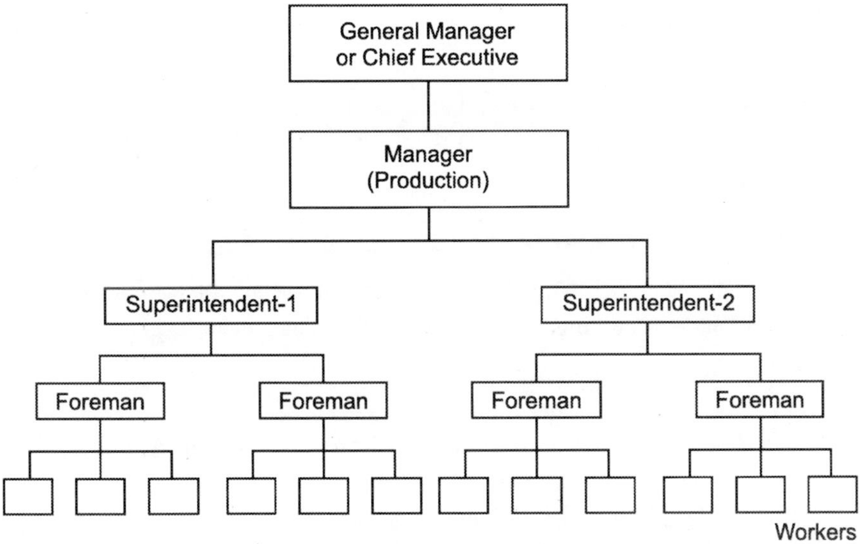

Line organization chart for a medium size manufacturing company

Advantages

- Simple and easy to understand.
- Flexible, easy to expand and contract.
- Makes clear division of authority.
- Clear channel of communication with no confusion.
- Encourages speedy action.
- Strong in discipline as it fixes responsibility on an individual.
- Capable of developing the all-round executive at the higher levels of authority.

Disadvantages

- Neglects specialists.
- Overloads a few key executives.
- Requires high type of supervisory personnel to meet the challenges imposed in the absence of specialists as advisors.
- Limited to very small concerns.
- Encourages dictatorial way of working.
- Provisions are seldom made to train, develop and replace top executives.
- Due to task of specialisation, perhaps there is more wastage of material and man hours.
- Rigid and inflexible.

Applications

Line organization is suitable for

(a) Small concerns free from all complexities.

(b) Automatic continuous process industry such as paper, sugar, textile etc.

4.4.2 Functional Organization (Staff organization)

F.W. Taylor suggested functional organization because it was difficult to find all round persons qualified to work at middle management levels in the line organization.

Functional authority is the right which is delegated to an individual or a department that authorizes control of specified processes, practices, policies or other matters relating to activities undertaken by personnel in other departments. If the principle of unity of command were followed without exception, authority over these activities would be exercised only by their line supervisors. But numerous reasons including lack of special knowledge, lack of ability to supervise processes and danger of diverse interpretation of policies explain why they occasionally are not allowed to exercise this authority. It is delegated by their common superior to a staff specialist or a manager in another department.

As the name implies the whole task of manufacturing and direction of subordinates should be divided according to the type of work involved. For example almost all business organizations have separate departments to look after production, sales and the general office. The functional manufacturing carries this idea to its logical limit of dividing up management into a number of functions such as production, R & D, personnel, purchasing, finance, office management and sales. Each one of these departments would serve the rest of the organization. The personnel department for example, would recruit train and deal with the people required for all other departments, the purchasing department would handle purchasing for the entire organization. While dividing management into such departments care should be exercised to see (1) that the entire work has been divided into various departments, so that there is no one activity which has not been allotted to one department or the other. (2) there should be no duplication in the sense that an activity should not be allotted to more than one department. (3) the work allotted to one department should consist of interrelated jobs.

At the higher levels of organization, functional departments are divisions and all related and similar work is placed in one department or division under one executive.

Need : The functional organization was developed so as to achieve complete organization on the basis of various functions performed by the enterprise. Also in order to get a thorough knowledge of exact procedure or greater effectiveness in a particular area or field, it was necessary that the organization structure should be based on the functions performed by the individuals.

Advantages

- It is a logical reflection of functions.
- It ensures a greater division of labour and enables the concern to take advantages of specialisation of functions.
- It makes for a higher degree of efficiency as the workers and others in the organization have to perform limited number of operations.
- It facilitates mass production, through specialisation and standardisation.
- It relieves pressure of need to search a large number of all round executives.
- Quality of work is improved.
- Simplifies training.
- Furnishes means of tight control at top.

Disadvantages

- Coordination of the efforts of various functional foremen is difficult.
- It is unstable because it weakens the disciplinary controls by making the workers work under several different bosses.
- It makes it difficult for the management to fix responsibility for unsatisfactory results.
- Workers always remain confused about the authority, activity of each supervisor, hence it makes industrial relationship more complex.
- Responsibility for profit is at the top only.
- Makes economic growth of company difficult.
- Limits development of general managers.

Functional organization is the most widely employed basis for organizing activities and is present in almost every enterprise at some levels in the organization structure. On the whole, this system has been quite successfully followed in big concerns for division of work at the top but for division of work in various departments themselves the system has not been found to be very successful because there is no clear line of authority.

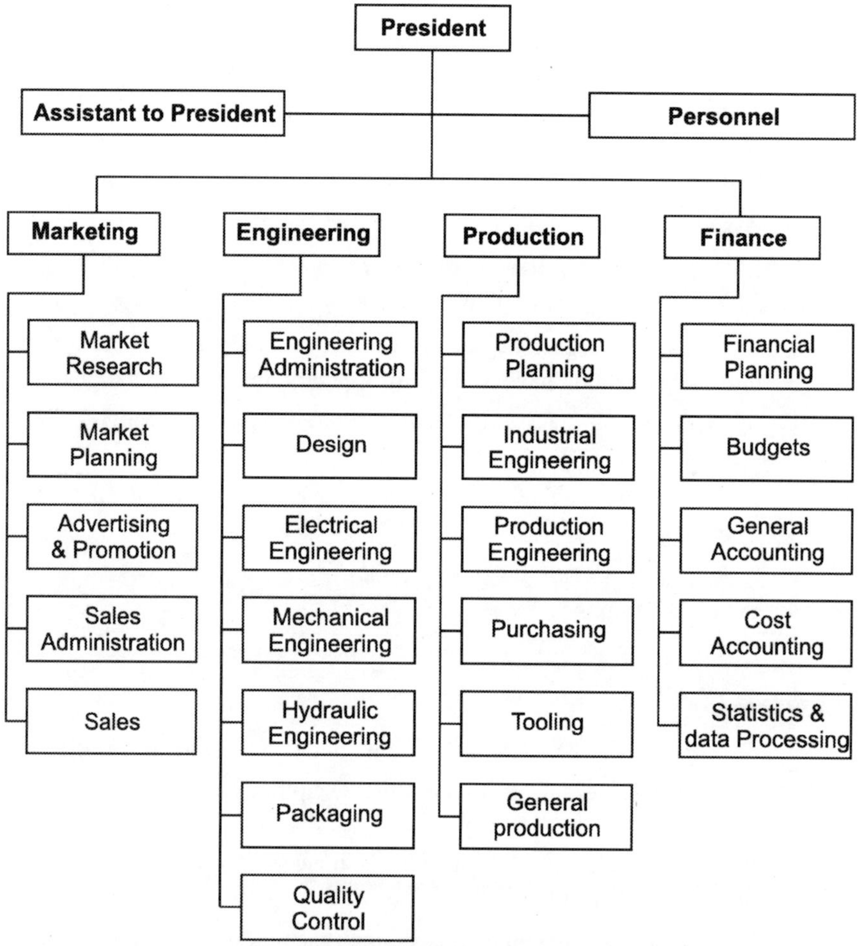

Functional Organization

Functional Authority of line Departments

A variation of line staff organization is line functional organization in which the staff or specialist executives has full authority (i.e., a higher degree of authority than in a line and staff organization) over his particular function which may be inspection work, study, purchasing; employment etc.

4.4.3 Line and staff Organization

The line organization gradually developed to shape as the line and staff organization. Taylor's functional organization heartened its development. As the industry grew in size and complexity, the line executives could not perform properly all other functions (besides looking after production, sales) such as R & D, planning, distribution, legal, public relations, purchasing, accounting, quality control etc. This necessitated the employing of special executives to assist line executives and they were known as 'staff' as they were recruited to perform staff or specialist functions. One widely held concept of line and staff is that line functions are those that have direct responsibility for accomplishing the objectives of the enterprise while staff functions to help the line to work most effectively in accomplishing the primary objectives of the enterprise. Line authority gives a supervisor a line of authority and control over a sub ordinate while nature of the staff relation ship is advisory. The function of people in a pure staff capacity is to investigate, research and give advice to line managers to whom they report. The final decision whether to accept/implement the recommendation of the staff executives remains in the hands of the line executive.

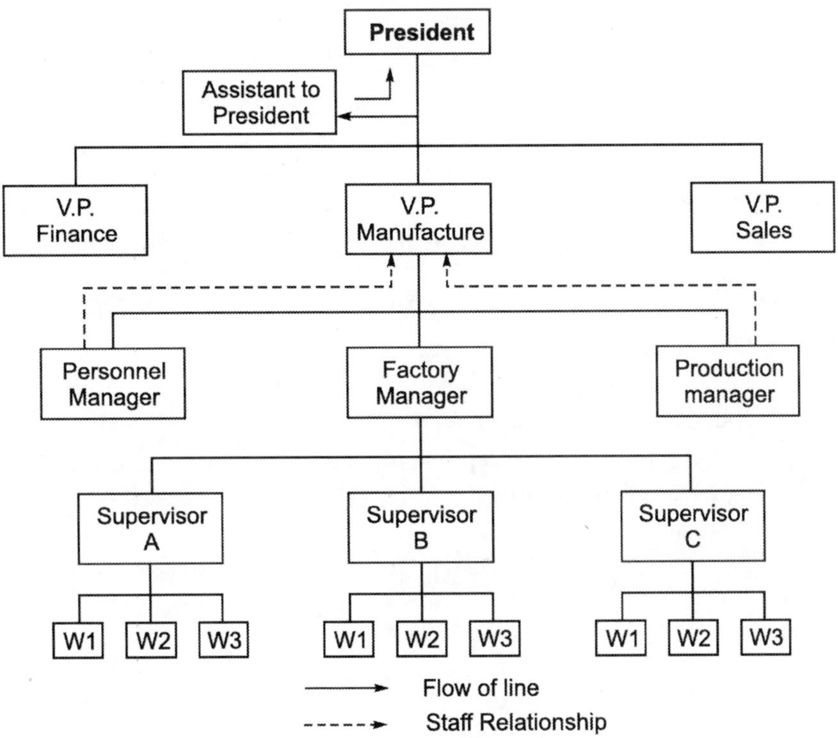

Line and Staff Organization

It is thus often stated that staff officers are assigned an 'authority of ideas' and line officer an "authority of command" i.e., the line executives function is to act, the staff executives' function is to think. Supervisors and sub ordinates must know whether they are acting in a staff or line capacity. A staff officer's job **is** to advice and not to command, then line supervisor must take decision to issue instructions through the scalar plan. Frequently, line and staff are regarded as different types of departments. Although a department may stand in a predominately line or staff position with respect to other departments, we distinguish line and staff by authority relationship.

Advantages

- Expert advise from specialist staff executive can be made use of
- Line executives are relieved of some of their loads and are thus able to devote more attention towards production.
- Less wastage of material, man and m/c hours.
- Quality of product is improved.
- There is no confusion as exists in functional organization.
- Line and staff organization possesses practically all the advantages of both the line and functional organization.
- It provide greater chances of advancement to able employees by making more jobs available.

Disadvantages

- Product cost will increase because of high salaries of staff executives.
- Line and staff organization may bring in confusion in case functions are not clear.
- Friction and jealousies will develop between staff and line executives and may cause harm to enterprise.
- If line executives start depending too much on staff executives, they may loose their initiative.
- Complex in nature.
- May not be effective for small organization.

Applications

It is very common in the medium and large enterprise.

4.4.4 Committee organization

In the modern complex business world, some of the administrative tasks cannot be performed by a single person alone. Such situations may call for two are more persons to perform such tasks. This calls for a committee organization. A committee is a group of people pooled to carry out a defined objective.

The various functions of a committee are:

(i) Collect the necessary information from different sources and arrange them in order.

(ii) The collected information is critically examined and analysed.

(iii) Draft a detail report containing the recommendations for the purpose of implementation.

(iv) Framing the policies of the organization.

(v) Selection of personnel, directing and controlling the officers at regular intervals to achieve the goals.

Advantages of committee organizations

(i) Committees can take valuable decisions. Hasty decision can be avoided.

(ii) The committee members can use their expertise while taking decisions.

(iii) Committee decisions are many times better.

(iv) As a member of a committee, a manager has to accept the decision and implement it faster.

(v) Communication of decision is faster with the involvement of members from different groups.

(vi) Coordination among departments is made easy, since managers of various departments are involved in decision-making.

(vii) Committee members have authority to implement the decisions.

(viii) Decisions are generally widely accepted since they are taken in a democratic process.

(ix) Decision is based on vast experience of the members.

Disadvantages

(i) Many times decisions are delays due to the heterogeneous group in the committee.

(ii) Increased administrative expenses.

(iii) In the absence of concurrence of ideas, sometimes decisions cannot be arrived.

(iv) Secrecy of decision cannot be maintained.

(v) Sometimes decisions are taken on compromise.

(vi) Sometimes expressing ideas may lead to heated arguments.

(vii) Dominating nature people influence more in decision-making.

(viii) Since committee takes decisions, intuition of individuals will deteriorate.

(ix) Responsibility cannot be fixed on any individual if a decision does not produce expected favourable results.

4.4.5 Matrix organization

There are several departments under matrix organization. Each department is assigned with a specific task. The available resources can be effectively used by each department with the coordination of other departments.

It is defined as "Any organization that employees a multiple command structure but also related support mechanisms and an associated organizational culture and behaviour pattern".

This type of organization is best suited where large number of small projects are to be managed.

For the matrix organization to function effectively, the following conditions should prevail.

(i) Scalar chain of command is not followed. A project manager will give reports to several superiors.

(ii) The physical, financial and human resources are to be shared by people of different projects in a cooperative way.

(iii) Sharing the resources may lead to conflicts if not understood each other properly.

Advantages of matrix organization

(i) The matrix organization combines the advantages of functional and line organizations.

(ii) It ensures the achievement of objectives with technical specialization.

(iii) It ensures effective utilization of available resources.

(iv) It adopts itself easily to external charges.

(v) It is highly flexible.

(vi) Motivation can be effectively applied.

(vii) Makes room for training and development of people.

Disadvantages

(i) Since matrix organization does not follow scalar chain of command, it leads to confusions.

(ii) Since too may supervisors controlling an activity, work may be delayed.

(iii) Sometimes resources may not be made available owing to other priority projects.

(iv) May lead to conflicts owing to lack of unity of command in the organization.

4.5 DEPARTMENTATION

Horizontal differentiation of tasks or activities into discrete segments is called departmentation. There are several bases for departmentation depending upon the nature and size of organization, goals, strategies and environment.

1. Departmentation based on Products

This is more suitable for a large organization that manufactures a vast variety of products. Under this separate groups or departments are created and each department is controlled by a manager who will be responsible for all the activities of that sub group. Each subgroup will have its own facilities required for manufacture, purchase, marketing and accounting etc. This type is advantageous where variety of products are manufactured for example *(i)* Godrej, that manufactures soaps, cosmetics, refrigerators, machines, furniture etc., *(ii)* HMT that manufactures machines, watches, tractors, bearings etc. *(iii)* TATAs that make trucks, cars, steel, machines etc.

Advantages

- ➢ Top management is relieved of operational task enabling them to concentrate more on common goals.
- ➢ Performance of different product groups can be easily compared enabling the top management to invest more and more in profitable product groups and exercise better control on non performers.
- ➢ Managers of individual products put better effort to improve his area compared to others.

Disadvantages

- ➢ This calls for duplication of staff and facilities.
- ➢ Separate work force are required in sales, marketing and finance, resulting in extra expenditure.
- ➢ More managers are required.
- ➢ May result in under utilization of facilities and equipment.

2. Departmentation based on functions

The departmentation is based on each major function of the organization. Depending on the nature of organization the various functions are as follows:

Marketing, Engineering, Production, Finance, Personnel, Purchase etc. Functional departmentation is most widely employed basis of organising activities and is present in almost every organization at some level in its structure.

Advantages

- It is logical reflection of functions.
- Maintains power and prestige of major functions.
- Follows principle of occupational specifications and thereby facilitates efficient utilization of people.
- Simplifies training.
- Provides means of right control at top.

Disadvantages

- De-emphases overall company objectives.
- Leads to over specialization of people.
- Reduces coordination between functions.
- Slow adoption to changes in environment.
- Limits development of general managers.

3. Departmentation based on time

One of the oldest forms of departmentation, generally used at lower levels of an organization, is grouping of activities on the basis of time. The use of shifts is common in some organizations due to economic or technological reasons. For service organizations like hospitals, fire department, security, steel mills, chemical plants, round the clock work is essential. All these call for 3 shift working of organization. Then under such circumstance, the departmentation is made on the basis of shifts as first shift, second shift etc.

Advantages

- Service can be rendered, that goes beyond the normal 8 hours shift/ day.
- Facilitates use of processes that cannot be stopped or interrupted.
- Expensive capital equipment can be better utilized.
- Provides part time jobs for people who are otherwise busy during day time (students going for part time job etc.)
- Higher and continuous production per day.

Disadvantages

- Lacks good and efficient supervision during night shifts.
- Inconvenient for people to work in night shifts and more difficult during shift changes from day to night.
- Lack of effective coordination and communication from people of one shift to next shift.
- Loss of product or service may increase owing to higher payment/ over time payment during night shift.

4. Departmentation based on Territory and Geography

Departmentation by Territory is common in organizations that operate over a wide geographical area. The activities of an enterprise are divided into territories like, western region, northern region, eastern region, southern region etc. They may be further divided into sub regions in main regions like Karnataka region, Kerala region, Andhra Region, Tamil Nadu region within souther region etc.

Territorial departmentation is especially attractive to large-scale firms or other enterprises whose activities are physically or geographically spread over a large area. Banks, Railways and big manufacturing companies like petroleum companies (HP, Indian Oil etc.), cosmetic companies are some of the examples of this.

Advantages

- Places responsibility at lower level.
- Places emphasis on local problems and markets.
- Ensures a better coordination with-in a region.
- Facilitates direct communication within a region.
- Better involvement of people to achieve higher targets.
- Provides a region-wise comparison of performance.
- Takes advantage of economics of local operations.

Disadvantages

- Requires more persons with General Manager abilities.
- Requires to maintain similar functional people at all regions.
- Difficult to control from top management.

5. Departmentation based on simple numbers

This was one of the most widely used ancient methods of departmentation. This is achieved by tolling of persons performing the same job and grouping them together under one supervisor. This is not in common use now.

4.6 COMMITTEES

A committee consist of a group of people specially designated to perform some administrative acts. It functions only as a group and requires the free inter change of ideas among its members.

It must be remembered that there is no piece of work in a modern business house which does not affect the work in other departments. If the production management wants to change the product even slightly, the sales management would be deeply concerned because he has to convince his customers that the change is all for the good. Similarly the sales manager cannot follow a policy without consulting the finance manager or the production manager. In this manner it is necessary that important policy decisions in all the departments should be made not by each departmental manager alone but by a committee consisting of departmental managers. This committee should preferably be presided over by the G.M. This will ensure that when a decision is arrived at, all departments are consulted, so that when a decision is put into effect, all departments will cooperate.

A further advantage of setting up a committee is to widen the view points of departmental managers when important policy decisions are arrived at. Only through committees, the various departmental managers will automatically consider the view points of other departments. Committees are also useful for harmonizing the efforts of the staff and the line executives.

4.6.1 Principles

- The number of persons in a committee should depend upon need (about 5 to 10 persons).
- Responsibility, authority, objectives, duties of the committee should be clearly defined.
- Agenda of the committee should be proposed or communicated to the committee at least a week before they meet for discussions.
- Problems which can be taken care by an individual should not be included in the agenda of the committees .
- Committee meeting should begin and end on prefixed timings.

- Problems not related to the subject matter at hand should not be discussed because it will simply be waste of time.
- The recommendation made by committee should be published and circulated to interested and concerned persons.
- The committee should be appraised, if this action is taken based upon its recommendation.
- A committee must be dissolved after its purpose is over.

4.6.2 Types of Committees

There are many types of committees. They are basically classified according to the place and purpose they serve.

- **Standing or Permanent Committee :** This is needed in a complex organization experiencing multi-faced problems almost all the times Govt. enterprise like Railway Boards, Board of Revenue, Planning Commission, etc., are some examples of Standing Committees.
- **Temporary Committee:** Is formed to face and solve problems arising occasionally.
- **General Advisory Committee:** May advise the management on important matters relating to the organization. Some examples are Business enterprise, Board of directors, Executive Committee.
- **Joint Consultative Committee:** Consisting of the representatives of labour and management, may promote better relation between management and labour by discussing matters of common interest.
- **Academic Committee:** Non-business institutions like Universities councils, Board of studies, Development committee etc.
- **Religious Committee:** Trust, Temple organization etc.
- **Educational:** Aids in getting information about company problems, policies, projects to major individual concerned.

Advantages

- Provides opportunities for pooling of idea and leads to integrated group judgement, two heads are better than one.
- Coordinates the efforts of the .departments which are represented eg: sales, production and engineering.
- Committees receive cooperation of various parts of the organization in the execution of plans.

- Committee meetings may be called to train younger executives and give them a keener insight into the operation of the business.
- Provide a safe guard against the ends of the concentration of power in one individual and bring about dispersal of authority.
- Blurred responsibility.
- Helps in achieving optimum decision.

Disadvantages

- Committee operations are slow and committees tend to hang on for a considerable time.
- No individual can be held responsible for wrong decisions.
- Committee decisions represent generally a compromised position and do not truly reflect the real feelings of the individual committee members.
- There is a tendency to indulge in irrelevant discussion, members trying to impress supervisors and tendency to jump to conclusions.
- Often influenced by political activities.
- There is a fear of dominating by a single person.

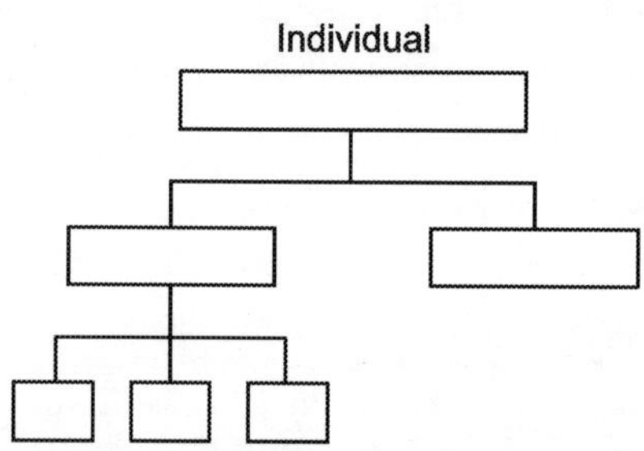

Line & Functional Organisation

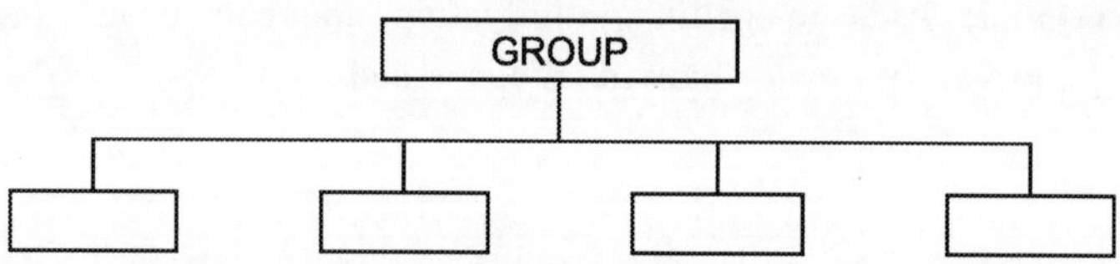

Committee

4.6.3 Designing an Organisational structure

Organization chart: Organization chart shows the structure of an organization. It portrays graphically the structural relationship among the different departments and the position in the enterprise, who are responsible for these functions.

It is also known as organization tree and is nothing but a map or drawing of the organization. It shows

- The inter relationship and relative position of each department of the company.
- The types of command i.e. authority, responsibility.
- Relation ship between different managers by virtue of their status in the organization.
- Kinds of managerial relationship which exist (line, staff and functional).
- Some times the name of manager along with the number of persons they supervise.

They are three major types of chart according to which one can view his own organization structure.

4.6.3.1 Paramedical structure chart

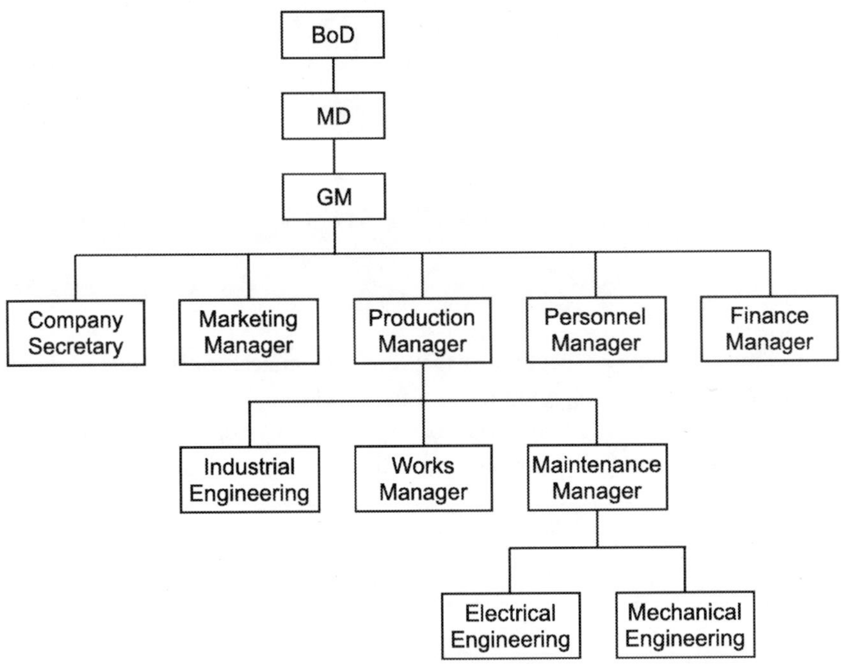

It is the most widely used type of chart. It shows the vertical flow of authority and communications.

4.6.3.2 Horizontal chart

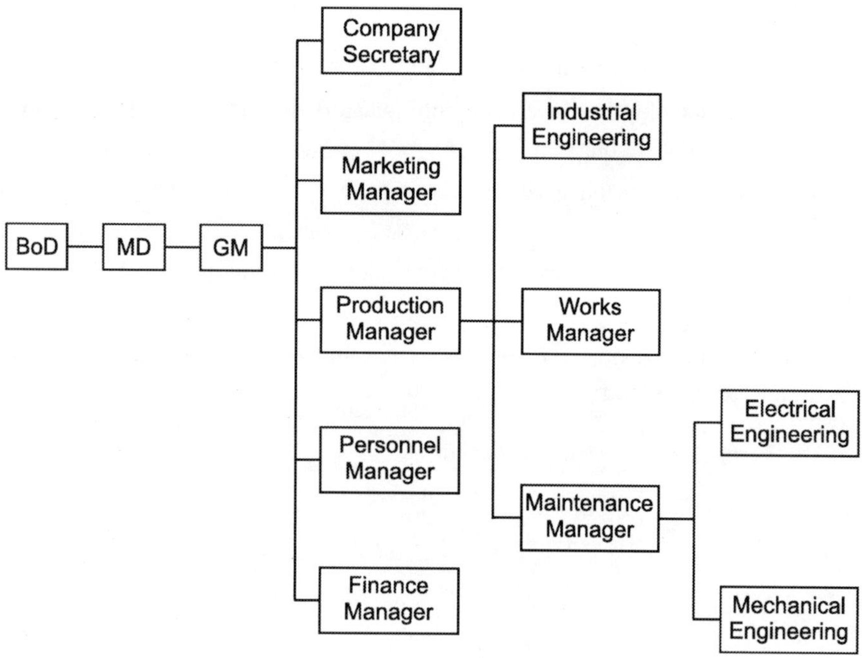

It moves from left to right hence it is in accordance with the normal left to right reading habits.

4.6.3.3 Concentric chart:

It shows the chief executive in the centre of concentric circles, each of which depicts the next succession level in the hierarchy. It's advantage is that it tends to de-emphasize vertical authority relationships. It also shows the outward flow of authority from chief executive though it appears to be complex.

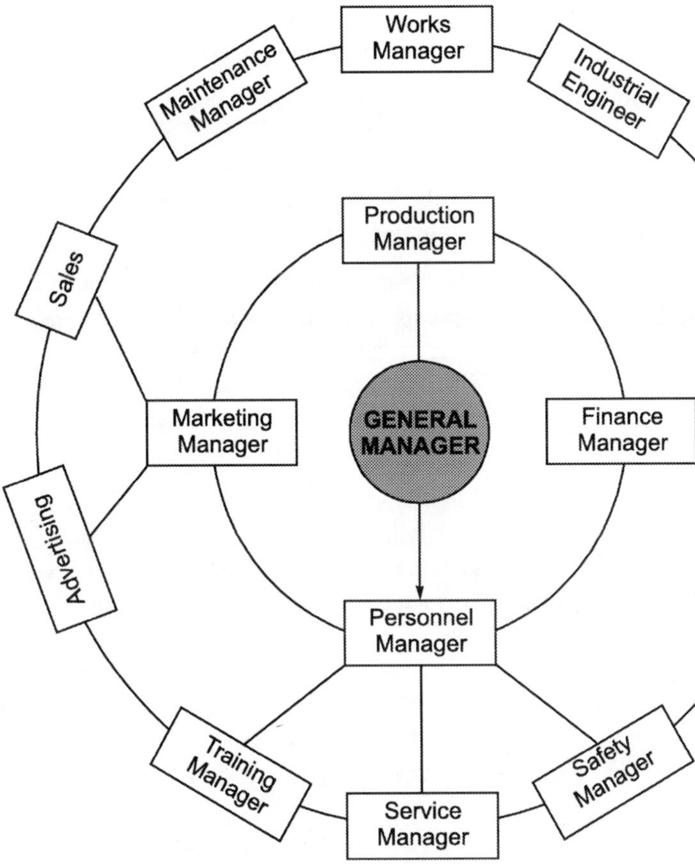

4.6.4 Advantages of Organization chart

- It tells quickly as to who is responsible for a particular function.
- It pin points the weakness of organization.
- It supplies the details available in organization manual.
- Can serve as a training device or as a guidance in planning for expansion.
- Useful in showing the nature of organization changes, if any in existing staff and the new comers.

4.7 CENTRALISATION VS DECENTRALISATION

4.7.1 Concept of Centralization and Decentralization

Organization authority is merely the degree of discretion conferred on people to make it possible for them to use their judgement by giving them power to use their own decisions and issue instructions, how much authority should be concentrated or dispersed throughout the organization.

Decentralization is the tendency to disperse decision, making, authority in an organization structure. It is a fundamental aspect of delegation, to the extent the authority is not delegated it is centralized. There can be absolute centralization of authority in one person; this implies that no subordinate managers, and therefore no structured organization.

Some decentralized authority exists in all organizations. On the other hand there cannot be absolute decentralization, for if managers, should delegate all their authority, their status as managers would cease, their position will be eliminated and again there would be no organization structure. Centralization and decentralization are qualities with various degrees in practice.

When work of an executive increases so much in volume that he cannot hope to cope with it, he has to divide it among his subordinates. In doing so he naturally expects that each subordinate will do the job as he himself would have done. This process of dividing the job is referred to as ‘delegation’. Delegation is simply a matter of entrusting part of the work operations or management to others. “It is the ability to get results through others” - “It is the dynamics of management”. It is a process a manager follows in dividing the work assigned to him so that he performs that part which only he, because of his unique organizational placement, can perform effectively, so that he can get others to help him with what remains. The primary purpose of delegation is to make organization possible.

Just as no one person in an enterprise can do all the job necessary for accomplishing a group purpose, so it is impossible as an enterprise grows for one person to exercise all the authority for making decisions. There is a limit to the number of persons that a manager can effectively supervise and for whom they can make decisions. Once this limit has been passed, authority must be delegated to subordinates, who will make decisions within the area of their assigned duties.

4.7.2 The process of Delegation

- Authority is delegated when superior gives a subordinate, discretion to make decisions. The entire process of delegation involves:
- Determination of results expected (MBO)
- Assignment of tasks.
- Delegation of authority for accomplishing these tasks.
- Holding of people responsible for accomplishment of tasks.

In practice it is impossible to split this process, since expecting a person to accomplish goals without the authority to achieve them is meaning less, as the delegation of authority without knowing for what results it will be used.

4.7.3 Clarity of Delegation

Delegation of authority can be specific or general, written or unwritten. If the delegation is unclear, a manager may not understand the nature of the duties or the results expected. Specific written delegations of authority are extremely helpful both to the manager who receives them and to the person who delegates. Sometimes, especially, in the upper levels of management, it is too difficult to make authority delegation specific and the subordinate, robbed of flexibility, will be unable to develop in the best way.

4.7.4 Recovery of Delegated Authority

A manager who delegates authority, does not permanently dispose it off; delegated authority can always be regained.

A shuffle in an organization means that rights are recovered by the responsible head of the firm to a department and then re-delegated to new managers to modified departments, so that head of a new department may receive the authority held by other managers.

4.7.5 Difficulties in delegation

Although delegation is apparently a simple process, but in practice certain difficulties do generally crop up, hampering the process. They are as follows:

(i) On the part of the boss

- "I can do it better myself" feeling.
- Lack of ability to direct.
- Lack of confidence and trust in subordinates.
- Absence of control that warns of coming troubles.
- Conservative and canvas temperment.

(ii) On part of the subordinates

- Over dependence on boss for decisions.
- Fear of criticism.
- Lack of information and resources to do a particular job effectively.
- Lack of self confidence.
- In adequate positive incentives.

4.7.6 Principles of Delegation

(i) Receptiveness

An underlying attribute of managers who will delegate authority is a willingness to give other people's idea a choice.

(ii) Willingness to let go

A manager who will effectively delegate authority, must be willing to release the right to make decisions to subordinates.

(iii) Willingness to let others make mistakes

As everyone makes mistakes, a subordinate must be allowed to make them, and they must be considered upon investment in personal development.

(iv) Willingness to trust subordinates

Trust is the basis of all coordination.

(v) Willingness to establish and use broad controls

To ensure themselves that the authority is being used to support enterprise or department goals and plans.

4.8 ORGANIZATION LEVELS AND SPAN OF CONTROL

Span of management or control refers to the number of subordinates who report to a manager or the number of subordinates a manager can effectively supervise. It is also called span of supervision. A manager should not have more subordinates, looking to him for guidance, than he can effectively manage. Because there is a limit to the number of persons a manager can supervise with effect, even though this limit varies depending on situations, the result is the existence of organization levels. The relation ships between the span and organization levels are shown in figure. A wide span of management is associated with few organizational levels; a narrow span results in many levels.

The major problem in this regard is to decide how wide a span should be i.e., to decide how many subordinates a superior can manage. If the span is small, an executive may tend to over supervise and may even do spoon feeding to his subordinates. On the other hand if the span is large, executive may not be able to supervise the subordinates effectively and they may start thinking that they are too remote from the point of control and may tend to become careless or may feel that they are impersonal and unimportant part of the organization machinery.

Research Studies of management have found that this number (span) is usually 4-8 subordinates at the upper levels of organization and 8-15 or more at the lower levels. However this is nothing definite. The relative advantages and disadvantages of narrow and wide spans are show below.

4.8.1 Organization with Narrow span

Advantages

- Close supervision.
- Close control.
- Fast communication between subordinates and superiors.

Disadvantages

- Superior tend to get too much involved in subordinates work.
- Many levels of management.
- High cost due to many levels of management.
- Excessive distance between lower level and top level.
- Complicates planning and control process.

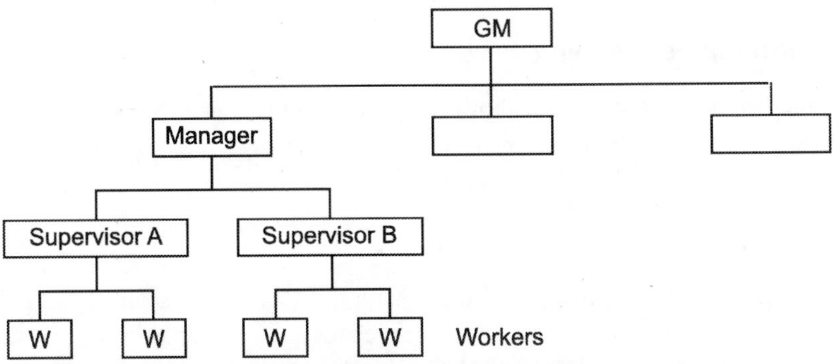

Organisation with Narrow span

4.8.2 Organization with Wide span

Advantages

- Superiors are forced to delegate.
- Clear policies must be made.
- Subordinates must be very carefully selected.

Disadvantages

- Tendency of overloading superiors to become decision bottle necks.

- Danger of superior's loss of control.
- Requires managers with exceptional qualities.

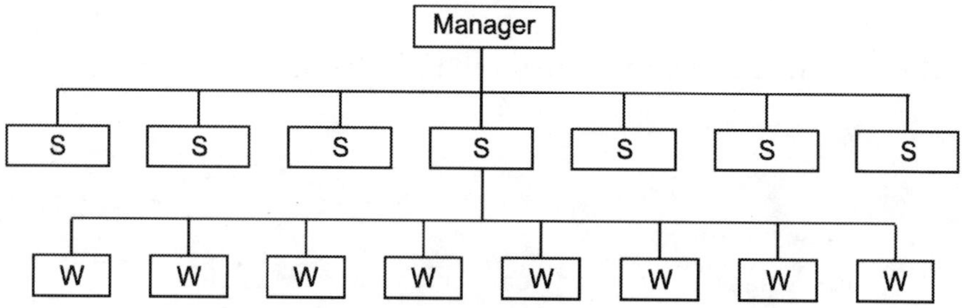

Organization with Wide span

4.8.3 Factors determining an effective span

The most important determinant factor is the manager's ability to reduce the time the superior spends with the subordinates. This ability naturally varies with managers and their jobs. The 7 general factors materially influence the number of frequency of such relation ships are explained below:

(i) Subordinate Training

The better the training of subordinates the less the impact of necessary superior-subordinate relationship. Well trained subordinates require not only less of their managers time but also less contact with them.

(ii) Clarity of delegation of authority

The most serious symptom of organization affecting the span of management is inadequate or unclear authority delegation. If a manager clearly delegates authority to undertake a well defined task, a well trained subordinate can get it done with minimum of superior time in attention. But if the subordinate's task is not one that can be done, if not clearly defined, or if the subordinate does not have the authority to under take it effectively, either the task will not be performed or the manager will have to spend a disproportionate amount of time supervising and guiding the subordinates efforts.

(iii) Clarity of Plans

Much of the character of a subordinate's job is defined by the plan to be put into effect. If the plans are well defined, if they are workable, if the authority to undertake them has been delegated and if the subordinate understands what is expected of him, little of supervisors time will be required. On the other hand, where plans cannot be drawn accurately and where subordinates must do much of their own planning, then their decisions may require considerable guidance (resulting in a lesser span).

(iv) Use of objective standards

A manager must find out by either personal observation or by use of objective standards, whether sub ordinates are following plans. Obviously good objective standards reveal with ease any deviation from plans, enable managers to avoid many a time-consuming relationships and to direct attention to exception at points critical to the successful execution of plans.

(v) Rate of change

Certain enterprises change much more rapidly than others. The rate of change is important in determining the degree to which policies can be formulated and the stability of policies maintained. It may explain the organization structure of companies e.g. rail, road, banking and public utility companies operate with wide span of management. On the other hand the very narrow span of management was used by General Eisenhower during World War II.

(vi) Communication Technique

The effectiveness with which communication techniques are used also influences the span of management. Objective studies of control are a kind of communications device, but many other techniques reduce the time spent with subordinates. If every plan, instruction, order or direction has to be communicated by personal contact, a manager's time will obviously be heavily wasted. Written recommendations by subordinates, summarizing important considerations frequently speed up decision making. An ability to communicate plans, instructions clearly and concisely also tends to increase a manager's span.

(vii) Amount of personal contact needed

In many instances in management face to face meetings are necessary. Many situations cannot be handled by written reports, memorandums, policy statements, planning documents or other communications not calling for personal contact. In such cases the span of management tends to be narrow.

There should be a proper balance between span and levels considering all the factors. The basic principle of span does exist and is useful in guiding manager towards ably managing more subordinates and simplifying the organization.

4.8.4 Authority

It is the formal right given to an individual to command (the action of others). According to Koontz, it is the tool by which a manager is able to exercise discretion and to create an environment for individual performance.

An authority may be defined as the "right to act". It may also be referred to as the power to take necessary steps or decisions in order to achieve organization's goals.

An enterprise may have the best of plans, sound organization structure and efficient management, yet nothing happens or is achieved. As nothing is done i.e., the 'act' is missing and it is the act that influences in the body structure. Thus, "Authority is the right to act" the most appropriate definition given to it.

Enterprise and types of authority

An enterprise can be of various types. For each of that types there are different types of authority.

Enterprise	Authority
1. Public Organization	Share holders, Board of directors.
2. Partnership firm	All the members who are partners
3. Private Ltd.	Director / Directors, M.D.
4. Proprietor ship	Proprietor of the firm.
5. Government / Institutional Organization	Committees, Council, Board of Directors.

4.8.5 Responsibility

It is also called as Accountability or Answerability. It may be considered as the obligation of a subordinate to his superior to do a work assigned to him. Each person who is given responsibility must recognise that the executive above him will hold him responsible for the .quality of his performance.

Authority and responsibility exist together in a business organization. They represent the two sides of the same coin while authority is right to command; responsibility is an obligation to performance as someone with authority has directed. It accompanies the assignment of work to a subordinate and becomes increasingly important at successive higher levels in the hierarchy. It is not merely a desire to cooperate or to advance group objectives but is a recognition of the obligation to perform managerial functions.

One major and important aspect of responsibility is that a manager can part with authority but not with responsibility, which is an inherent property of his position in the organization.

The terms "responsibility"' and "accountability" are often used dischargeably. Strictly speaking accountability is used to denote a special kind of responsibility. As employed in military, an officer is said to be "accountable" for equipment, but responsible for the action of troops reporting to him.

4.8.13 Scalar Principle

It is also referred as 'chain of command' or 'scalar chain of command' or 'line or authority.'

An organization level consists of levels of authority arranged in a hierarchy from with the Chief executive at the top and the workers at the bottom. The scalar principle holds that these levels represent gradation of distributed authority, each successive level downward representing a decreasing amount of authority, a decreased scope of authority and often a different kind of authority. This is the chain of command.

The scalar principle refers to the chain of direct authority relationships from superior to subordinate throughout the organization. It is stated by Koontz that "The clearer the line of authority from the top manager in an enterprise to every subordinate position, the clearer will be the positions responsible for decision making and the more effective organization communication will be" (A clear understanding of the scalar principle is necessary for proper functioning of organization, because subordinates must know who delegates authority to them and to whom, matters beyond their own authority must be referred). Although the chain of command may be safely detoured for purposes of obtaining information, for proposes of decision making tends to destroy the decision making system and by doing so, to undermine managership left. The scalar principle is an important concept as it throws light on the way in which the differential parts of an organization are created and held together. The scalar levels also play an important role in communication by providing the home work for the transmission of authority in an organization.

4.9 MANAGEMENT BY OBJECTIVES (MBO)

Management by objectives (MBO) is also referred as results management or management by results. Its main aim is to increase the effectiveness of managers by placing responsibility. It is very popular because of its advantages.

MBO is a process, in which the General Manager and his subordinates of an organization jointly identify the common objectives, define individual's responsibility, and use these measures as guides in achieving the company goals/targets.

Unless clear defined objectives are set, it is not easy to attain company goals. The objectives set must meet the following. requirements-

- Work in the same direction for achieving company goals.
- Clearly define and communicate to all.
- They can be easily attained.
- Flexible for making adjustments.

The nature of the objectives can be of the following types

- *Short term:* Short term objectives are those which are set to bring effect within a short time, For example, expediting, (follow-up) of the works lagging behind the schedule.
- *Long term:* Long term objectives are set to achieve things in a longer duration. For example, planning for a project.
- *Specific:* Specific objectives are related with the nature of goods, customers, type of production, deciding the prices, etc.
- *General:* General objectives are concerned with the nature of business, economic matters, social survival, profit and growth of company.

Advantages of MBO

- It provides a basis for planning and development of policies, budgets and procedures.
- It is a powerful tool for the management to achieve a higher productivity.
- It gives proper direction and necessary responsibility to the people in an organization.
- It coordinates the efforts of various departments of an organization.
- It prevents waste efforts and unnecessary expenditures.
- It provides motivation to people.
- It leads to better understanding between superiors and subordinates.
- It improves employee morale and discipline.

Limitations of MBO

The major limitation is that, the management working by objectives may be rigid in action. For the MBO to be successful, the management thinking should be flexible, but should not affect the decided objectives.

4.10 MANAGEMENT BY EXCEPTION (MBE)

The principle of management by exception was first given by F.W. Taylor in 1919. According to this principle, only unusual or exceptional items of major deviations in daily activities should be brought to the notice of the manager. It states that non deviations from standards should not be brought to his attention.

The theory behind this principle is that once a standard is set for a particular activity, and if it is going on smoothly, there is no point in informing this to the manager, as this is a mere waste of his time as well as the messenger's time. If something in the activity goes wrong and affects the smooth functioning of the progress, and the deviation is such that it could not be solved at the lower level, then that matter should be brought to the notice of the manager and his expert opinion can be sought in resolving the problem.

Advantages of Management by Exception

- Much of the Managers time is saved. It would be, a waste just to listen about the routine standard activities.
- Manager finds more time and feels comfortable to think of improvements.
- Subordinates feel free and take responsibility of the work.
- Because of practice, people at lower level also think and take corrective action for minor problems.
- This principle brings confidence among workers in their work.

Disadvantages of Management by Exception

- Under this principle there is a possibility of misusing the authority by the subordinates. If the subordinate is not a better judge of a minor problem, it might grow to a huge one by the time it is informed to the manager. Also people may not work promptly as they feel more free.

Six Phases of Management by Exception.

(i) Assignment of values, often numbered to past and present performances. Otherwise, it would be impossible to identify the exception.

(ii) Projection of meaningful measurements to business objectives and extend to future.

(iii) Make observation. It is the phase of measurement that informs management about the current state of performance.

(iv) Comparison of actual performance with expected performance to identify those exceptions that require the attention of management.

(v) Reporting the balance to management.

(vi) Decision making: This prescribes the action to be taken to control the performances, adjust exceptions to changing conditions or utilize opportunity.

REVIEW QUESTIONS

1. Explain the nature and purpose of organization.
2. State and explain the principles of organization.
3. What are various types of organizations?
4. What is organization chart? Explain.
5. What are advantages of line and staff organization?
6. What are the functions of staff people?
7. Explain with sketch the line organization.
8. Explain with sketch line and staff organization.
9. Explain functional organization.
10. What is departmentation. Explain the types of departmentation.
11. What are committees? Explain the principles of committees.
12. How committees can be classified?
13. Explain the various types of organization structures.
14. Enumerate the merits and demerits of centralization and decentralization.
15. Explain the process of delegation.
16. What are the difficulties in delegation?
17. Explain span of control.
18. What is management by objectives? Explain MBO.
19. What is management by exception? Explain MBE.
20. Differentiate between MBO & MBE.

CHAPTER 5

STAFFING

Staffing is defined as "filling and keeping filled, positions in the organization structure". It is also known as "human resource management". This includes identifying the requirement of work-force, taking inventory of people available, recruiting, selecting, placing, promoting, appraising, planning the employee's careers, training them to suit the job, developing the staff to carry out the defined job effectively and efficiently.

5.1 NATURE AND IMPORTANCE OF STAFFING

A business cannot be successfully run without the right kind of people. It is very important to fill the jobs with suitable people who will carry out the job effectively. The staffing is very important because of following reasons.

(i) It helps in discovering talented and competent workers and developing them to move the organization ladder.

(ii) Staffing is important to put the right person at right job which results in increased production.

(iii) It avoids sudden disruption of the production due to shortage of workers, since it plans and fills the positions.

(iv) It maintains harmony and creates healthy atmosphere in any organization by planning the promotions, training needs and additional skills required.

(v) It plans the requirement of man power at various time and levels of a project and cater to it.

Elements of staffing:

While carrying out the staffing function, the management should ensure that right people are engaged for a job. The jobs cannot be changed to suit the people. The main elements involved in staffing are:

(i) Proper placement of people.

(ii) Rational recruitment and selection.

(iii) Proper positioning and fixation of salaries.

(iv) Providing necessary training for the people to carry out the job.

(v) Good promotional policies and retirement scheme.

Functions of staffing:

Staffing plays a vital role in organization. It has key roles to play for the well being of any organization. The following are some of the functions of staffing.

(i) Man power planning:

The first function of staffing is to plan the requirement of man power in various levels of organization to achieve the objectives of the organization. Man power planning involves short term and long term. Short term is the immediate requirement of man power to reach the targets where as long term planning involves the requirement of people for future proposed projects.

(ii) Development:

Development means preparing the people of an organization to develop required skills to perform their tasks. This involves training of people.

(iii) Fixing employment standards:

The staffing defines and fixes the responsibilities of people. The specification and qualifications of people to be put on a particular job are prepared.

(iv) Sources of selection:

The staffing identifies and specifies sources of selection like internal or external sources. A position may be filled by people from internal source available with in the organization either by transfer or promotion. External sources may be considered for filling a position from outside organizations.

(v) Selection:

After having identified the sources of selection, next function is selection process. People are selected as per specifications and qualifications set earlier and recruited. The selected people are placed on the job.

(vi) Training:

If required, the selected people are given necessary training to carry out the specific job.

(vii) Routine functions:

In addition to the above functions, the staffing also involves in promotion, transfer, punishment, motivation, welfare, coordination, retirement etc.

5.2 SELECTION

Selection of personnel for the organization is one of the most important managerial responsibilities.

According to the requisition, a primary selection is done for the suitable candidates, to be called for the interview. The final selection is done by the executives in the case of higher posts and for lower posts recruitment, the personnel officer is present in all selections and keeps an eye on the recruitment activities with an aim:

- To find out whether the candidate can be suitable employee. For this, the candidate should be clearly told about the nature of the job, terms and conditions.
- To know the suitability for the particular jobs, he can be cross questioned and thus the suitability can be judged.
- If the selection of the worker, admitted to the firm is not working skillfully then the result will be, either there will be a poor level of work or there will be a high rate of labour turnover. Both will be harmful to the firm in the long run. Therefore every effort should be made to make proper selection.

5.2.1 Techniques of selection

- Application Banks
- Preliminary or Initial Interview
- Interview
- Group discussion
- Employment tests.

(i) Application Bank

It is invariably used as one of the selection tools and can be helpful at the interview stage. It provides actual information needed for evaluating the candidate's suitably. It is also used as a basic record of his personnel data is about educational qualifications, training, experience etc. Many large companies use such application forms which determine, whether the candidate possesses the basic minimum requirement about the Qualifications, Knowledge and Skills or not.

Generally they seek information in the following areas:

- Personnel data such as age, sex, marital status.
- Family background, such as father's and mother's occupation and earnings.

- Educational background including training.
- Employment record including details about previous employment if any and present employment.
- Name and address of few persons usually other than relation to whom references can be made.
- Membership of professional organization.
- Reason for seeking job in the organization.

(ii) Preliminary or Initial interview

This interview is usually of short duration and is aimed at obtaining certain basic information with a view of identifying the knowledge and other information not present in application.

The candidate is asked about his educational skill, knowledge, job experience, minimum salary acceptable etc. Sometimes he is also asked that why he is applying for job in that particular organization. If the candidate seems to be possessing the basic minimum requirement for efficient performance, he is given an application form to fill in.

(iii) Interview

It is one of the least reliable and valid selection techniques. It relies upon a considerable extent in accepting or rejecting a candidate. The interview is left with the inevitable personality variables and for this he has nothing to depend upon except his subjective judgement. The interview may follow a structural pattern or an unstructural pattern.

- **In structural pattern or directive pattern:** In structural pattern of Interviewing, a list of questions based on job specification is prepared in advance. The interview may be occasionally separated from the prepared list of questions and put other questions.

  The candidate is supposed only to answer the questions and the interviewer can learn a lot about the candidate's ability and knowledge, but this technique imposes serious limitation in drawing out his personality. It is not very effective.

- **Unstructural or non-directive or unpatterned :** It is one of the most effective interviewing technique. The interviewer, instead of asking too many questions initiates the candidate to create a kind of permissive atmosphere in which the candidates talks usually quite revealingly about his experiences, aspirations, fear, weakness etc. This kind of interview requires a high degree of interviewing skill and it can therefore be conducted by only trained interviewers.

  In some large organizations, the candidate has to go through a review of two or three panel interviewers. After each panel interviewer some candidates are eliminated and only those candidates, who succeed in the first interview are sent on to the second interviewing panel and so on.

(iv) Group Discussion

In this technique candidates are brought together in group of 6 or 8 persons for informal discussion and the selectors observe them and evaluate them. There are two kinds of group discussions, one where a problem is given to a group to discuss and the individual member is free to choose his own approach. In the second type, each individual is given an initial position and supplied with supporting information to defend his own position.

(V) Employment tests

Most of the large companies use one or other kind of employment tests. Before a company use employment test it should take following points into account.

- Since the tests are aimed at predicting future success in a job situation, they should be selected or designated on the basis of a sound job analysis programme.
- In deciding upon the test to be used as a selection tool, its specialty should be taken into considerations.
- Tests should be valid. Before a test is selected for use as an employment, its validity should be determined in relation to the specific job.

Tests are only one of the techniques of selection. They are not fool proof and therefore instead of using single test, often a batch of tests is used. A variety of test are used as selection tools.

The object of these scientific methods of selection is to ensure that a person selected possesses those physical and mental qualities in required degrees which are essential if he is to become an efficient and successful worker.

- **Intelligence Test:** It is a measure of an individual's capacity of reasoning and verbal comprehension. It is used in the selection and classification of workers for almost every kind of job from the unskilled to the highly skilled, administrative and professional jobs.
- **Vocations Aptitude Test :** Physical strength and general intelligence are not enough to enable a person to perform a task efficiently. Besides, he must posses the ability for the performance of that job. Infact from the point of view of future achievements, a person of high natural ability is likely to prove more successful than one who

through training and experience has gained more knowledge but possesses less natural ability. If this is correct, then it makes it necessary to find out whether the applicant possesses the necessary vocational aptitude or not.

- **Analytical Test:** In this method, a job is analysed in terms of key qualities or abilities as speed and quality of observations, ability to keep one's head and not get confused when a quick decision is called for. A test or a combination of tests are then taken which measure the degree to which these abilities are present or lacking in the candidate.
- **Synthetic Test:** In case of jobs which are complex and for which the analytical tests can't be performed, synthetic tests may be adopted. It presents the candidate a complex situation more or less similar to the one normally present in actual task and his success or failure in the test is accepted as the possession or absence of the required vocational aptitude.

5.3 RECRUITMENT

It is an important step in the employment of labour. Haphazard recruitment of labour brings in a measure of chances and uncertainty in an industry and may result in inefficiency and loss of production. This means that systematic steps should be taken to ensure that right type of persons are available to the concern in right number.

The numbers of workers required by a concern depends on

- The scale of production.
- The degree of mechanization.

Following are the various sources from where the personnel may be recruited:

- Applications introduced by friends and relatives.
- Consulting agencies.
- Campus recruitment.
- Casual callers
- Through advertisement.
- Field trip and college recruitment
- Employment exchange.
- Labour contractors.

- **Applications Introduced by friends and relatives:** Often the employees introduce their relative's application to find a good job for them. Many companies prefer to take such candidates because their background can be known. In this way a good worker can bring a good worker. However this may lead to nepotism and favouritism.

- **Consulting agencies:** A consulting agency is commonly utilised to find specialised executive personnel. It either helps the personnel department by supplementing its efforts or work on its behalf. In such a situation, the agency must understand and estimate correctly the client's past experiences, history and future projections.
- **Campus recruitment:** As a large numbers of management institutes like IIM, XLRI, IIT etc., are engaged in giving the professional training, many companies find it easier to pick up the best talent straight from the institute to fill its managerial position. In fact these professional institutes have provided recruitment source to firms.
- **Casual callers:** Sometimes on his own initiative, the applicant sends his application for the job. The personnel office keeps the record of applications and the suitable candidates can be selected from the callers.
- **Through advertisements:** Companies advertise in the newspaper for their vacancies. Generally the senior posts are filled by this method when they can't be filled by promotions. The advertisement gives a wide range of choice. It also depends upon the employers fame. If the name is not reputed one some of the good personnel do not apply.
- **Field trips and college recruitment:** This method is being used for private industrial firms. These firms send their selecting teams to respective colleges and universities, interview the candidates who are nearing completion of their studies and make selection. This is no doubt very expensive and time consuming but has the advantage of choosing the cream from the lot.
- **Employment exchange:** The recruitment is also done through the employment exchange of the persons who are enrolled in the exchange. The main function of the exchange are:
  - To supply informations about persons in need of jobs and about jobs that are available.
  - To direct persons to factories where suitable jobs exist.
  - To develop job specification.
  - To procure information about current wage rate.
  - To introduce selected employees with personnel department and policies of the company.
  - To follow up the new recruits for initial adjustments.

- To look-after the employee canceling and operating the system seriously.
- To keep records of employees, hired, resigned, discharged and transferred.

Labour Contractors: The casual vacancies may be filled up by the company through labour contractors. Usually unskilled candidates are appointed in this manner.

REVIEW QUESTIONS

1. Explain the nature and importance of staffing.
2. What are the various elements of staffing? Explain.
3. Explain the techniques of selection.
4. What are different types of interview techniques?
5. Explain group discussion.
6. What is recruitment? Explain various sources of recruitment.
7. Differentiate between recruitment and selection.

CHAPTER 6

DIRECTING

6.1 MEANING AND NATURE OF DIRECTING

Direction means issuing of orders, leading and motivating subordinates as they go about executing orders. It is also defined as the process and techniques used for issuing instructions to carry out a job and making sure that the operations are carried out as per the plan.

Directing is the interpersonal aspect of managing by which subordinates are led to understand and contribute effectively and efficiently to the attainment of enterprise objectives. The direction has two major activities namely *(i)* giving orders to employees and *(ii)* leading and motivating them to accomplish the goals.

Definition of direction:

"Directing is the interpersonal aspect of managing by which subordinates are led to understand and contribute effectively to the attainment of enterprise objectives. (Harold D Koontz & O'Donnel)

"Directing consists of the processes and techniques utilized in issuing instructions and making certain that operations are carried on as originally planned". (Haimann)

"Direction is telling people what to do and seeing that they do it to the best of their ability. It includes making assignments, corresponding procedures, seeing that mistakes are corrected, providing on-the-job instruction and issuing orders". (Ernest Dole)

"Directing is the guidance, the inspiration, the leadership of those men and women that constitute the real core of the responsibilities of the management". (Urwick and Breach)

Principles of Direction:

The role of a manager is to understand the needs, motives and attitudes of his subordinates. He should use appreciate strategies according to the people and situations. The following are some of the principles of effective direction:

(i) Harmony of objectives:

For an organization to function well, it the goals of company and goals of individuals are in complete harmony. It is very uncommon for such a situation to exist in any organization. Individual goals may differ from the goals of the organization. The manager should coordinate the individual goals to be in harmony with the goals of the organization.

(ii) Unit direction of command:

This principle implies that an employee should receive orders and instructions only from one supervisor or boss. Otherwise, there may be indiscipline and confusion leading to conflicting orders, divided loyalties and reduced results.

(iii) Efficiency:

If the superior consults with the subordinates in decision-making, then there would be a sense of commitment. This makes the direction easy and improves the efficiency of subordinates.

(iv) Direct supervision:

Managers should have direct face-to-face contact with the subordinates. Personal touch with subordinates will ensure successful direction.

(v) Effective communication:

The supervisor must have good communication skills. He must clearly communicate the plans, goals, policies, responsibilities and the duties to the subordinates. In communication, comprehension is more important than the content.

(vi) Effective control:

The management should monitor the behaviour and performance of subordinates to exercise effective control over subordinates.

(vii) Follow-through:

Direction is a continuous process. Having given the directions may not ensure carrying out them. Hence a manager should follow-through the performance of his subordinates. Follow up is very important function of direction.

6.2 LEADERSHIP

Leadership is an important aspect of managing. Leadership is defined as "Influence, that is, the art or process of influencing people so that they will strive willingly and enthusiastically towards the achievement of group goals". (Koontz and Weihrich) In other words, people should be encouraged to develop not only willingness to work but also willingness to work with zeal and confidence.

"The will to do is triggered by leadership and lukewarm desires for achievements are transformed into burning passion for successive accomplishment by the skilful use of leadership" (George R Terry).

"Leadership is the lifting of man's visions to higher sights, the raising of man's performance to a higher standard, the building of man's personality beyond its normal limitation". (Peter Drucker)

"Leadership is the ability to secure desirable actions from a group of followers voluntarily without the use of coercion." (Alford and Beatty)

"Leadership is the ability to persuade others to seek defined objectives enthusiastically. It is the human factor which binds a group together and motivates it towards goals". (Keith Davis)

6.3 LEADERSHIP STYLES

There are 3 widely used leadership styles or leadership approaches viz., Traits approach, Behavioural approach and Contingency approach.

6.3.1 Traits approach

Trait is basically a character and early notions about leadership dealt with personal abilities. It was believed that some people have leadership qualities by birth or god's gift. The traits that associate with leadership are identified as: mental and physical energy, emotional stability, knowledge of human relations, empathy, objectivity, personal motivation, communication skills, teaching ability, social skills, technical competence, friendliness and affection, integrity and faith, intelligence etc.

This approach has several drawbacks:

- ➢ It failed to identify right traits required for effective leadership.
- ➢ It is difficult to associate the traits with jobs to be carried out. A leader who is successful in one area may be a failure in different area.
- ➢ Since these are subjective, it is difficult to measure their effectiveness quantitatively.
- ➢ This approach implies that leadership is in-built quality and no training can make a person leader.

6.3.2 Behavioural approach

Several studies have been made did not agree as to which traits are leadership traits or their relationship to actual instances of leadership. It is found that most of these so called traits are really pattern of behaviour.

There are several theories based on leadership behaviour and styles. Some of them are:

(i) Leadership based on the use of authority.

(ii) Likert's four systems of managing.

(iii) The managerial grid and

(iv) Leadership involving a variety of styles and level of use of power and influence.

(i) Style based on authority: Based on how the authority is used, the leaders are styled into 3 groups.

- The first is "autocartic leader" who commands and expects compliance, is dogmatic and positive, and leads by the ability to withhold or give rewards and punishment.
- The second is "democratic or participative leader" who consults with subordinates on proposed actions and decisions and encourages participation from them. This type of leaders include the person who does not take action without the concurrence of subordinates and who makes decisions but consults with subordinates before doing so.
- The third type is "free-rein" leader who uses his power very little and gives a high degree of independence to his subordinates to carryout their work. Such leaders depend largely on subordinates to set their own goals and the means to achieve.

Figure below shows the flow of influence in the three situations of leadership.

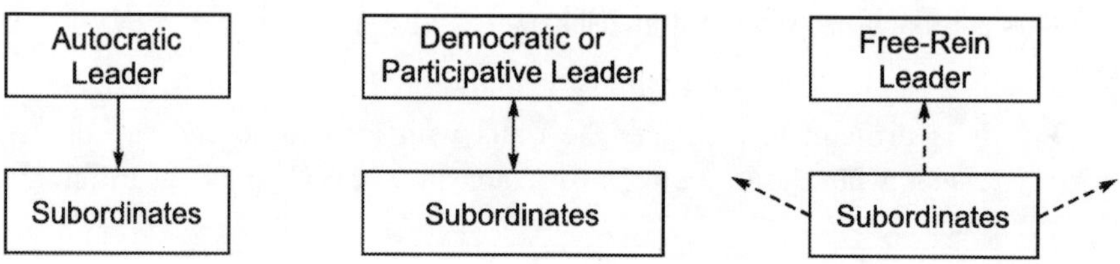

The flow of influence with three leadership styles

There are some variations within this simple classification of leadership styles. Some democratic leader may consult and listen to their followers ideas and concerns, but when decision is to be made, they make their own decision. A participative leader is the person who is supportive. They consult with their subordinates and take their opinions, feelings and suggestions before making decision.

The use of any style will depend on the situation. A manager may be autocratic in routine and emergency tasks. Leaders gain considerable knowledge and better commitment on the part of persons involved by consulting with subordinates whereas 'free-rein' type leadership works better in R & D organizations.

Comparison of leadership styles

Factor	Leadership style		
	Autocratic	**Participative**	**Free-Rein**
1. Decision maker	Leader only	Leader in consultation with subordinates	Subordinates only
2. Discipline	Obey the leader	Cooperative	Self-imposed
3. Delegation of authority	Rare	Good	Complete
4. Responsibility	Leader	Leader and subordinates	Individuals
5. Initiative	By leader	By team	Only by individuals
6. Communication	One way and downward	Both ways	Free flow
7. Motivation	Punishments	Rewards	Self motivated
8. Hierarchy of needs	Physiological and safety	Mixed	Self attenuation
9. Focus	Task oriented	People oriented	People

(ii) Likert's four systems of management: Prof. Likert had developed four systems of management based on his study of patterns and styles of leadership.

System 1: Management is described as "exploitive-authoritative". Its managers are highly autocratic, have little trust in subordinates. They motivate people through fear and punishment, only occasional rewards, engage downward communication and limit decision making to the top.

System 2: This is called "benevolent authoritative". Its managers have a patronizing confidence and trust in subordinates, motivate them with rewards and some fear and punishment, allows little upward communication, solicits some ideas and opinions from subordinates, allows some delegation of decision making but with close policy control.

System 3: This is referred to as "consultive" management. Managers in this system have substantial but not complete confidence in subordinates. They usually try to make use of the ideas and opinions of subordinates, rewards for motivation, occasional punishments, engage in communication in both up and down and act like a consultant to both top and subordinates.

System 4: This is most participative type and hence it is often called as "participative-group". These managers have complete trust and confidence in subordinates in all matters. The always get ideas and opinions from subordinates and use them for constructive purpose. They give monitory rewards, encourage decision making and work with subordinates as a group.

(iii) The managerial grid: A well-known approach to defining leadership styles is the managerial grid developed by Robert-Blake and Jane Mouton. Building on previous history which dealt with managers concerned with both people and production, they deviced a two dimensional grid based on people and production. "Concern for production" on X-axis of grid includes the attitudes of a supervisor towards a variety of things such as quality of policy decisions, procedures, creativeness, staff services, work efficiency, volume of output etc. "Concern for people" is taken on Y-axis of grid. This includes elements like degree of personal commitment towards good achievement, maintenance of self-esteem of workers, placement of responsibility on the basis of trust rather than obedience, provision of goal working conditions and maintenance of satisfying interpersonal relations.

The managerial grid is a useful device for identifying and classifying managerial styles, but it does not tell how to lead.

(iv) Leadership involving a variety of styles: This concept is also called as leadership continnum. It is seen that the leadership involves a variety of styles ranging from one which is highly boss centered to the other which is highly subordinate concerned. The style vary with the degree of freedom a leader or manager grants to his subordinates. Thus instead of suggesting a choice between two extreme styles of leadership autocratic and democratic, this approach offers a range of styles with no suggestion of what is right and what is wrong. This theory recognizes that which type of leadership is appropriate depends on the leader, the subordinates and the situation.

6.3.3 Contingency approach to leadership

The behavioural approach seems to suggest that the best style of leadership is one that combines both autocratic and democratic. There is no one best style of leadership under all conditions. Effective leadership style varies with situation. The effective leaders need to analyse the situation and find the most appropriate and best-suited style for a given environment. Contingency approaches have much meaning for managerial theory and practice.

6.4 MOTIVATION

6.4.1 Introduction

Management is an art of getting the work done by the people and thereby achieving the best results. Getting the work done, depends upon the inducement of the people to better their performance by inspiring the personnel with a zeal to do work for the accomplishment of objectives of the organization. It may rightly be called motivation of people, the most important function of the personnel management. Management should constantly provide for incentives or motivating forces to intensify their desire and willingness to apply their potentialities for the achievement of common objectives. Some people may be motivated by the intense outer pressures of reward while some others are self-motivated.

Motivation is derived from 'motive'. Motive means any idea, need, emotion or organic state that prompts a man to an action. Motive is an internal factor that integrates a man's behaviour. As the motive is within the individual, it is necessary to study the needs, emotions etc., in order to motivate him to do work. There are certain inducing factors which influence the man's behaviour and induce him for the best performance to meet his needs and emotions. So motivation is a process to get the needs of the people realised with a view to induce him to do work. Indeed motivation is nothing but an action of inducement.

Motivation has been defined by Edwin B. Flippo as follows:

- Motivation is the process of attempting to influence others to do your will through the possibility of gain or reward.
- Motivation is the process consisting of the three parts (a) motives, (b) the needs, drives, desires, aspirations ect., which are the motivating factors (c) attainment of the objectives.

6.4.2 Characteristics of Motivation

The following are the characteristics of motivation.

- **Motivation is a Psychological Concept:** Motivation should come from inside each individual. There are two desiring factors, in motivation:
  - (i) Fundamental needs, such as food, clothes and shelter and
  - (ii) Ego-satisfaction including self-esteem, recognition from others, opportunities for achievement, self-development and self-actualisation, which act as powerful, though unconscious, motivators of behaviour.
- **The whole individual is motivated, not part of him:** A person's basic needs determine to a great extent what he will try to do at any given time. All these needs are interrelated because each individual is an integrated organised whole.
- **Motivation is an unending process:** Man is a social animal. As a social animal he has innumerable wants which induce him to work. If one basic need is adequately satisfied for a given individual it loses power as a motivator and does not determine his current behaviour, but at the same time others needs continue to emerge. Wants are innumerable and cannot be satisfied at one time. It is an unending process so the process of motivation is also unending to induce the person to satisfy his innumerable wants.
- **Frustration of basic needs makes a man sick:** If anybody fails in trying to meet a need which he feels is essential for him, he becomes to some extent, mentally ill and such frustrated man cannot be motivated any further, until his essential need is satisfied.
- **Goal are motivators:** Goals and motives are inseparable. Man works to achieve the goals. As soon as the goal is achieved he would be no longer interested in work. Therefore, it is very essential for the management to know his goal to push him to work.
- **The self-concept as a unifying force:** Unifying force means the drive to actualise his own image of himself. The outlines of a person's self image are fairly well checked in early childhood and there after do not act inner change. For example, a child who easily seems himself as a leader, will if possible try to behave that way in later life. Thus, two things that individual is always trying to do are:
  - (i) to act like the person he thinks he is, and
  - (ii) to get what he thinks he can.

Motivation is an important function of personnel management because management of personnel means getting the work done by the people to achieve the organizational objectives. Motivation is one of the methods to induce the man on the job to get the work done effectively to have the best results towards the common objectives. Motivation is necessary for the better performance.

The expected results from motivation are as follows:

- **Best utilisation of Resources:** All other resources (except human resource) can produce no results unless the man tries to put them into action. Man should be motivated to carry out the plans, policies and programmers laid down by the organization by utilising the other resources to the best of their efforts.
- **Will to Contribute:** A distinction should be made between capacity to work and willingness to work. A man can be physically, mentally and technically fit to work but he may not be willing to work. Motivation concerns to create a need and desire on the part of the workman to present his better performance.
- **Reduction in labour problems:** All the members try to concentrate their efforts to achieve the objectives of the organization and carry out the plans in accordance with the policies and programmes laid down by the organization. If the management introduces motivational plans, it reduces the labour problems like labour turnover, absenteeism, in-discipline, grievances etc., because their real wages increase by the motivational plans.
- **Sizable increase in production and productivity:** Motivation induces the men to work hence it results in increased production and productivity because men try to put their efforts to produce more and more and thus their efficiency increases.
- **Basis of co-operation:** In a zeal to produce more, the members work as a team to pull the weight effectively, to get their loyalty to the group and the organization, to carry out properly the activities allocated and generally to play an efficient part in achieving the purposes which the organization has undertaken. Thus motivation is basis of cooperation to get the best results out of the efforts of the men on the job.
- **Improvement upon skill and knowledge:** All the members will try to be as efficient as possible and will try to improve upon their skill and knowledge so that they may be able to contribute to the progress of the organization.

6.4.3 Positive and Negative Motivation

Motivation is concerned with inspiring the man to work to get the best possible results. It may be done by two ways:

- by positive motivation and
- by negative motivation.

(i) Positive Motivation

In the real sense, motivation means positive motivation. Positive motivation makes the people induce to do their work in the best possible manner they can and improve their performance. It provides better facilities and rewards to them for their better performance. Such rewards and facilities may be financial and non-financial. Financial or monetary motivation may include different incentive wage plans, productive bonus schemes etc. Non-financial or non-monetary motivation may include promotion, praise for the work, participation in management, social recognition etc. Monetary incentives provide the worker a better standard of life while the non-monetary motivation satisfies the ego of the man.

(ii) Negative Motivation

Negative motivation aims at controlling the negative efforts of the workers and so inducing the man to work positively in the interest of the organization. It is based on the concept that if the man fails in achieving the desired results, he should be punished. Punishments, reprimands, fear of loss of job are some of the methods which are usually taken as a means to direct the man in the desired direction. Under this method man works in fear and tends to produce minimum enough to get by safety. The negative motivation may also be classified into monetary and non-monetary motivation. Wages may be cut in case he produces below the standard fixed, keeps himself away the work and creates indiscipline in the organization. The non-monetary negative motivation may include reprimands, cut in facilities and greater control on the activities etc. This is based on the presumption that man works because of fear.

Though both the methods of motivation – positive and negative aim at inspiring the will of the people to work but the two differ in their approaches. Positive approach has no place for punishment whereas the negative approach does not provide for rewards. In this sense both are opposite to each other and may be regarded as two ends of a rod.

6.4.4 Human Needs

The central problem of motivation, as far as management of an organization is concerned, is how to induce the people because the psychology and behaviour of people differ from one another. A manager should invariably, know before planning for motivation, why people work. In order to take effective motivational decision the manager should study and try to understand the behaviour of people at work and thus plan to motivate it in the desired direction.

For this purpose, manager must have knowledge of the motives of the worker which bring about purposeful behaviour and induce him to behave in a particular manner. These motives are known as 'needs' or 'wants'. These are drives to work. They have direct influence on the individual, since they determine in part his thoughts and actions.

Need can be defined as a condition requiring supply or relief, the lack of any requisite, desired or useful. A motivating situation has both subjective and objective aspect. The subjective side is a need, a drive or a desire. The objective side is called the incentive or goal. When the process of obtaining the incentive satisfies the needs, the situation is described as motivating.

6.4.5 Maslow's theory of motivation

Abraham Maslow was the pioneer in contributing a systematic scheme of need hierarchy. He arrived at a conclusion, after a proper research, that there are certain perceived needs of the employees which they expect to be satisfied by joining any organization. If the perceived needs are satisfied according to the satisfaction, they feel satisfied and motivated and if there is a gap between the two, they become slow or refuse to work,

Maslow's hierarchy of needs

Maslow has suggested that the underlying needs for all human motivation can be organised in a hierarchical manner on five general levels,

They are (i) Physiological needs (ii) Safety needs (iii) Social needs (iv) Esteem needs and (v) Self-actualization.

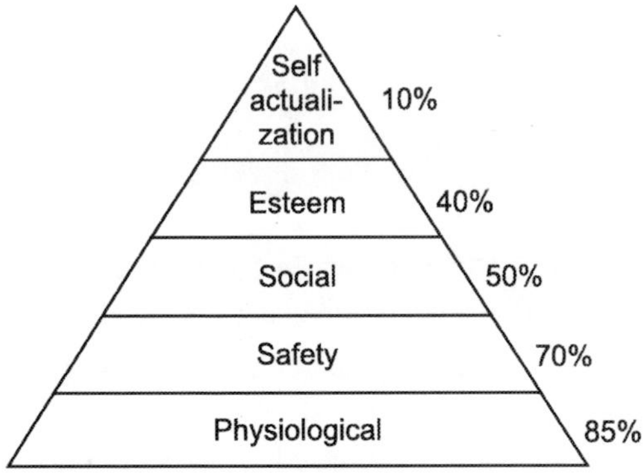

- **Physiological needs:** At the lowest order level are physiological needs which include the need for food, water, sex, clothing and shelter. For a human being who lacks every thing the major motivation would be such physiological needs.

If these needs are not satisfied, other needs will not emerge.

- **Safety needs:** When the physiological needs are satisfied, the safety needs become the most important in the hierarchy. These are the needs for protection against danger or loss of existing physiological needs.
- **Social needs**: The third level in the hierarchy comprises the social needs, that is the giving and receiving of love, friendship, affection, belongingness, association and acceptance. If the first two levels are fairly well satisfied, then a person becomes keenly aware of the absence of friends or of a sweetheart, and will be motivated toward affectionate relations with people in general.
- **Esteem needs:** At the fourth level in the hierarchy are the esteem needs (ego needs), which are generally classified in to two subsets. The first subset includes the needs for achievement, strength and freedom. In essence this is the need for independence. The second sub set includes the needs for status, recognition, and prestige. In essence this is the need for self-esteem or self-worth.
- **Self actualization:** The fifth and highest level in hierarchy is the self-actualization need. This is the need to realize one's potentialities for continued self-development and the desire to become more and more of what one is and what one is capable of becoming. This is also known as self realization or self attenuation.

  For Example: A musician must create music, an artist must paint, a poet must write in order to achieve ultimate satisfaction.

In 1943 Maslow arbitrarily suggested that in general, our physiological needs are generally 85% satisfied, the safety needs 70% satisfied, the social needs 50%, satisfied, the esteem needs 40% satisfied and the self actualization needs 10% satisfied.

6.4.6 Behaviour

Behaviour is basically goal oriented. In other wards, our behaviour is generally motivated by a desire to attain same goal.

The basic unit of behaviour is an activity. In fact any behaviour is a series of activities and motives. The motivation of people depends on the strength of their motives. Motives are defined as needs, wants, drives, with in the individual. Motives are the ways of behaviour. They arouse and maintain activity and determine the general direction of the behaviour of an individual.

6.4.7 Goals

Goals are out side of an individual. They are referred to as hopes for rewards towards which motives are directed. Managers who are successful in motivating employees are often providing an environment in which appropriate goals are available for need satisfaction.

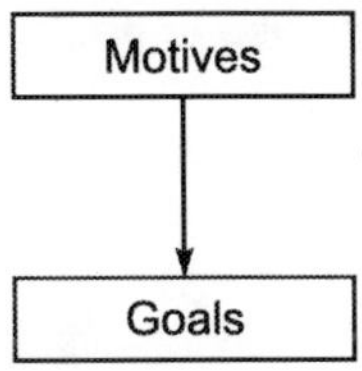

Motives are directed toward goals.

Motive Strength

This can be defined as the need which has the highest strength at any given time. If a need is satisfied the motive strength for the particular need will decrease at that particular time.

Changes in motive strength

A motive tends to decrease in strength if it is either satisfied or blocked from satisfaction.

Need Satisfaction

When a need is satisfied according Maslow, it is no longer a motivator of behaviour. High strength needs that are satisfied are some times referred to as "satisfied".

Example: If a high strength need is thirst, drinking tends to lower the strength of this need, and afterwards the other needs may now became more important.

Blocking need Satisfaction

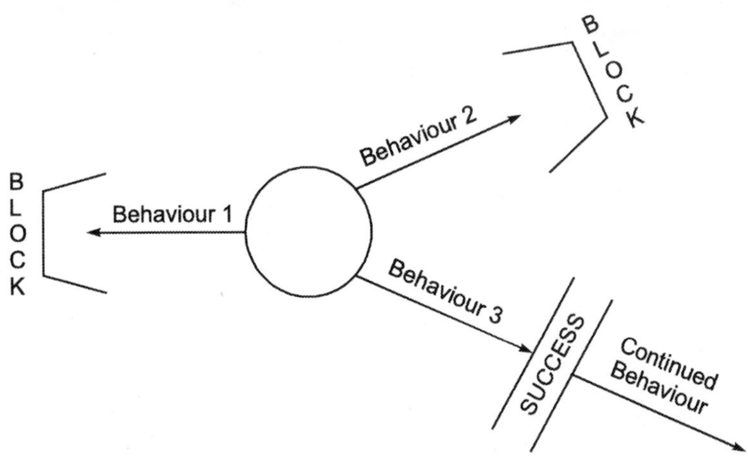

The satisfaction of a need may be blocked. If there is a high motive strength for attaining a particular goal the individual may behave in various ways to attain a goal. If all the ways are blocked either by imaginary or real barriers, then frustration can take place. Frustration can take in different forms.

Example : Regression, Fixation

Frustration

The blocking or thwarting of goal attainment is referred to as frustration. This is defined in terms of the condition of the individual rather than in terms of the external environment. A person may be frustrated by an imaginary barrier and may fail to be frustrated by a real barrier.

Aggression, Rationalization, regression, fixation and resignation are all symptoms of frustration.

Increasing Motive Strength

Behaviour may change if an existing need increases in strength. The strength of some needs tends to appear in a cyclical pattern.

Example: The need for food tends to recur regardless of how well it has been satisfied at a given moment.

Categories of activities

Activities resulting from high strength can be classified in to goal directed activity and goal activity.

- **Goal directed activity:** It is motivated behaviour directed at reaching a goal.

  Example : If one's strongest need at a given moment is hunger, various activities such as looking for a place to eat, buying food or preparing food would be considered goal-directed activities.

- **Goal-activity :** It is engaging in the goal itself.

  Example: In case of hunger, food is the goal and eating is the goal activity.

6.4.8 Motivating Situation

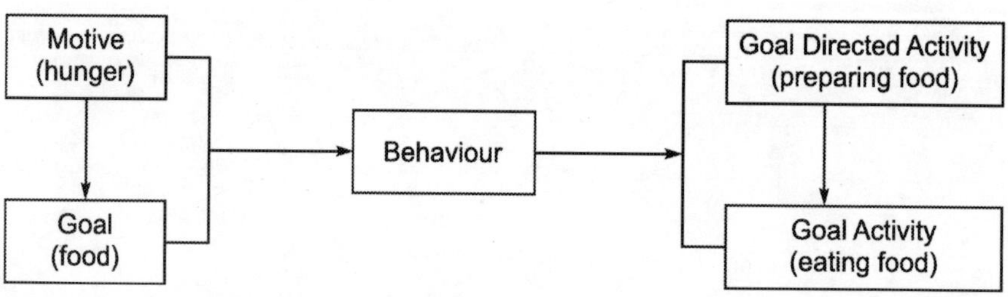

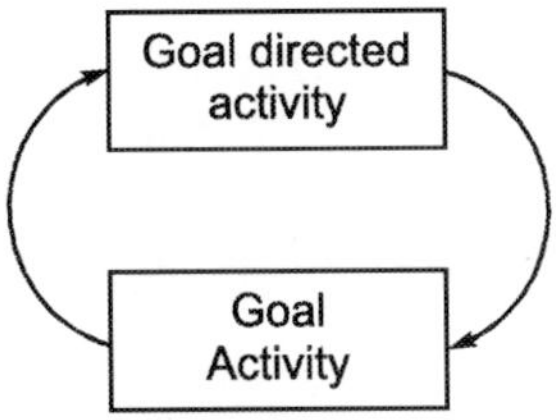

6.4.9 Expectancy and Availability

Two important factors that effect strength of needs are expectancy and availability.

Expectancy

It is the perceived probability of satisfying a particular need of an individual based on past experience. Expectancy can be either actual or vicarious. Vicarious behaviour comes form sources such as parents, teachers and books etc.

Example: Suppose a boy's father is a cricket star and the boy also wants to become a cricketer. In the beginning his motive strength will be very high, but if he is not selected year after year, then his expectancy of being a cricket star decision will slowly die and finally he may give up hopes of being a cricket star.

Availability

This reflects the perceived limitations of the environment. It is determined by how the goals that can satisfy a given need by an individual.

Example: If a person is watching a TV in the night and if current goes off he can not watch TV or read. This goal activity is limited by the external factors. So the individual may settle for sleeping. This availability is variable of environment.

In this situation there seems to be a general disregard for the welfare of the organization.

6.4.10 Goal oriented behaviour

Since in every human being there is some need or the other, there will also a goal for every human being. He works to achieves the goal. This is goal oriented behaviour.

An organization can be considered as collective of individuals with one particular goal. It may so happen very often that the goals of the management do not coincide with the goals of the individual. When this happens the organization will not prosper. If the goal of the individual can be made parallel to the goals of the organization then the organization will be profited. This can be represent by means of vector diagram as shown below:

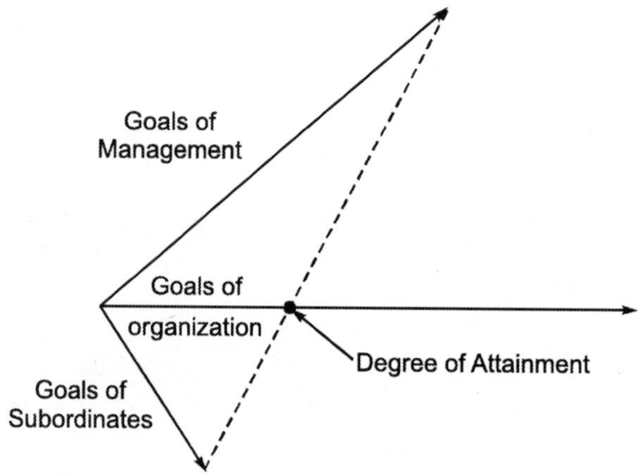

In this, the result of the interaction between the goals of management and the goals of subordinates is a compromise and actual performance is a combination of both. This situation can be much worse when there is little accomplishment of organizational goals.

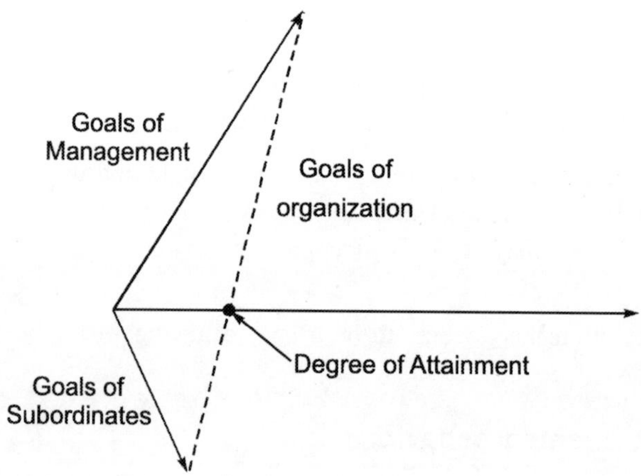

Both managers and workers see their own goals, conflicting with those of the organization.

In some cases, the organizational goals can be so opposed that no positive progress is obtained and resulting in losses.

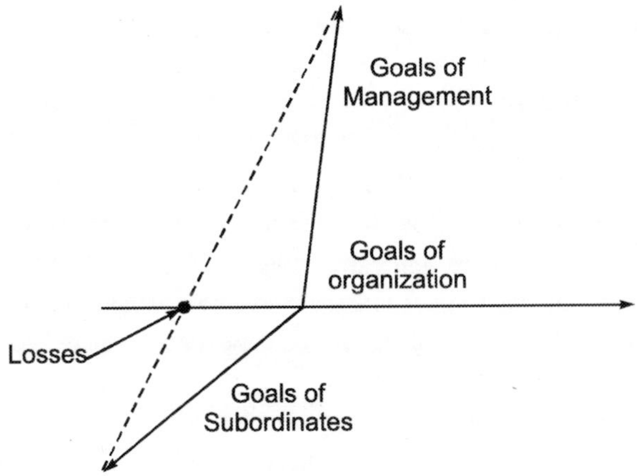

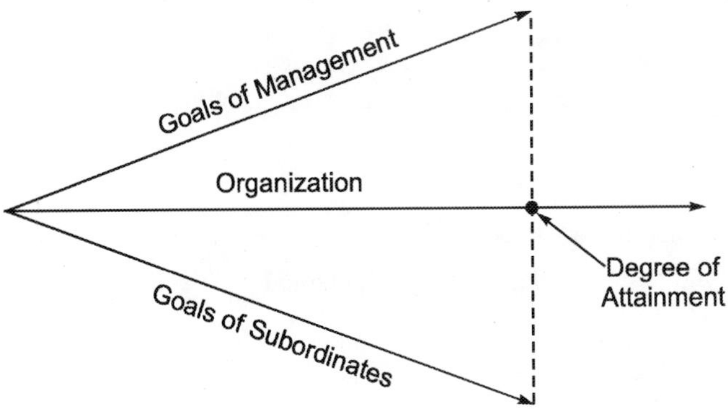

The hope in an organization is to create a climate in which the two things occurs. The closer we can get the individuals goals and objective to the organization goals the greater will be the organizational performance as shown here.

6.4.11 Integration of organizational goals and needs of an employee

The goals of organization mainly are increasing the production and process. The needs of the employee also must be the same as that of the organization. For this the basic needs must be satisfied i.e., the physiological, safety, and social needs must be satisfied.

- **Physiological needs:** Money is the goal; for this need money satisfies other needs as well. So workers will demand higher wages and other financial benefits.

- **Safety:** Free from hazards of life, accidents, diseases, wars, etc., are the goals for the need of safety. Insurance for life, accident, health, promise for retirement benefits etc., are the best measures to satisfy the need of safety. Security of job is a very important goal.
- **Social need:** This is expressed in the form of co-operation tendency of workers. They join groups of similar belief oriented people.
- **Esteem:** Which are generally classified into two subjects. The first subject includes the needs for achievement, strength and freedom. In essence this is the need for independence. The second sub-set includes the needs for status, recognition, and prestige. In essence this is the need for self-esteem or self-worth.
- **Self actualization:** This is the need to realize one's potentialities for continued self-development and the desire to become more and more of what one is and what one is capable of becoming.

6.4.12 Needs of an employee

Maslow told motives are those which are still not satisfied. So accordingly the workers want the following:

- Full appreciation of their work
- Feeling in the things
- Sympathetic understanding of personal problems
- Job security
- Good manager
- Good wages
- Promotion and growth with company
- Management loyalty with workers
- Good working conditions
- Tactful discipline

6.4.13 Hawthorne Studies and its findings

In 1924, experts at a Hawthorne plant of the Western Electric Company, USA., decided to study the effect of illumination on productivity. It is one of the most famous studies in the history of human relation.

In the beginning of studies the efficiency experts assumed that the out put increases with illumination for that the expert selected two groups of employees: Control group and the Test group.

The control group worked under normal lighting. The test group worked under various light conditions. As the lighting was increased the out put of the test group also increased as expected. But the out put of the control group also increased. But this was unexpected. The experts could not explain this. Elton Mayo of the Harward University tried to explain this:

They increased and improved the working conditions of the workers in the control group and the output was correspondingly high. After one and half years the team suddenly brought the conditions back to normal. They expected to have a negative psychological impact on the women workers and reduce the output. But the out put jumped to all time high.

So, Hawthorne research found out that the workers were motivated to work more when the benefit was decreased. The workers wanted to get the same level of benefit so they work hard to get the benefit and therefore production increases or this can also be due to level of self actualization, in which case the workers realized their true potential and did their jobs perfectly. From these researches, they concluded that there is something more than Maslow's hierarchy of needs which motivates the person. They found this to be another theory and later experts like Douglas Mc Gregor called the same as Theory – X and Theory – Y and Chris Argyrious also exposed it as Maturity and Immaturity Theory.

6.4.14 Theory X and theory Y

The findings of Elton Mayo helped Douglas Mc Gregor to form his theory of human nature which is called Theory X and Theory Y.

Theory X assumed that the most people are not willing to assume responsibility. They do not like to work and they like to be directed. After defining theory X, he then questioned whether these views of human nature are correct and if management practice based upon it are correct.

Basing his analysis on Maslow's hierarchy of needs, he concluded that the theory X is wrong. Therefore he developed another theory. This is called Theory-Y. This assumed that people are not lazy by nature. The work is as natural as play and people can work naturally if motivated properly.

Theory X

- Work is inherently distasteful to most people.
- Most people are not ambitious, have little desire for responsibility and they prefer to be directed.
- Most people have little capacity for creativity in solving organization problems.
- Motivation occurs only at the physiological and safety levels.
- Most people must be closely controlled or often forced to achieve organization objectives.

Theory Y

- Work is as natural as play if the conditions are favourable.
- Self control is often responsible in achieving organization goals.
- The capacity for creativity in solving organization problems is widely distributed in population.
- Motivation occurs at the social esteem and self-actualization levels as well as physiological and security levels.
- People can be self directed and creative at work if properly motivated.

The idea one may get that theory X is manager is usually direct. They like controlling people and they supervise people very closely. Theory Y manager is directly opposite to the theory X manager. They are more supporting and appreciative.

Let us not assure that theory is X good and theory Y is bad or vise verse. For the particular given situation and particular worker for a given job, a manager should choose either theory X or theory Y.

A manger who adapts theory X will be of the type who orders people and is more task oriented. A manager who adopts theory Y will be more relation oriented and will care for worker. But only a combination of both theory X and theory Y will give a manger good control over his group. So a manager should adopt theory X with a particular person and theory Y with the another and so on.

6.4.15 Immaturity – Maturity theory

This theory was developed by Chris Argyrious of the Harward University. This theory is better than Douglas Mc. Gregor's Theory X and Theory Y.

According to him, a person will develop from immaturity to maturity in the following seven stages:

- People become adults from infants.
- They become from a dependent to relatively independent persons.
- They are at this state behaving more like adults and less like infants.
- Their interest as adults increases till their interest as children become very little.
- They develop longer time perspective than children.
- They become independent form depending stages.
- They develop awareness of self.

Maturity Theory	Immaturity Theory
Active	Passive
Independence	Dependence
Capable of behaving in many ways	Behave in a few ways
Deeper and stronger interest	Erratic shallow interests
Long time perspective	Short time perspective
Equal or super ordinate position	Subordinate position
Awareness and control over self	Lack of awareness of self.

6.4.16 Motivation-Hygiene Theory

This theory was developed by Frederick Herzberg of the University of Utah was the basis of effective utilization of human resources. Herzberg began collecting information on job attitude from over 200 engineers and accountants from various industries in Pittsburgh area. In this interview the people were asked about what kinds of things on their jobs made them dissatisfied or unhappy and what made them satisfied or happy.

In analyzing the data he came to a conclusion that people can be divided into two categories dissatisfied and satisfied. When people are satisfied they are concerned with work it self. He called this as motivation factor. While when they were dissatisfied, they were concerned about the environment in which they were working. He called this as hygiene factor.

Hygiene Factors

Company policies, administration supervision, money status, security etc., may be thought of as hygiene factors. These are not an integral part of the job but are related to the conditions under which a job is performed. Hygiene factor has not produced a growth in worker's output capacity, but only prevent output losses in worker performance due to work retraction.

In analysis of the data, it was concluded that the people have two categories of needs. The following is the comparison between hygiene factors and motivators.

Hygiene Factors	Motivating Factors
Environment	The job it self
Policies and administration	Achievement
Supervision	Recognition for accomplishment
Working conditions	Challenging conditions
Inter-personal relations	Increased responsibility
Money, status, and security	Growth and development.

Motivator

Feeling which produces feelings of achievement, recognition in jobs can be called motivator. These motivators often increase the productivity. If the motivation hygiene theory is applied to Maslow's hierarchy of needs, one will come to a situation of the type shown below:

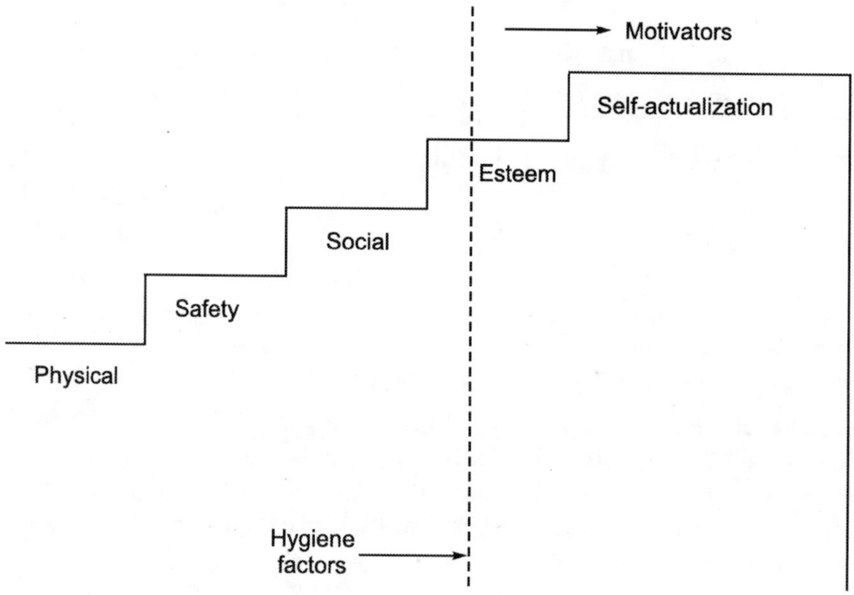

As be seen from the above figure, the lower of Maslow's hierarchy of needs came under hygiene factors, i.e., physiological safety, social needs are completely by hygiene factors, while esteem is half hygiene and half motivating factor. Self actualization is a completely motivation factor.

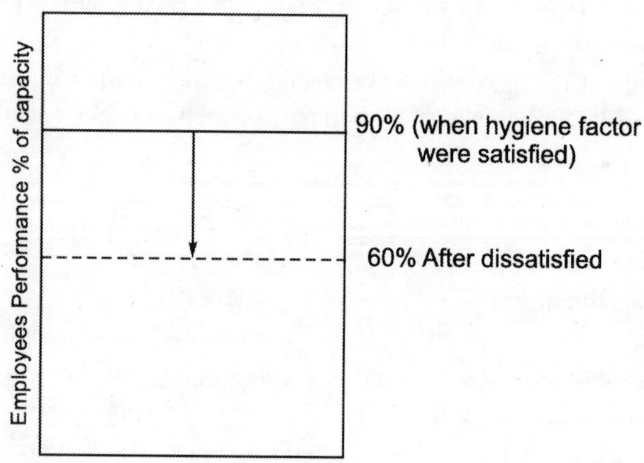

Effect of dis-satisfying Hygiene

Let us assume that a man is highly motivated and is working at a 90% capacity. He has good working relationship with his supervisors. He will be satisfied with his working conditions. Let us also assume that his supervisor is suddenly transferred and a person who is unable to work with him becomes his supervisor, then the man is dissatisfied. His capacity for work falls to 60%.

6.5 COMMUNICATION

Communication is the process of transmitting ideas or thoughts from one person to another, for the purpose of creating understanding in the thinking of the person receiving the ideas or information.

It can also be said that communication is an exchange of facts, ideas, opinions or emotions by two or more persons. The effectiveness of communication largely depends upon the proper understanding of what is being communicated and what is being received at the other end. The correct interpretation and understanding of the messages is important from the point of view of organizational efficiency. As such the greater the degree of understanding present in communication, the more likely-hood that the human action will proceed in the direction of accomplishing organizational goals.

6.5.1 Systems of communication

- According to organizational structure.
  (a) Formal and (b) Informal
- According to direction of expression
  (a) Downward (b) Upward (c) Horizontal
- According to the way of expression
  (a) Oral or verbal (b) Written.

(i) Formal Communication

Such communications are those which are associated with the formal organizations structure. They travel through the formal channels. These communications include orders, instructions, decisions etc., of the supervisor. Thus it is a deliberate attempt to regulate the flow of organizational communication so as to make it orderly and thereby to ensure that the information flows smoothly, accurately and timely. This officially prescribed communication network may be designed on the basis of single or multiple channel. A single channel network prescribes only one path of communication for any particular position and all communications have to necessarily flow through one path only. This path is the line of authority linking its line supervisor and it is commonly referred to as "through proper channel". Its implication is that all communication to and from a position should flow through the line supervisor and subordinates only.

Merits

- **Maintenance of authority of the officers:** It helps in exercising control over subordinates and fixation of responsibility in respect of activity to be carried out by a person in the organization.
- **Sound and proper communication:** An immediate supervisor has a direct contact with his subordinates. He/She understands their attitudes, wants, level of intelligence and capacities. He/She can determine efficiently as to how, what and when the information is to be communicated to whom. It is easy to maintain and is orderly in nature.

Demerits

- **Overload of work:** In a modern business organization, there is a lot of information, messages and other things to be communicated. All these, if transmitted through formal line of authority only, it will increase the work level on the line officers and they will not be able to perform their duties well.
- **Decay in accuracy:** It provides bottlenecks in the flow of information. It exhausts the original distance also and channels of more information at various positions, recode the accuracy of message.
- **Over look by the line officers :** Communication through chains of command is not suitable for upward communication at all. Line officers do not take any interest in their subordinates. They do not like to forward the suggestions to the top management given by their subordinates. This bias changes the nature and characteristic of information at all levels when it reaches its final destination.

Limitations

- The formal communication is useful only in downward communication. One way of overcoming this limitation is to provide a number of communication channels linking one position with various other positions. Thus the system of multiple channels may improve the situation in some cases, but an unlimited use of this may cause confusion and also undermine the supervisors authority. So along with formal communication, the informal channel should also be developed for efficient and effective communication within the enterprise.

(ii) Informal communication

It is also known as grape wine communication. The communication to be made through informal channels of communication is called informal communication. It is not the result of official action but of the operation of personnel, social and group relationship of people. Apart from these formal organizational relationship, people have got social or personnel relationship, membership of some club or organizations from same place.

Such channels of communication serve as a quick vehicle for messages. While formal communication exists to meet the utility and needs of the organization, informal communication is the method by which people carry on their non programmed activities within the formal boundaries of the system. Such type of communications are very fast, spontaneous and flexible. It is a very active channel of communication through which the information is carried immediately.

Merits

- It performs a positive service to the organization.
- It operates with much greater speed.
- The informal communications fulfil needs of various person in the organization, more particularly those persons who freely mix up with others and rely upon informal relationship.
- A typical informal committee network involves people within the same level of an organization.

Demerits

- It is less orderly and less static.
- Messages communicated through informal channels, sometimes are very erratic and uncertain, and any action taken based upon these may lead to difficult situation to the organization.
- Often it carries incinerate information, half-truths, rumours and distorted information.
- Origin and direction of the flow of information is hard to pin point.
- There is a chance that by the time a communication completes a complex journey it may be distorted.

Limitations

- The informal communication is the part and parcel of the organizational process. The only thing the management can do in this respect is to take suitable actions to minimise the adverse affect of such channels. Proper analysis of informal communication and a suitable classification in this respect would be helpful in making its use towards organizational efficiency.

iii) According to the direction of communication

Downward Communication: Communication which flows from supervisor to the subordinate is known as downward communication. They include orders, rules, instructions, society directions etc. Their nature is directive. It would be impossible to manage an enterprise without downward communication.

Upward communication: This is just the reverse of the downward communication. It flows from subordinate to supervisor. Each communication includes reactions and suggestions from workers, their grievances etc. The contents of the upward communication are reports, suggestions, reaction, statements and proposals prepared for submissions to the supervisors. There was very little application of this forms of communication sometime before as it does not fit into the traditional theory of organization. But in modern times upward communication is considered to be main source of motivation to employees.

Horizontal communication: When communication takes place between two or more persons who are subordinates of the same person or those who are working on the same levels of the organization, this communication is known as horizontal communication or lateral communication or cross communication. The communication between functional managers, among superintendents working under some supervisor, meetings of General Manager's of various factories are some of the examples of such communication. This type of communication may be oral or written.

(iv) According to the way of expression.

Oral or vertical communication: In this type of communication both parties to the process of communication exchange their ideas orally either face to face or through devices like phone, intercoms etc., meetings, conference, lectures, interviews or other ideas.

Written communication : In this type of communication, written words, graphs, diagrams, pictures, etc., are used. They may take forms of circulars, rules, manuals, reports, porters, memos etc.

6.5.2 Barriers to successful communication

- More levels in organization structure through which an information has to pass.
- Long and instructured channels of communication.

- Heavy work loads at certain level of organization.
- Prestige and superiority complex.
- Sender unable to symbolise the information correctly.
- Prejudicial and biased attitude of the receiver.
- Receiver ignoring conflicting information.
- Receiver tending to evaluate information from his own angle.

6.5.3 Techniques to overcome barriers and improve communication

- Sending direct and simple messages using many channels
- Feedback system to know whether the manager has been understood correctly or not.
- Adopting face to face communication.
- Time the message carefully, communicate when the receiver is motivated to listen.
- Be sensitive to the private world of the receiver, try to predict the impact on his feeling and attitude and tailor the message to fit receivers vocabulary, interests and values.
- Introduce a proper amount of redundancy of in the message i.e., some amount of repetitions of information so that it is not misunderstood.

6.6 COORDINATION

6.6.1 Meaning

Various departments of an organization will be performing different tasks as assigned to them on the basis of their specialisation. It is essential to coordinate these activities to achieve common objectives collectively. Coordination is the process which ensures smooth ensuring of the functions of management with the increase in the departmentation, coordination has become important.

Definition: The following are definitions given by some management pioneers.

"To coordinate is to harmonise all the activities of a concern so as to facilitate its working and success. In a well coordinated enterprise, each department or division works in harmony with others and is fully informed of its role in the organization". – Henri Fayol.

"Coordination deals with the task of blending efforts in ordered to ensure the successful attainment of the objective. It is accomplished by means of planning, organizing, actuating and controlling" – G.R. Terry.

"Coordination is regarded as the essence of managerialship for the achievement of harmony of individual efforts towards the accomplishment of group goals as the purpose of management. Each of the managerial function is an exercise in coordination". – Koontz and O'Donnel.

Thus coordination is the management of interdependence in the work situation. It is the orderly synchronization of the interdependent efforts of individuals in order to attain a common goal. In any modern organization consisting of number of departments such as purchase, finance, production, designs, personnel, sales etc., there is a need for all of them to perform their tasks properly and timely for achieving the targets. This calls for coordination between the various departments of any organization.

Characteristics of coordination

(1) **Not a separate function of management:** It is necessarily in all the functions of management and not a separate one.

(2) **Managerial responsibility:** Every departmental head is responsible to coordinate the efforts of his subordinates and also coordinate with his counter parts of other departments.

(3) **Unity of action:** Unity of action is essential to reach common goals. Coordination brings about unity of action.

(4) **Coordination is part of all levels of organization:** It is to be built in activity at all levels of organization.

(5) **It is relevant to group efforts:** Coordination brings about group efforts than individual efforts. It guides the individuals towards group efforts to reach the targets.

(6) **Continuous and dynamic process:** It is continuous and dynamic process. Managers should continuously monitor and coordinate between people and activities.

(7) **System concept:** Any organization starts is a system of cooperation. Each department functions are different in nature and interdependence in the organization system. The organization runs smoothly with the help of co-ordination. Thus coordination is a system concept.

6.6.2 Importance of coordination:

The coordination is important because of the following factors:

(i) **Unity in diversity:** There are large number of employees each with different ideas, views or opinions and interests. This results into a diversified activity in any organization. It is necessary to bring them together to accomplish the common objective. Hence coordination is the main element to bring unity in diversity.

(ii) Specialisation: In the modern industrial organizations, there is a high degree of specialization. Though specialists are well aware of their tasks and perform their tasks very effectively, they lack the knowledge of job of others and the importance of others activities. This will lead to misunderstanding and dispute among the specialists. Coordination plays important role in bringing them together and explaining the importance of each others activities.

(iii) Team work: Coordination help converging the diversified efforts of various groups to achieve the objectives. It promotes teamwork and avoids duplication of work.

(iv) Large number of employees: Large organizations employ large number of employees. They have different habits, behaviour and approaches in a particular situation. Many times they don't work in harmony. Coordination is necessary to bring harmony among them.

(v) Empire building: Empire building refers to top level of line organization. The line officers expect cooperation from staff officers, but the line officers are not ready to extend their cooperation to staff officers. This creates conflicts between line and staff officers. Therefore, coordination is necessary to avoid conflicts between line and staff officers.

(vi) Functional differences: The functions of organization are divided section wise. Each section performs different jobs. Each department tries to perform its function in isolation from others. Coordination is necessary to integrate the functions of the related department.

(vii) Recognition of goals: There are general goals of an organization. In addition, each department has its own goals and the individual employees also have their own goals. The individual employees give more importance for their own goals than the organizational goals. Even the departmental heads give priority for departmental goals than the goals of organization, Coordination plays important role to reconcile both the employees goals and departmental goals with organizational goals.

(viii) Communication: Coordination ensures the smooth flow of information one direction to other direction.

(ix) **Interdependency**: The need for coordination in an organization arises of the interdependence of various units. The greater the interdependence of units, the greater the need for coordination.

6.6.3 Techniques of coordination

The following are some important techniques of coordination:

(i) **Effective chain of command or hierarchy:** In any organization hierarchy or chain of command decides who is responsible to whom. If the line of authority and responsibilities are clearly defined, then the manager can access control over subordinates. This would bring about better coordination.

(ii) **Harmonious rules, policies and procedures:** Rules and regulations, policies and procedures are used as guidelines for decision making in a consistent manner. It ensures uniformity in action and decision at every level of management.

iii) **Clearly defined objectives:** Every organization has its own objectives. The objectives should be clearly defined so that the employees of the organization will understand them well. Unity of the purpose is essential to achieve coordination.

(iv) **Coordination through liaison officer:** A liaison officer is one who acts like a link between two people or departments. For effective coordination between interdependent departments like production and sales, organization and government etc., a liaison officer plays very important role.

(v) **Effective communication:** Effective communication promotes mutual understanding and cooperation among the people of an organization. Quick and direct communication facilitates between understanding and coordination.

(vi) **Sound organizational structure:** Sound organizational structure integrates the activities of different units of an organization, resulting in better coordination.

(vii) **Coordination through committees:** Committee or participative group decision-making is another common coordinating device. This helps in reducing the rigidity of hierarchical structure.

(viii) **Incentives:** The term incentive includes only monitory incentives. The incentives are increment in pay, bonus, profit sharing etc. These schemes of incentives promote better spirit and cooperation between employees and workers, between workers and supervisors. Mutuality of interest reduces strife and ensures better coordination.

6.6.4 Principles or Requisites of Effective Coordination

In order to ensure effective coordination it should be based on certain principles as listed below:

(i) **Early start**: The coordination should be started from the early stages of planning and policy making. The plan is to be prepared in mutual consultation. By this, the task of implementation and any change or adjustment in the plan can be easily carried out.

(ii) **Direct contact**: Direct personnel contact, ideas, ideals, goals and views can be discussed and misunderstanding, if any, can be clarified much more efficiently. An agreement may be arrived at on methods and actions through personnel contact in achieving the goals.

(iii) **Continuity:** Coordination is a continuous process and it must go on at all stages of management. It starts with planning and ends with controlling.

(iv) **Dynamism:** Coordination should not be rigid. The change in internal and external environments calls for change in type of coordination. The coordination should change with charges in circumstances.

(v) **Simplified organization:** Simplified organization facitates effective coordination. The departments can be rearranged so that better coordination can be achieved. Similar departments or functions can be put under one supervisor, as this would bring out better coordination. It is further suggested that all interfacing departments may be brought under one boss for ensuring effective communication.

(vi) **Self coordination:** Self-coordination with in each depart will bring about over all coordination of entire organization. Hence it is essential to have self-coordination.

(vii) **Clear-cut objectives:** Clear-cut objectives are very essential for an effective coordination. The management should take necessary steps to explain the objectives to the departmental heads. Clear cut objectives and clear explanation of objectives are bound to produce uniformity in action.

(viii) **Clear definition of authority and responsibility:** The management should clearly define the authority and responsibility of each individual and each department. This will facilitate effective coordination. It will also reduce conflicts among the individuals and between departments. The department manager has clear authority to exercise over the subordinates who are violating the rules.

(ix) **Effective communication:** Effective communication is essential for proper coordination. Through continuous exchange of information, individual and departmental differences can be easily resolved. Policy changes, any adjustment in programmes etc., can be discussed.

(x) **Effective supervision and leadership:** Top executives should supervise the work of subordinates to ensure successful performance of a plan. When a top executive finds any deviation, they may take immediate steps to correct them with the help of supervisors. Hence, there is a need for coordination between supervisors and between top management and supervisors. Thus supervisors play important role in coordination.

6.6.5 Types of coordination

Coordination may be classified as internal and external coordination.

(i) **Internal coordination:** Coordination among the employees of the same department or section, among workers and managers at different levels, among branch offices, plants, departments and sections is called internal coordination. Internal coordination is subdivided into two types.

   (a) ***Vertical coordination:*** Vertical coordination refer to the one in which a departmental head coordinates his work with that of his sub-ordinates and vice-versa.

   (b) ***Horizontal coordination:*** Horizontal coordination refers to the coordination taking place sideways, i.e., the relationship between the persons of same status. It exists between heads of different departments, or supervisors or co-workers.

(ii) **External coordination:** Coordination with customers, suppliers, government and other outsiders with whom the organization has business connections is called external coordination.

6.6.6 Coordination and co-operation

Coordination and cooperation are two terms widely used in a business organization. Though they sound similar they differ with each other. The differences are explained below:

Coordination	Cooperation
1. It is a management function.	1. It is not a management function.
2. Coordination is an orderly arrangement of group efforts.	2. Cooperation is willingness to work or help others.
3. Coordination is obtained officially.	3. Cooperation is a voluntary service.
4. Achievement of objectives is directly linked to coordination.	4. There is no direct link between cooperation and objectives.
5. The success of an organization depends upon the degree of coordination.	5. Cooperation forms the basis of coordinating.

REVIEW QUESTION

1. Explain meaning and nature of directing.
2. Define directing.
3. Give principles of directing.
4. Define leadership.
5. Explain types of leadership.
6. Differentiate between Autocratic, Participative and Free-Rein styles of leadership.
7. Define motivation and give its characteristics.
8. List and explain the results of effective motivation.
9. Explain positive and negative motivations.
10. Write about Maslow's theory of motivation.
11. Explain Behaviour and Goals.
12. Write about Hawthorne studies and its findings.
13. Explain Mc Gregor's theory X and theory Y.
14. What are hygiene factors?
15. Explain Herzberg theory of motivation.
16. Define communication. Explain different systems of communication.
17. Differentiate between formal and informal communication.
18. Differentiate between vertical and horizontal communication.

19. What are barriers of successful communication?
20. Explain the meaning of coordination.
21. What are various characteristics of coordination? Explain.
22. Explain the importance of coordination.
23. What are various techniques of coordination?
24. What are requisites of effective coordination?
25. Differentiate between coordination and cooperation.

CHAPTER 7

CONTROLLING

Controlling is the last function of management. The main objective of control is to identify the variations between the set standards and actual performance and then to take necessary steps to correct it and prevent such deviations in future.

7.1 DEFINITION

"Control is checking current performance against predetermined standards contained in the plans with a view to ensure adequate progress and satisfactory performance" – E.F.L. Brech.

"Control consists of verifying whether everything occurs in conformity with the plans adopted, the instructions issued and principles established. It has for its object to point out weaknesses and errors in order to rectify them and prevent recurrences" – Henri Fayol.

"Controlling is determining what is being accomplished, that is, evaluating the performance and if necessary, applying corrective measures so that the performance takes place according to the plans" – George R. Terry.

"Controlling is the measurement of accomplishment against the standards and the correction of deviations to assure attainment of objectives according to plans" – Koontz and O'Donnel.

7.2 STEPS IN CONTROLLING

Control points out the deviations of the plans and suggests remedial action to improve future plans. There are three steps in control process.

(i) Establishing standards

(ii) Measuring and comparing actual results against standards

(iii) Taking corrective action

(i) Establishing standards: The first step in any control process is to establish standards against which results can be measured. Standards are criteria of performance. Standards may be qualitative or quantitative. Standards like, costs should be reduced, communication is to be faster, goodwill, employees morale etc., are some examples of qualitative standards. Number of units produced, profit percentage, standard hours, total cost incurred, overheads etc., can be expressed quantitatively.

Standards are to be flexible in order to adapt to changing conditions. Standards should emphasise the achievement of results more than the conformity to rules and methods. The standards could be of physical standards, cost standards, revenue standards, capital standards, intangible standards etc.

(ii) **Measuring and comparing actual results against standards:** The second step in control process is to measure the performance and compare it with the set standards. Measurement of performance can be done by personal observation or by a study of various summaries of figures, reports, charts and statements. Comparison is very easy if the system of control is well defined. Several established techniques are available for quick comparison. Some variations are desirable like excess production, reduced expenditure than standard etc. When the actual performance matches with standards, no corrective action is required. However, if the standards are not achieved, then the management should initiate necessary corrective action. If the deviations are beyond the reasonable limits then they should be reported to the top management.

(iii) **Taking corrective action:** After comparing the actual performance with the set standards and noticing the deviations, the next important step is to take corrective action by managers. The causes of deviation may be due to ineffective communication, defective system of wages, wrong tools and machines, negligence from worker, lack of training, ineffective supervision, inadequate facilities etc. The management has to take necessary corrective action based on the nature of causes of deviation.

Managers may correct deviations by redrawing their plans, or by modifying goals, they may use their authority through reassignment of job to others, or by putting additional staff, or providing extra training, better tools and by better leading.

7.3 ESSENTIALS OF A SOUND CONTROL SYSTEM

The essentials of a sound control system are as follows:

(i) ***Feedback:*** Feedback is the process of adjusting future actions based upon the information regarding past performance. Feedback makes the control system very effective.

(ii) ***Objective:*** Control system should be objective and understandable. Objective controls specify the expected results in clear and definite terms and leave little scope for argument by the employees. They avoid aristocracy.

(iii) ***Suitability:*** The control system should be appropriate to the nature

and needs of the activity. The controls used in production are different than the one used in finance and personnel. Hence every organization should evolve suitable control system that serves specific needs.

(iv) ***Prompt reporting:*** The control system should provide for prompt and timely reporting without any delay. Delayed reporting may lead to ineffective control actions. Prompt reporting will help the managers to take immediate corrective action before the problem occurs.

(v) ***Forward looking:*** Effective control system must focus on how the future actions will conform to plans.

(vi) ***Flexible:*** The standards will be altered from time to time. Hence the control system should be flexible in accordance with the modified standards.

(vii) ***Economical:*** The benefits derived from the control system should be more than the cost involved in implementing it.

(viii) ***Simple:*** The control system should be simple to understand and implement.

(ix) ***Effective and operational:*** A control system should not only detect deviations but should also provide solutions to the problems that cause deviations. It must disclose where and how the failures are occurring, who is causing them and how they should be dealt with.

(x) ***Motivation:*** A good control system should motivate people to achieve higher performance. The control is to be so designed that it induces positive reactions from employees. The purpose of control is to prevent and not to punish.

7.4 METHODS OF ESTABLISHING CONTROL

Various methods are used by the management for controlling the various deviations in the organization. Some of the important methods of establishing control are discussed below:

(i) ***Personal observation:*** This is the oldest and simple method of control. The manager personally observes the operations in the work places. Any deviations observed are corrected immediately then and there itself. However, this is a time consuming technique and may not be liked to be observed by workers.

(ii) ***Budgeting:*** A budget is a statement of anticipated results during a designated time period expressed in financial and non-financial

terms. The budgeting process typically involves the use of cost standards. Budgets are made for a specific period like monthly, quarterly or annually. The budgets are prepared on the basis of the purpose like sales budgets, capital expenditure budget, advertisement budget, R and D budget etc.

(iii) ***Cost accounting and cost control:*** Profit of any business depends upon the cost incurred to run the business. Profits are increased by reducing costs. Hence, much importance is given for cost accounting and cost control.

(iv) ***Break-Even analysis:*** The point at which sales is equal to the total cost is known as Break-Even Point (BEP). At this point there will be no loss or no profit. The total cost is the sum of fixed cost + variable cost. Fixed cost is fixed irrespective of production but variable cost changes according to the volume of production. This analysis helps in determining the volume of production or sales and the total cost which is equal to the revenue. The excess of revenue over total cost is profit.

(v) ***Standard costing:*** Standard costing is used to control the cost. The objective of standard costing is the same as budgetary control. The system compares the actual with standards and variance is noted. The following are the steps involved in standard costing.

(a) Setting the cost standards for various components like labour, material, machine hour rate etc.

(b) Measurement of actual performance and comparing with standard cost.

(c) Find the variance of actual cost compared to standard cost.

(d) Taking corrective measures to avoid such variances to occur in future.

(vi) ***Return on investment (ROI):*** Ratio of net profit to the total investment or capital employed in the business is termed as return on investment, generally expressed as percentage.

$$\text{ROI} = \frac{\text{Profit}}{\text{Total Investment}}$$

Using this the percentage of profit is identified. The amount of profit earned by a company is different from the rate of profitability.

(vii) ***Responsibility accounting:*** It is defined as the system of accounting under which each departmental head is made responsible for the

performance of his department. Under this system, each department is made a profit center. The individual department is responsible for its own operation.

(viii) ***Management audit:*** Management audit is an independent process that aims at pointing out the inefficiency in the performance of functions of management such as planning, organizing, staffing, directing, controlling and suggesting possible improvements. It helps the management to handle the operations effectively.

(ix) ***Internal audit:*** Internal audit is conducted by an internal auditor who is an employee of an organization. He makes an independent appraisal of financial and other operations. He identifies the defects and deviations and reports to management.

(x) ***External audit:*** External audit is an independent appraisal of the organization's financial accounts and statements. The purpose of external audit is to safeguard the interests of shareholders and other outside parties concerned with the company. It is also known as statutory audit control. The external auditor certifies the compliance of all accounts. The external audits are conducted by qualified auditors.

(xi) ***Statistical control reports:*** This type of reports are prepared and used by large organizations. They are quantitative in nature. These reports are very useful in sales, production, etc. There are various statistical tools available for this purpose.

(xii) ***Gantt milestone chart:*** This technique was proposed by Henri I. Gantt. This is basically a time based production control technique. This is widely used to monitor the progress of projects. This a two dimensional chart with activities on vertical and time on horizontal scale. This is basically a schedule of activities against time.

(xiii) ***Production control:*** Production control technique is necessary for smooth functioning of an organization. Production control involves forecasting and planning of production, inventory control, scheduling, selection of process etc.

(xiv) ***Programme Evaluation and Review Techniques (PERT):*** This was developed during 1957-58 for US Navy. This is primarily oriented towards achieving better managerial control of time spent in completing a project. A project is split into activities and all the activities are integrated in a highly logical sequence to find the shortest time required to complete the entire project. PERT was created primarily to handle R & D projects.

(xv) ***Critical Path Method (CPM):*** This technique also follows the principles of PERT. This concentrates mainly on cost rather than duration like PERT. The use of both PERT and CPM has grown rapidly today in controlling time bound projects such as repairing a weak bridge, construction of huge buildings etc.

REVIEW QUESTIONS

1. Define controlling.
2. State and explain the steps in controlling.
3. What are the essentials of sound controlling?
4. Explains the methods of establishing sound controlling.
5. What is the need of fixing standards?

CHAPTER 8

MARKETING MANAGEMENT

8.1 INTRODUCTION

Marketing management is one of the important functions of management which involves

(a) Analysis

(b) Planning

(c) Implementation

(d) Control

of programmes designed to bring about the desired exchanges with target markets for the purpose of achieving the goals/objectives of the enterprise.

8.2 FUNCTIONS OF MARKETING

Marketing involves certain activities (functions) in order to move goods from producers to consumers. All these functions can be grouped into three major functions.

Facilitating functions or supporting activities

- Collecting market information and market research.
- Market finance.
- Marketing risk bearing.

Exchange functions and merchandising

- Product planning.
- Standardising and grading.
- Buying and assembling.
- Advertising and selling.

Physical supply functions or Physical distribution

- Storage
- Transportation

8.3 MARKET RESEARCH

Like any other type of research, Market research is a scientific search for knowledge especially in the areas related to functions of marketing. Market research is the essential ingredient of marketing intelligence. In modern industries market research has become an important segment since it is just as valuable to the manufacturer as the technical research and it ensures the continued vitality of business. The current century implied its horizon in marketing and hence market research has been receiving a great amount of importance.

8.3.1 Definition of Market Research

American Marketing Association has defined Market Research as the gathering, recording and analysis of the data about the problems related to the marketing of goods and services.

Market research can also be defined as spanished approach which includes all research activities and marketing problems such as:

- Process of gathering, recording and analyzing of the utility and marketability of the product.
- Research on the nature of the demand.
- Research on the nature of the competition.
- Research on the methods of marketing.

8.3.2 Objectives of Market Research

Research in market must have certain objectives. The understanding of these objectives will also help appreciate the need for and the importance of market research.

Following are some of basic objectives of market research.

To know about the persons who buy company product

This will include the number of persons who buy, the frequency of their buying, sources of their buying, their regional location and the social category of the buyer.

To findout the impact of promotional efforts

The company may adopt different strategies to promote a product and there are possibilities that some aspects of promotional strategy are more effective than the rest. Research in this area will enable the researcher to find out strength and weakness of the promotional mix.

To know consumer response to the product

The basic objective of this approach is to know what consumer feels about the product and will help to determine the degree of satisfaction derived by the consumer. The research in this area may also reveal the need for importance in quantity, design, size and packing, distribution method etc. This kind of information is essential for product planning.

To measure the effectiveness of channels, price policy and personal selling

There is no meaning in spending effort and money through a particular media if it does not contribute any significant thing towards the marketing effort. Thus research in this area will help to know the correct mode of selling products and their correct price.

To know the marketing cost and profit

The main objective of this research is to get the valuable information about the distribution market cost. Marketing cost is the difference between the cost of production and the final purchase price. This research will help to find out the percentage of such cost and tries to minimise it which may be due to improper channel members, transport, storage, advertising or packaging. This research will also help to know the contribution of different products to the total profit of the company.

To study the external forces

Research in this field will help the company to provide reliable information about the competitors moves and share of the Market, Government policies, consumers income and spending new products and substitutes entering the market and their impacts over the company product etc.

To forecast

Research in this field area will help the company to forecast the future of existing product and their future sales, demand etc.

To explore (Search and Examine)

Research in this area will provide the company to explore new market, new products and help to develop the new better and effective ideas.

To determine overall effectiveness

Market research measures the effectiveness of advertisement rules, promotion techniques, marketing policies, after sales-service etc. Also it measures the consumers and dealers relations.

To keep close watch

Market research will keep a business in touch with its market. It will also study profitability, liking of the product and safeguards the company against unforeseen changes in the markets.

8.3.3 Process of Marketing Research

To carry out market research, the following procedure or process and steps are to be followed.

- ➢ Define the objective and the problem.
- ➢ Collect the necessary data required for the purpose.
- ➢ Process or analyse the data collected.
- ➢ State the outcomes of results of research or state whether the project under consideration is feasible economically or not.

8.3.4 Method of data collection for Market Research

The methods of data collection for market research are of the following two types.

Primary Data

This refers to all the data collected specially for the problem under study. The methods as follows:

(1) Survey method
- ➢ Personnel interview
- ➢ Telephone interview
- ➢ Mail interview

(2) Experimental method

(3) Questionnaire method

Secondary Data

This refers to the use of the already gathered statistical information for some other purpose and which may be useful for the problem under study. The methods are as follows:

(1) Desk research
- ➢ Scales interview
- ➢ Correlation studies
- ➢ Ratio analysis

(2) Statistical method
   - Bar chart
   - Histogram
   - Frequency polygon
   - Frequency histogram

8.4 EVALUATION OF CONSUMER WANTS

In order to evaluate consumer wants, usually techniques of market research are applied. The evaluation is done by adopting certain steps and procedure. Although no set rules or steps can be laid down to evaluate the consumer wants (because it often depends upon the nature of market, products etc.) the general steps which can be followed are as follows:

- Define the problem and objective.
- Conduct survey and collect the relevent data.
- Process the data and analyse it.
- Prepare the questionnaire.
- Test the product in small scale.
- Evaluate the reaction.
- Make decision and implement the decision.

The above steps can be best explained by taking an example of one product such as toilet soap or a biscuit item. Example: Let us assume that a new variety of toilet soap is chosen as the product.

Step 1: Define the problem of objectives

Here in order to carry out evaluation one must answer following question before starting the process.

- What is the market of product?
- Where it should be marketed?
- What should be its price?
- What should be its colour? etc.

Step 2: Conduct the survey and collect the data:

This is also called as pilot survey in which all the facts and information about the product is collected. This information can be collected by

- Personal interviews – Questions are asked in personnel.
- Telephone interviews – Questions are asked by Telephone.

- Mail interviews – Questions are asked through mail.

Thus all necessary information and data are collected.

Step 3: Process the data and analyse it.

The collected data is then processed, analysed and interpreted. Finally a written report is prepared regarding its possible/predictable market demand.

Step 4: Prepare Questionnaires:

Once it is found that there is a possibility of success of the product, a questionnaire is prepared. It consists of all important questions pertaining to data and very specific in nature. A consumer just has to give answer in short and sometimes in Yes/No preference. A certain group of people to whom these questions are to be asked is prepared and thus only some class of people is interviewed.

Step 5: Test the sample scale and evaluate.

Once after getting the source of answers that people give in response to the questionnaires prepared, we can test one product in very small area, quantity, group etc., and after the completion of this process we evaluate the responses.

Step 6: Decision

From the evaluation, we can judge the fixed trend of the customer, their likes and dislikes and a decision is made and implemented whether to launch the product or not.

REVIEW QUESTIONS

1. Explain the functions of marketing.
2. What is market research?
3. What are the objectives of market research?
4. Explain the process of market research.
5. How the wants of consumer are evaluated?
6. How is the data collected for market research?

CHAPTER 9

PRODUCT DEVELOPMENT

Once any company has carefully segmented the market with one product, it has to develop and launch appropriate new products. Every company must carry on with new product development. Replacement products must be created to maintain sales. A company can add new products through acquisition or through new product development. The acquisition can be of three forms: (i) The company can buy other companies, it can acquire patents from other companies, (ii) it can buy licence (iii) in can take franchise from other companies.

The new product development is of two forms: the company itself can develop new products within its own Laboratories or R & D centers or it can engage independent researchers to develop new products for the company.

The success factor of new product is unique superior product. Another key success factor is a well-designed product concept prior to development, where the company carefully defined and assessed the target market, product requirements, and benefits before proceeding. The other success factors are technological and marketing synergy, quality of execution in all stages and market attractiveness.

It has been identified that for successful launching of a product, the following factors have influence. They are deeper understanding of customer needs, the higher the performance-to-cost ratio, early introduction of product ahead of competitors, the greater the expected use, better top management support and effective cross functional team work. The team work aspect is particularly very important. New product development is very effective when there is team work among R & D, engineering, manufacture, purchase, marketing and finance departments from the beginning till the launch.

Failure of New Product:

A new product may fail due to the following factors

(i) A top executive may push his favourite idea inspite of not required in the market.

(ii) Product idea may be good, but market is over estimated.

(iii) Product is not well designed.

(iv) Not correctly positioned in the market, insufficient advertisement or over priced.

(v) Development costs are higher than expected.

(vi) Competitors fight better.

9.1 NEW PRODUCT DEVELOPMENT PROCESS

New product development process involves eight stages.

- idea generation
- idea screening
- concept development and testing
- marketing strategy developed
- business analysis
- product development
- Market testing and
- Commercialization.

9.1.1 Idea generation

New product development process starts with the search for the ideas. New product idea can come from many sources: customers, scientists, employees, competitions and top management. Although ideas flow from many sources, their chance of receiving serious attention often depends on someone in the organization.

A number of creative idea – generating techniques can help individuals and groups generate ideas. They are:

(i) ***Attribute listing:*** This technique calls for listing an existing product and major attributes and then modifying each attribute in the search for an improved product.

(ii) ***Forced relationship:*** In this technique, several objects are considered in relation to one another to create new product. For example, a mobile phone, a MP3 player and a FM radio combined into one single unit with all features.

(iii) ***Morphological Analysis:*** This method calls for identifying the structured dimensions of a problem and examining the relationships among them with a hope to find novel combination.

(iv) ***Need/problem identification:*** The previous idea generation techniques are not based on customer input. In this, customers are asked about needs, problems and ideas. Based on this new product idea is generated.

(v) ***Brainstorming:*** Group creativity can be simulated through brain storming techniques. The usual brain storming group will have about 6 to 10 people who sit isolated and discuss a specific problem. The ideas start flowing and one idea trigger another idea. The ideas are recorded for further screening.

9.1.2 Idea Screening:

The company should motivate its employees to submit their ideas to an Idea Chairman in written form. These ideas should be reviewed periodically and sorted into three groups: promising ideas, marginal ideas and rejects. Each promising idea should be thoroughly studied by a committee and then they are moved to a full scale screening process. The company should offer payments or rewards to the employees submitting the best ideas. In screening ideas, the company must avoid two types of errors. A "drop-error" occurs when the company dismisses an otherwise good idea. A "go-error" occurs when the company permits a poor idea to move into development and commercialization. The purpose of screening is to drop a poor ideas as early as possible.

9.1.3 Concept development and testing:

Attractive ideas must be refined into testable product concepts. Any product ideas can be turned into several product concepts. This is called concept development. Then the concepts developed are to be tested. Concept testing calls for testing product concepts with an appropriate group of target consumers, then getting those customers' reactions. In past, creating physical prototypes was costly and time-consuming. But today with the help of computers, the concepts can be turned into models and can be tested with ease.

9.1.4 Marketing strategy development

After testing the new-product the manager must develop a preliminary marketing strategy plan for introducing the new product into the market. It includes deciding of target market's site, planned price of product, distribution strategy, advertising and marketing budget etc.

9.1.5 Business Analysis:

Management has to prepare sales, cost and profit projections to determine whether they satisfy the objectives of the company. Then only the concept can be considered for product-development.

9.1.6 Product development:

If a product concept is accepted and satisfies business analysis and objectives, then it moves to R & D or Engineering Department for developing the physical product. The R & D department will develop one or more physical versions of the product concept. The lab scientists or R & D engineers must not only design the product with required or specified functional characteristics but also know how to communicate its psychological aspects. When the prototypes are ready, they must be put through rigorous functional and consumer test. Any modifications based on testing may be incorporated.

9.1.7 Market testing:

After the management is satisfied with the product's functional and psychological performance, the product is ready to be given a brand name, packaging, price and market launching. The amount of market testing is influenced by the investment cost and risk and research cost.

9.1.8 Commercialisation:

Market testing presumably gives management necessary information to decide whether to launch the new product or not.

In commercializing a new product, the critical points like market-entry time, whether to launch in one region or several regions etc., and target market prospects and how to introduce into the markets. To sequence and coordinate the many activities involved in launching a new product, network planning techniques like critical path scheduling can be used.

9.2 PRODUCT LIFE CYCLE

The companies normally reformulate their marketing strategy several times during a product's life. Economic conditions change, competitors may launch new products, change in buyers interests and requirements. Consequently a company must plan strategies appropriate to each stage of product's life cycle. Product life cycle (PLC) is an important concept that provides insights into product's competitive changes.

To understand that a product has a life cycle is to assert four things:

- Products have a limited life.
- Product sales pass through distinct stages, challenges, opportunities and problems.
- Profits vary at different stages of product's life.
- Products need different marketing, financial, manufacturing, purchasing and human resources in each stage of the life cycle.

Product life cycle is a bell-shaped curve drawn for sales and profits vs time and is shown as figure below.

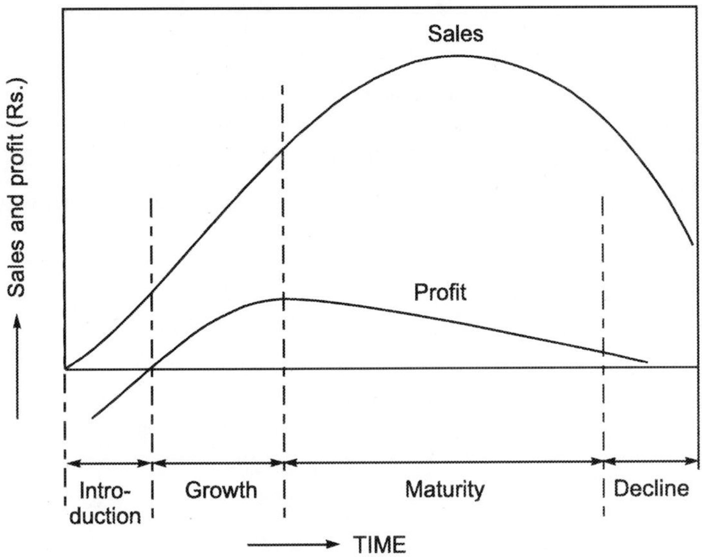

Product Life Cycle

This curve is typically divided into four stages: Introduction, growth, maturity and decline.

Introduction: It is the period of slow sales growth as the product is introduced in the market. Profits are nonexistent in this stage because of heavy expenses incurred with product introduction.

Growth: A period of rapid market acceptance and rapid increase in sales. Hence profits also improve substantially. This is called growth since there is growth in both sales and profits.

Maturity: After sometime, when the market saturates with a particular product, the sales slow down. This is because the product has achieved acceptance by most potential buyers. Profits stabilize or even decline because of increased marketing outlays to defend the product against competition. Competitors might have introduced similar products with better features. Buyers tastes and needs would have changed.

Decline: Finally the sales show a downward drift and come down drastically. The profits will erode and reduce to bear minimum.

It is very difficult to designate where each stage begins and where ends.

Usually, the stages are marked where the rates of sales growth or decline is noticed. These stage must be reviewed periodically. Increased competition leads to shorter product life cycles.

REVIEW QUESTIONS

1. Explain the steps in new product development process.
2. Explain the various idea generating techniques.
3. Explain the stages of product life cycle.

CHAPTER – 10

SALES MANAGEMENT

10.1 INTRODUCTION

Sales forecasting is a practice of rapidly growing importance. It is considered as the basis of all industrial activities. Example: The first step in any budgeting is sales forecasting. It furnishes many important informations such as capacity of the plant to be installed, the capital and raw materials that will be required, the stock and the distribution to be achieved, the size of the operation to be conducted in general and many more important factors.

It is simply an estimation of type, quantity or future work. It is defined by American Market Association as "an estimation of sales in dollars or physical units for a specified future period under a proposed marketing plan or program and under a assumed set of economic and other forces outside the unit for which the forecast is made".

Sales Management is important because it provides information regarding:

- An economic foundation for operations planning, scheduling on action etc.
- Some work of corporate investment planning, sourcing, capital, investment proposal such as modernizing, expansion, diversification etc.

10.2 METHODS OF SALES FORECASTING

There are various methods (techniques) of forecasting. All these techniques can be grouped under two types, one for new product and another for established products.

10.3 SALES FORECASTING TECHNIQUES

For New Product	For Established Product
1) Direct survey method	1) Projection method
2) Indirect survey method	2) Related information method
3) Comparing with established products	3) Market research
4) Limited market trial	4) Jury of executive opinion method
	5) Sales force composite method.

10.4 SALES FORECASTING FOR NEW PRODUCTS

Forecasting the demand for new product is a difficult task since, in such cases, past information on which future can be predicted is not available. Some of the techniques used for forecasting a new product are as follows:

Direct survey Method

In this method the prospective consumers are approached and are asked what they intend to buy. Generally sampling technique is adopted for this purpose in which a sample of customers is questioned and with some degree of certainty it can be predicted how the population will respond.

Application: This method is used for a product:

- When the products are totally new and whose past information is not available.
- If introduced in a small critical trial area.
- Whose first-hand information is required.

Example: New soaps, Powders, Shaving cream etc.

Indirect survey Method

In this method the attitude and behaviour for the product is predicted through salesman, intermediate selling agents, wholesalers and retailers etc.

Applications

- For a product which may not be possible to carry from house to house.
- For a product for which less time, money and effort is available.

Comparing with established products

In certain situation, it may be possible to compare the new product with the existing product, and so the sales figure can also be predicted on that basis.

Applications

- If a new product is a substitute for a competitor's product.
- If a new product is more or less similar type (in functioning, nature, application etc.) as that of existing product.
- If a new product can be assumed to be equally good saleable and popular (Brand name, company's name etc.) to that of existing product.

Limited market trial method

To predict the acceptance of product by potential customers limited market trial method. Sometimes limited selling techniques are also used when industrial goods are marketed. It is called as market probe.

Applications

- When a company desires to have a market test before attempting sales. Forecast is based on expert opinion or executive opinion.
- Usually used by customers goods marketers.

10.5 SALES FORECASTING FOR ESTABLISHED PRODUCTS

Following methods are adopted for established products.

Projection method

This method is based on the historical data. Here sales forecast can be predicted, to some extent by projecting the previous data into the future. Here a line drawn through known information is projected into forecast area to project what the sales volume will be for future period. Some of the important methods are:

- Time series analysis.
- Correlation analysis.
- Exponential smoothing.
- Least square method.

Applications

- When a reliable and accurate past data is available.
- When forecasting needs simple and easier approach to the problem.
- For regular, continuous and popular product.

Related information method (Comparison method)

In this method a predictor which varies directly with sales volume is found.

Example: The actual birth rates might be used to project the sales of baby foods.

Applications

- The products having an accurate, a reliable past data and which can be related with the present products forecast.

- For the product having a direct relation or effect on the other products and factors.

Market research method:

Though the critical analysis of marketing forces, changing patterns of socioeconomic pressures, political changes, etc., we can predict the future demands of the product.

Applications

- To know consumers behaviour (reaction)
- To know what product to be sold, where, in what quantity, of what quality to whom show and when

Jury of executive opinion method:

In this method opinion of executives, exports are invited about the future sales. This method is neither scientific nor accurate.

Applications

- When huge volume of statistical data of complicated calculations is not involved.
- To get fast and inexpensive results.

Sales-force composite method:

In this method views of salesmen, traders and middlemen are grouped and estimates are made accordingly. Also, often company keeps records of such views and whenever the forecast has to be made on this basis, such past data is referred and results may be then predicted.

Applications

- To have a rough idea about the product.
- To test the opinion of the above group of people.

10.6 SALES PROMOTION

Sales promotion is highly specialised function of marketing. All activities that go into the development of sales are those that are intended to raise the demand level for a product very quickly and grouped under this title. As defined by American Marketing Association, Sales promotion means "Those marketing activities, other personnel selling, advertising and publicity that simulate consumer purchasing and dealer effectiveness such as display shows, demonstration and various selling efforts not in the ordinary routine."

Today sales promotion is an urgent necessity and not a luxury. It is an investment and not an expenditure that yields highest dividends in the days to follow. It is needed for the following:

- To bring about effective communication so that consumers are persuaded to buy the products with least resistance.
- To attract the consumers, so that a lowerness can survive keen (sharp) and cut throat competition.
- To fill in the gap between the time when advertisements are given and people act on it.

10.6.1 Methods of sales promotion

There are various methods of sales promotion and it can be achieved by providing the following:

Service to the salesman

- By assisting the salesman
- By training the salesman
- By analyzing specific problem and suggesting sound solution.

Service to the dealers

- By provision of management aids
- By training dealers
- By effective attraction of terms of deal.

Direct publicity and package

Incentives to the dealers and users

Specialty publicity devices

Another way of classifying various methods of sales promotion is as follows:

- Consumer promotion
- Trade promotion
- Sales force promotion

10.6.1.1 Consumer promotion

This is one method of sales promotion in which a consumer or buyer is motivated to buy manufacturer's product by attracting through some attractive and tentative offer. Following are the methods of sales promotion by means of consumer promotion method / procedure

(1) Sample
(2) Coupon
(3) Bonus offer (Premium)
(4) Money return offer
(5) Price off promotion
(6) Contests / Prizes
(7) Trading Samples
(8) Demonstrations

Sample

This involves distribution of free samples. For this purpose, a manufacturer uses either a regular size purchase or special simple size package of a product, distributes it to the buyer free of cost. The sample might be delivered door to door or offered in a retail store. Example: A biscuit manufacturer distributing a sample of new variety of biscuit.

Merits

- Very powerful tool
- Suitable for new products
- Very effective and easy

Demerits

- Expensive
- Limited to low price, smaller size and movable items.

Coupon

A coupon is a certificate that entitles the consumer a specified saving on purchase of specific product. These coupons are issued by manufacturers either directly, by mail or through retailers.

Merits

- Less expensive.
- Simple in nature and easily available.

Demerits

- Imparts more burden to the retailers
- There is no guarantee that the retailers will buy back the company coupons only against the purchase of manufacturers brand issuing the coupon .

Premium or Bonus offer

In this method an offer of a certain extra product is given at no extra cost to consumers who buy a new of product which is nothing but a bonus of premium on purchase of that stated amount of product .

Merits

- It can boost the product in the situations where heavy competition is involved.
- Attracts a buyers if the premium offered is very useful item.

Example: A silver spoon is offered as a bonus on purchase of economy size Horlicks bottle.

Demerits

- Not efficient from net profit point of view but helps in maintaining increasing sales.

Money return offer

Here manufacturer states that the he will return the purchaser's money if he is not satisfied with the product and return it with in the stated period.

Merits

- People are attracted to buy the product.
- Very rarely, the buyer will ask for money return.
- Increased popularity, if the product satisfies the consumer.

Demerits

- Involves risk of misuse.
- Sales return is a costly affair.

Price off Promotion

This involves an offer to the buyer a certain amount of 'Money off' on the regular price of a product prominently printed.

Merit

- The only, merit is that people feel that the company has discounted the items and the same product can be now purchased at little lower price.

Demerits

- Not very effective

- Does not import much impact if the price off is very little when compared with total marked price.

Contest or Quizzes

This is a new and effective technique to promote sales. Here the consumers, on purchase of items, are provided with an opportunity to participate in a contest, game or a quiz, with a chance of winning costly prizes like free air trips or some regularly usable house hold items.

Contest: It calls for matching an appropriate pairs, places etc. This was done by Wills Cigarettes : 'Made for each other'.

Quiz: Here a buyer is asked to complete and return, best slogan, missing letter etc., is selected for awarding prize.

Merits

- Highly effective.
- Buyer can always give a try to his luck.

Demerits

- Needs proper calculations and amount.
- If a product fails, then a company may incur a loss.

10.6.1.2 Trading promotions

In this method of sales promotion, usually a dealer, retailer or a wholesaler is offered some discount. Thus the manufacturer can achieve more sales through some of the methods:

- Buying allowances
- Co-operative advertising
- Buy back allowances
- Dealers listed promotion
- Free goods
- Push money or PM's
- Merchandise allowances
- Sales contest

Buying allowances

Here the buying allowance is offered to the dealer to induce him to buy a new product introduced by the manufacturer. This involves an offer to dealer of a percentage of each minimum quantity of product purchased during the stated period of time.

Buy back Allowances

Under this method, the manufacturer offers a certain amount of money for additional new purchases based on the quantity of purchases made on the first trade deal. Thus this allowance goes to strengthen a buyers move to cooperate on the first trade deal also.

3) Free goods

This is also buying allowance but in the form of offer. Here an offer is made of a certain amount of a product, to wholesaler's and retailers at no extra cost, on the purchase of a stated amount of the same or another product.

Merchandise Allowances

Here the retailers are given / offered an allowance to compensate expenses incurred by them for him. Here the manufacturer offers advertising allowance, display allowances, etc.

Cooperative advertising

Under this method, a manufacturer agrees to pay an advertising allowance to retailers for each unit of product purchased on a contract for a specified period.

Dealer listed promotion

Here the advertisement or other publicity materials like calendars issued by the manufacturer carries also the names and addressees of retailer who stock the product or who are operating in promotion.

Push Money or PMs

This is an incentive payment in cash or gift to the retailers to push the manufacturer's brand at so many rupees per article sold. It is an expensive method.

Merits

- Motivates retailers to promote the product's sales
- Reduces problems and botheration on the part.
- Gives extra push to product.
- Effective in case of heavy competitions.

Demerits

- Reduces profit per product (item).
- Requires accurate accounting.

10.6.1.3 Sales force Promotions

This is the method which promotes personal selling as in the case of salesman, sales representative etc. Nowadays this method has been in wide use. This includes

- Bonus to sales force
- Sale force contest
- Sales meeting, sales man's conference, etc .

Bonus to sales force

This is a very effective technique and here a quota is set for a year or for a short period. Then bonus is offered on sales in excess of the quota. This bonus could be in terms of gift, promotion or cash. Generally it is in terms of cash reward. This technique, motivates salesman to sell more than the quota and hence to earn more.

Sales force contest

In this method salesmen are offered an opportunity to participate in a contest a certain target of sales is achieved and the winner in the contest may be offered a free ticket (for his family) and a week holidays or certain holidays to certain hill stations.

Sales meeting conference

In this method salesmen are gathered periodically and are inspire to sell more by providing them with knowledge of new selling techniques and strategies, often they are also offered a promotion if the sales target is achieved.

Merits

- Incredible increase in sales
- Increase in overall profit
- Benefits to all manufacturing retailers and the salesman.

Advertising

Advertising is a salesmanship in print and it can also be referred as a form of paid publicity. It is one of the important components of company's promotional mix. It is common technique for mass selling and has a strong persuasion role.

Definition

"Advertisement is a purchased publicity, directed according to a defined plan to secure, maintain and increase the distribution and consumption of a product".

10.7 ADVERTISING

- Makes the buyer aware of the product and its brand.
- Helps selling on mass scales both by persuading new buyers in a given region and by extending persuasion to new regions.
- It helps the retailers to stock goods, which are better known and have better sales possibilities.
- It promotes competition.
- It helps salesman while making personal causes.

10.7.1 Advertising Strategies (Media of Advertising)

Advertising strategies are nothing but the measure of the medium through which a sales message is delivered. Thus these strategies are the means through which an advertising information is passed on to the customers.

- Indoor Advertising
- Outdoor Advertising
- Direct Advertising
- Promotional Advertising (Display advertising) .

10.7.1.1 Indoor Advertising

- Mass media: Newspaper and Magazines
- Radio Advertising
- TV Advertising
- Film Advertising.

Mass Media

It covers newspapers and magazines.

Newspaper: Although many media are available to advertise, the newspaper continues to remain the most powerful and effective selling force. It is a backbone of advertising programme.

Merits

- Low cost for reader
- Assured readership

- Quick response
- Flexible and speedy

Demerits

- Shorter life
- Low ton of próduction
- Waste of circulation

Magazine: Magazines are the periodicals published monthly or weekly, to be read, normally in easy cost. It provides light and leisure reading.

Merits

- Longer life
- Visible display
- Attractive colour representation.

Demerits

- Rigid and high cost per reader,
- Unsuitable for small waits
- Time consuming.

Radio Advertising: It can he described as "word of mouth advertising on a whole sale scale". This is because advertiser delivers his message orally and not visually. The advertisements through this media make it (products) to the ear than to eyes. It has a great impact when broadcast through popular stations such as voice of America, BBC, All India Radio, Local FM Stations etc., with the advent of TV's this is slowly loosing its importance.

Merits

- Human appeal
- Variety of programmes
- Message at home
- Flexible and timely

Demerits

- No pictorial presentation
- High cost of time
- Not covering all
- Wasteful.

TV advertising: This media has been declared as the most effective powerful media in the recent years. TV advertising is probably most significant single new thing that has happened in advertising in this century.

Merits

- It gives a better and more effect.
- All merits of radio and pictorial advertising are combined in this.

Demerits

- It is costly.
- Has limitation of time.

Film Advertising: This is another medium of advertising which is more effective, since it comprises sound, motion, visual and time lines. It can be considered as TV advertisements, extended to larger and larger expanded screen.

Merits

- Dramatic impact and appeal to audience
- Mass publicity
- Reliable means of communication.

Demerits

- Costlier
- Limited spread

10.7.12 Outdoor Advertising

- Posters display
- Traveling display
- Electric signal
- Sky writing
- Sandwitch

Merits

- Widest appeal
- It hides ugliness (Hide damage walls)
- Flexible
- Durable
- Best type of advertising.

Demerits

- Only reminder publicity
- Lack novelty
- Costlier.

REVIEW QUESTIONS

1. Explain various sales forcasting techniques for now products.
2. Explain various sales forecasting techniques for established products.
3. What is the need of sales promotion. Explain various methods of it.
4. Explain Advertising need and stratigies.
5. Explain briefly sales management.

CHAPTER 11

COST ACCOUNTING

11.1 NEED FOR COST ACCOUNTING

Cost Accounting is a branch of accounting. It has been developed due to limitations of financial accounting. Financial accounting is primarily concerned with record keeping directed towards the preparation of Profit and Loss Account and Balance Sheet. It provides information regarding the profit and loss that the business enterprise is making and also its financial position on a particular date. This information concerning the business enterprise is helpful to the management to control in a general way the major functions of a business viz., finance, administration, production and distribution etc., with out this it becomes difficult to evaluate operating management performance, to guide management decisions or lay down management policies and thus fails to serve the management in discharge of its function.

11.2 MEANING OF COST, COSTING AND COST ACCOUNTING

- **Cost:** It may be defined as that which is given or is sacrificed to obtain something. The cost of an article consists of actual out goings or ascertained charges incurred in its production and sale. This word represents the cost to make and sell, but because of varieties of meaning, it is always advisable to qualify the word cost, or show exactly what it means. Example prime cost, factory cost, etc.
- **Costing:** It is the technique and process of ascertaining costs. The technique in costing consists of the body of principles and rules for ascertaining the costs of products and services. The technique is dynamic and changes with the change of time. The process of costing is the day-to-day routine of ascertaining costs.
- **Cost Accounting:** It is the· process of accounting for cost which begins with recording of income and expenditure and ends with the preparation of statistical data. It is the formal mechanism by means of which costs of products or services are ascertained and controlled. Cost accounting is thus the provision of such analysis and classification of expenditure as it will enable the total cost to be constituted. It is not sufficient to know that the cost of one article is Rs. 4 but the management is also interested to know the value of material

used, the amount of labour and other expenses incurred so as to control and reduce its cost. Thus cost accounting is a quantitative method that collects, classifies, summarises and interprets information for product costing, operation planning and control and decision making.

11.3 ADVANTAGES OF COST ACCOUNTING

- Establishment of more accurate unit costs, a knowledge of which results in the establishment of fair selling prices and in the elimination of unprofitable lines of product.
- Development of cost comparisons, enabling the management to note unfavorable developments and to institute procedures for their elimination. Such comparison may be made, from period to period, of the figures in respect of the same unit or of several units in an industry by employing uniform costing and inter-firm comparison methods.
- Elimination of inefficiencies in plant operation. These inefficiencies are costly and are caused by material wastage, use of obsolete machinery, poor planning, or assignment of men to work for which they are not qualified.
- Presentation of more frequent and more accurate financial accounts with the help of perpetual inventory system of stock control.
- Establishment of increased operating efficiency through the use of standards and subsequent analysis and comparison of actual performance with established standards.
- Establishment of control over material, labour and overhead expenditures. The facts of the day-to-day operation of the business are disclosed, and prompt remedial action can be taken to correct adverse trends. Moreover, introduction of a cost reduction programme combined with operational research and value analysis leads to considerable economy.
- Assisting in developing cost calculations for new products and designs to guide management in its efforts to determine the profitableness of proposed changes in products and designs.
- The establishment of an effective costing system prevents manipulation and fraud and assists in furnishing correct and reliable cost data to the management as well as to other interested parties such as the shareholders, the consumers and the Government.

11.4 ELEMENTS OF COST

The following are the various elements of cost. Each element of cost is examined in detail:

11.4.1 Direct Materials Cost

Direct materials cost is the cost of materials, which can be identified with, and allocated to cost centers or cost units. Direct material is that material which becomes a part of the product. There are some materials which become a part of the product, but are used in comparatively small quantities and have very negligible costs. Under such circumstances, instead of making a futile effort to make an analysis of them for the purpose of a direct charge, they are conveniently grouped under indirect material as part of overhead. Thus in the manufacture of shoes it would be futile to count the number of nails or quantity of thread used in a particular shoe. The cost of glue in cardboard boxes, through a part of the box, is conveniently treated as an item of overhead. The following are the examples of direct material:

- Materials, including component parts, specially purchased or requisitioned for particular job, order or process.
- Material passing from one operation or process to another.
- Primary packing materials such as cartons, cardboard boxes etc.

The following terms are used in the same sense as direct material cost: Prime cost material, process material, production material, requisitioned material.

11.4.2 Direct Wages

Direct wages (labour cost) are the wages, which can be identified and allocated to cost centres and cost units. Payment of direct labour and in some cases payment of indirect labour fall within the definition of direct wages. Direct wages are the labour expenditure incurred in altering condition, conformation or composition of the product. There are some cases where wages of indirect labour may be treated as direct wages. The wages of foremen, inspectors, etc., whilst not directly expended in altering the condition or composition of product, are specifically connected with such activity and can be accurately identified for costing purposes, and as such are considered as a direct charge to products. Such variation in practice is allowed for accuracy, in cost finding and cost control.

Payment of the following routs of labour fall within the definition of direct wages :

- Labourers engaged in altering the condition, conformation and composition of the product.

- Inspectors, analysts etc., specifically required for such production.
- If specifically identified, the wages of foremen, shop clerks, the wages of internal transport personnel etc.

The following terms are used in the same sense as direct wages: direct labour, prime cost labour, process labour cost, operating labour cost.

11.4.3 Direct Expenses

Direct expenses are the expenses (other than direct material, cost of direct wages) which can be identified with and allocated to cost centres or cost units.

The following groups of expenses fall within the definition of direct expenses.

- Cost of special designs, drawings or layout.
- Hire of special tools or equipments for a particular job.
- Maintenance costs of such tools and equipments.

The following terms are used in the same sense as direct expenses: chargeable expenses, process expenses, productive expenses, prime cost expenses.

11.4.4 Production or Factory Overhead

Production or factory overhead includes all indirect material cost, indirect wages and indirect expenses incurred in the factory from the receipt of the order until its completion and ready for dispatch.

The following groups of indirect items fall within the category of factory overhead:

- **Indirect material:** In the strict senses, indirect material is the material that cannot be traced in the finished products such as consumable stores, e.g., lubricants, cotton waste, grease, oils, small tools, belt fasteners and work stationery. However, some minor items of material which enter into production and form part of it are conveniently treated as indirect material, such as, cost of thread in shirt-making, cost of glue in cardboard boxes, cost of nails in shoe-making etc. All indirect materials costs relating to factory become part of factory overhead.
- **Indirect Wages**: Wages that are not charged directly are indirect wages. In general, salaries or wages of the following are treated as direct wages; foreman, supervisor, inspectors, general labour, maintenance labour, clerical staff, watch and ward, indirect labour in drawing and design office, internal transport, tool room and other services.

- **Indirect expenses:** Expenses (other then indirect material and labour) that are not charged directly to production are indirect expenses. The following are treated as indirect factory expenses: Rent, rates and insurance in relation to factory, depreciation, power and fuel, repairs and maintenance of plants, machinery and buildings, sundry expenses for other services including employment office, first aid, rewards for suggestions for welfare, etc.

The following terms are used in the same sense as production overhead, factory overhead, works overhead, factory on cost, works on cost.

11.4.5 Administration Overheads

Administration overhead includes all indirect material cost, indirect wages and indirect expenses incurred in the direction, control and administration of an undertaking.

The following groups of indirect items fall within the definition of administration overhead:

- Cost of indirect materials such as printing and stationery.
- Indirect wages such as office salaries including salaries of administrative directors, secretaries, accountants, credit approval, cash collection and treasurer's department.
- Indirect expenses such as rent, rates and insurance of general offices, lighting, heating and cleaning of general offices; bank charges; depreciation and repairs of office buildings and equipment; legal charges; audit fees; etc.

11.4.6 Selling Overhead

Selling overhead includes all indirect material cost, indirect wages and indirect expenses incurred in promoting sales and retaining customers.

The following groups of indirect items fall within the definition of selling overhead:

- Cost of indirect materials such as printing and stationery, mailing literatures, catalogues, price-lists etc.
- Indirect wages such as salaries, commission, etc., of salesmen, technical representatives and sales managers, selling department salaries.
- Indirect expenses such as advertising, rent, rates and insurance of showroom and sales offices; bad debts and collection charges, cash discount allowed, after sales services etc.

11.4.7 Distribution Overhead

Distribution overhead includes all indirect material cost, indirect wages and indirect expenses incurred with making the packed product available for dispatch and ends with making reconditioned returned empty packages available for reuse.

The costs of the following groups of items fall within the definition of distribution overhead :

- Cost of indirect materials such as packing cases, oil, grease, spare parts used in upkeep of delivery vehicles.
- Indirect wages such as wages of packers, van drivers, dispatch clerks, etc.
- Indirect expenses such as carriage and freight outwards, rent, rates, depreciation and insurance of warehouses, depreciation, running expenses of delivery vehicles etc.

11.5 METHODS OF COSTING

Different methods of cost finding are used because businesses vary in their nature and in the type of products or service they produce. The output has to be costed, so the costing methods to be employed are also determined with due regard to the method of production and the unit of cost used. The two main systems of cost finding which have been evolved are Job costing and Process costing.

11.5.1 Job costing

This method is applied where the items of prime cost are traceable to specific jobs or orders, as in house-building; ship building; engine and machinery construction and repair; contractor's work, e.g., making reinforced concrete structures; garage and repair shops etc.

Job costing may include the following terms:

- **Contract costing:** In the building trade, a contract is treated as a whole job and is costed in total.
- **Terminal costing:** This method emphasizes the essential nature of job costing, i.e., the cost can be properly terminated at some point and related to a particular job.
- **Batch costing:** A batch of similar products is regarded as one job, and the cost of this complete batch is collected. It is then used to determine the unit cost of the article produced.

It should be noted that when the articles lose their identity in manufacturing operation, the process costing methods should be adopted.

11.5.2 Process costing

This method of costing is used where it is impossible to trace the items of prime cost to a particular order because its identity is lost in volume of continuous production.

In oil refinery works, for example, we cannot trace the prime cost of specific order, (say for 50 kg. of oil) where several tones of oil are being produced at the same time. Accordingly, the procedure would be to divide the cost of production during a certain period by the total number of tones of oil produced during that period, in order to find out the cost per tone of oil. Process costing is extensively used in paint manufacture, paper manufacture and soap manufacture, textile and chemical industries.

The following additional terms are used instead of process costing, but each is basically process costing.

- **Single, output or unit costing:** This is used where a single article or service is produced. The whole production cycle is costed as a process or series of processes, and division by the total number of units produced yields the average final cost per unit. This method is applied to marble quarry, mining, steel works and breweries.
- **Operating or operative costing:** This is applicable where services are rendered rather than goods produced. This procedure is same as in single costing. Operating costing applies to railway undertakings, road transport, telephone services, hospital services etc.
- **Operation costing:** This is a method of unit costing by operation connected with mass production and repetitive production.

11.5.3 Multiple or Composite costing

Some products are so complex (e.g., motorcars, aero planes, etc.) that no single system of costing is applicable. Where total cost is ascertained by aggregating component cost which are collected by both job and process costing, the system is termed as multiple or composite costing. Multiple costing applies to agricultural machinery, general hosiery, electrical accessories etc.

11.6 CLASSIFICATION OF COST

Cost classification is the process of grouping costs according to their common characteristics. In order to identify costs with cost centres or cost units, a suitable classification of costs is of vital importance. Costs may be classified according to their nature, i.e., material, labour and expenses and a number of other characteristics, such as, function, variability, controllability and normality.

11.6.1 Function

Under this, costs are classified according to the purpose for which they are incurred. Functional classification leads to the grouping of costs according to broad divisions of activity into-

- **Production cost** - The cost of the process which begins with supplying materials, labour and services and ends with primary packing of the product. Under this head all expenses are collected and further subdivided to arrive at the production cost.
- **Administration cost** – The cost of formulating the policy, directing the organisation and controlling the operations of an undertaking, which is not related directly to research, development, production, distribution or selling activity or function.
- **Selling cost:** The cost of seeking to create and stimulate demand (sometimes termed 'marketing') and of securing orders.
- **Distribution cost:** The cost of the sequence of operations which begins with making the packed product available for despatch and ends with making the reconditioned returned empty package available for reuse.

11.6.2 Variability

Under this, costs are classified according to their behaviour in relation to changes in the volume of production. Considering the variability, costs may be grouped as:

- **Fixed cost:** A cost which tends to be unaffected by variations in volume of output. Rent, insurance, etc., remain the same whether we produce different units in different months. It is also called 'capacity cost' or 'period cost'.
- **Semi fixed cost:** A cost which is partly fixed and partly variable. The semi-fixed or semi-variable cost varies at certain levels and also remains fixed at other levels of activity.
- **Variable cost:** A cost which tends to vary directly with volume of output.

11.6.3 Controllability

Under this, costs are classified according to whether or not they are influenced by the action of a given member of the undertaking. The broad divisions under this are:

- **Controllable cost:** A cost which is influenced by the action of a given member of an undertaking.

- **Uncontrollable cost** - A cost of which is not defined by the action of a given member of an undertaking.

11.6.4 Normality

Under this, costs are classified according to whether they are costs which are normally incurred at a given level of output in the conditions in which that level of output is normally attained. The broad divisions under this are :

- **Normal cost:** A cost which is normally incurred at a given level of output in the conditions in which that level of output is normally attained.
- **Abnormal cost:** A cost which is not normally incurred at a given level of output in the conditions in which that level of output is normally attained.

11.7 OVERHEADS

Overhead is defined as the cost of indirect material, indirect labour and such other indirect expenses incurred in the organization activities. Therefore, overheads are all expenses other than direct expenses. The main groups into which overheads fall are:

- Production overheads - Building rent, indirect labour, fuel, power, etc.
- Administration overheads - office rent, wages to clerks, telephone etc.
- Selling Overheads - Advertising, salaries to sales personnel, sales, office rents, etc.
- Distribution Overheads - Warehouse rents, goods freights, loading-unloading expenses, etc.
- R & D Overheads - Expenses on R & D materials, equipments, salaries to R & D personnel etc.

Factory cost

It is the cost of a product spent directly on manufacturing it includes the production overheads.

Factory Cost = Prime Cost + Production overheads

Total cost

This cost includes the manufacturing costs and all other overheads, both direct and indirect.

Total Cost = Factory Cost + All overheads

Note: All overheads includes Selling, Administration, Distribution, R & D overheads.

Selling Price

It is the total cost of the product with the profit added.

Selling Price per product = Total Cost + Profit.

11.7.1 Allocation of Overheads

An uniform overhead can be charged in an industry if it is manufacturing only one type of product. But, if a number of different products are manufactured then each product variety should be allocated with a fair and reasonable share of the overhead costs. The overhead costs are allocated on the basis of responsibility and relative benefits concerned in the manufacture of a product. The important methods of allocating overheads are:

- Percentage of direct labour cost
- Percentage of direct material cost
- Prime cost percentage rate
- Labour hour rate
- Machine hour rate
- Production unit method.

11.7.1.1 Percentage of Direct Labour Cost Method

This method makes use of the cost of direct labour charged to a particular product as a basis for allocating the overhead rate for the product.

Percentage of Direct Labour Cost = Percentage of overheads

$$= \frac{\text{Factory overhead for budget period}}{\text{Direct labour cost for budget period}} \times 100$$

Advantages

- The method is easy and economical.
- It gives highest efficiency under uniform conditions (like wages, machines, workers etc.).
- This method is more suitable where the products are manufactured using manual operations.

Disadvantages

- The method ignores the variations in machinery used for different production operations.
- The method is not equitable, as it charges higher overheads to jobs performed by workers receiving high wages.

11.7.1.2 Percentage of Direct Material Cost Method

In this method overheads are allocated on the basis of the cost of direct material used for production.

Percentage of Direct Material Cost = Percentage of overheads

$$= \frac{\text{Factor overhead for budget period}}{\text{Direct material cost for budget period}} \times 100$$

Advantages

- The material and method of manufacture are common to all products.
- The expenses on direct material constitute the factor determining the total cost, as in foundries.

Disadvantages

- Suitable only for common manufacturing methods with same materials.
- This method is not accurate when applied where different types of materials are used for production.

11.7.1.3 Prime Cost Percentage Rate Method

Prime cost is the sum of direct labour cost, direct material cost and direct expenses. This method allocates overheads on the basis of these costs.

Prime cost Percentage rate = Percentage of overheads

$$= \frac{\text{Factory overhead for budget period}}{\text{Prime cost for budget period}} \times 100$$

Advantages

- Method is more suitable where prime costs are more prominent in determining the total cost.
- Gives higher efficiency under uniform conditions of man, materials, and expenses.

Disadvantages

- Allocation of overheads is not equitable.

- Ignores variations in operating conditions.
- Not suitable where different materials and operations are involved for production.

11.7.1.4 Labour Hour Rate Method

In this method Labour hours form the basis for allocating the overheads. It is more accurate than direct labour cost method. Overhead rate per hour of direct labour is given by

$$\frac{\text{Factory overhead for budget period}}{\text{Direct labour hours for budget period}}$$

Advantages

- It is the most balanced method of allocating, overheads.
- It is suitable where manual labour operation are involved.

Disadvantages

- It ignore variations in type and size of machinery used.
- It requires additional clerical records.
- It is inaccurate if the products arc manufactured using both machine and hand operations.

11.7.1.5 Machine Hour Rate Method

In this method the number of machine hours are considered for allocating the overheads.

$$\text{Machine hour rate} = \frac{\text{Factory overhead for budget period}}{\text{Machine hours for budget period}}$$

Advantages

- This method is more accurate because in modern processes the overheads of machines are more than any other sources.
- This is suitable where machines constitute more important and costly element than manual labour.

Disadvantages

- It is not applicable where the products are a combined result of machine and manual operations.
- It requires maintenance of clerical records.

11.7.1.6 Production Unit Method

One of the simplest method of allocating overheads is on the basis of number units produced such as kg, tones, liters etc.

$$\text{Overhead rate per unit} = \frac{\text{Factory overhead for budget period}}{\text{Production in units for budget period}}$$

This method is simple and easy for use. It is suitable for industries manufacturing one type of product and of one size only.

11.8 STANDARD COSTING

Standard costing is the process of determining the cost per unit in advance, based on the management's standards of efficient operations and relevant expenditures.

Standard cost is the estimated cost per unit of output for labour, materials and overheads, based on the prediction of material prices, labour rates and overhead expenses for a given period.

Standard costs represent the best estimate that can be made of what costs should be for material, labour and overhead after eliminating inefficiencies and wastes.

However, any deviation from the standard of the materials used will deviate the standard cost of the product.

Advantages of Standard Costing

- Standard costing represent management's best measure of efficient plant operation.
- Based on standard costing the manufacturing process can be best controlled.
- Standard costs bring about a more systematic and thorough analysis of costs.
- Standard costs reduce the variations in final product price to a minimum.
- Standard costs can be used to fix the selling price of a product and for cost control.

REVIEW QUESTIONS

1. Differentiate between cost, costing and cost accounting.
2. What are the advantages of cost accounting?
3. State and explain the various elements of cost.
4. Enumerate various methods of costing.
5. Given the classification of cost.
6. What are various overheads?
7. Explain standard costing.

CHAPTER – 12

ENTREPRENEURSHIP

12.1 INTRODUCTION

Entrepreneurship is a trait possessed by an entrepreneur. The spirit of enterprise makes a person an entrepreneur. Entrepreneur thus is an innovator, who carries out new combinations in ever-changing environment to initiate and accelerate the process of economics, social and technological development.

"An entrepreneur is one who always searches for changes, responds to it and exploits it as an opportunity" – Peter F. Drucker

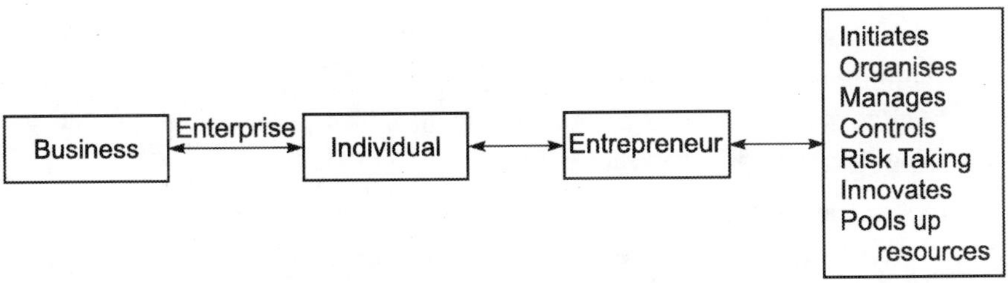

A model of entrepreneurship

An entrepreneur is an economic agent who plays an important role in the economic development of a country. He possesses required knowledge, skills, initiative, drive and spirit of innovation and aims to achieve goals. He identifies opportunities and grabs them for economic benefits.

Entrepreneurship is a dynamic activity which helps the entrepreneur to bring changes in the process of production, innovations in business, new ideas and usages of resources, establishing new markets etc.

12.2 ENTREPRENEUR

12.2.1 Meaning and evolution of concept:

The term "Entrepreneur" is defined in variety of ways. It varies from country to country, time to time and the level of economic development. The word "entrepreneur" is derived from the French verb "entreprendre" which means "to undertake". In 16th century, the Frenchmen who organized and led military expeditions were referred to as "entrepreneurs". In early 18th century

French economist Richard Cantillon used the word entrepreneur to business. Since then the word entrepreneur is used to one who takes the risk of stating new organization or business or introducing a new idea, product or service to society.

According to Joseph Schumpeter "An entrepreneur in an advanced economy is an individual who introduces something new in the economy a method of production not yet tested by experience in the branch of manufacture concerned, a product with which consumers are not yet familiar, a new source of raw materials or of new markets and the life". Accordingly to him the functions of an entrepreneurship are:

- Introduction of new product
- Introduction of new methods of production
- Development of new markets and finding fresh sources of raw materials and
- Making changes

Cantillon defined entrepreneur as "The agent who buys factors of production at certain prices in order to combine them into a product with a view to selling it at uncertain prices in future".

To summarise, "an entrepreneur is the person who bears risk, unites various factors of production, to explore the perceived opportunities in order to evoke demand, create wealth and employment".

12.2.2 Characteristics of Entrepreneur:

An entrepreneur is a highly goal oriented, enthusiastic and energetic individual. A good entrepreneur should posses the following characteristics.

(i) Action-oriented, highly motivated and ready to take risk at all levels to achieve the goal.

(ii) Should have unwavering determination and commitment.

(iii) Creativeness and result oriented, hard working.

(iv) Accepts responsibilities with enthusiasm.

(v) Self confident, dedicated and self disciplined.

(vi) Both thinker and doer, planner and worker.

(vii) Future vision, intelligent, imaginative and self-directed.

12.2.3 Qualities of an entrepreneur:

The important qualities of an entrepreneur are:

(i) Success and achievement: The entrepreneurs are self directed to achieve goals.

(ii) **Risk bearer:** He accepts risk, understand and manage risk.

(iii) **Opportunity explorer:** He always identifies opportunities and explores them.

(iv) **Planner:** He is a good planner and doer. He plans and follows the plans sincerely to achieve the goals.

(v) **Stress taker:** He should accept and bear any amount of stresses that may evolve in the business.

(vi) **Facing uncertainties:** They should face the uncertainties and unexpected outcomes and accept them.

(vii) **Independent:** He is an independent person and likes to be his own master. He is a job given and not job seeker.

(viii) **Flexible:** He is an open minded person, flexible to adopt to demanding situational changes.

(ix) **Self-confident:** He directs his abilities towards the accomplishment of goals.

(x) **Motivator:** He initiates and influences people, motivates the people to accomplish the goals.

12.3 FUNCTIONS OF AN ENTREPRENEUR:

An entrepreneur performs all the necessary functions that are essential from the point of establishing and developing the enterprise.

The functions are broadly classified into three groups.

- Primary functions
- Other functions and
- Functions important for developing countries.

The various functions and their sub functions are mentioned in the following table.

Functions of Entrepreneur

PRIMARY FUNCTION	OTHER FUNCTIONS	FUNCTIONS IMPORTANT FOR DEVELOPING COUNTRIES
1. Planning	1. Diversification of production	1. Management of scarce resources
2. Organising	2. Expansion of the enterprise	2. Dealing with public
3. Decision making	3. Maintaining cordial employer and employee relations	3. Engineering

4. Management	4. Talking labour problems	4. New product development
5. Innovation	5. Coordination with outside agencies	5. Parallel opportunities
6. Risk bearing		6. Marketing
7. Leading		7. Management
8. Controlling		8. Customer relation

Primary Functions

(i) **Planning:** Like in any other activity, planning is a first step of entrepreneur. He prepares his plan of proposed project or business in a very systematic way. Planning involves

- ➢ Study of various ideas
- ➢ Scanning and selecting the best idea
- ➢ Selection of product line and location of plant
- ➢ Deciding the type of business organization
- ➢ Preparation of budget and identifying capital sources
- ➢ Studying the government rules, regulations and policies
- ➢ Study and selection of work force
- ➢ Study and selection of marketing strategies

(ii) **Organisation:** An entrepreneur coordinates and supervises the various tasks of organizing for optimal utilization of resources.

(iii) **Decision making:** He has to take effective decisions with regard to business objectives of the enterprise, arrangement of resources and facilities like men, material, machines, money, methods, technology etc., development of a market for the product and maintain good relationship with others.

(iv) **Management:** It refers to managing of the day-to-day problems. These include future expansion and policies in long run.

(v) **Innovation:** He should be innovative in launching of new product, introduction of new technology in production line, creation of new market, new or better source of raw material.

(vi) **Risk bearing:** He should undertake responsibility of risk due to unforeseen situations.

In addition to these primary functions, entrepreneur has to perform other functions and functions important for developing countries.

The other functions are: diversification of production, expansion of the enterprise, maintaining cordial relations with employer and employees, attending to and resolving the labour problems and coordination with outside agencies for the well being of the enterprise.

The functions of an entrepreneur with reference to the underdeveloped countries include wide range of activities like: management of scarce resources, dealing with public, engineering, new product development looking out for parallel opportunities, marketing, management of customers and supplier relations etc.

12.4 TYPES OF ENTREPRENEUR

The entrepreneurs have been broadly classified according to the type of business, use of professional skill, motivation, growth and stages of development as given below:

(a) According to the type of business

(i) Business entrepreneur

(ii) Trading entrepreneur

(iii) Industrial entrepreneur

(iv) Corporate entrepreneur

(v) Agricultural entrepreneur

(vi) Retail entrepreneur

(vii) Service entrepreneur etc.

(b) According to the use of technology

(i) Technical entrepreneur or non technical entrepreneur

(ii) Professional entrepreneur

(iii) Low tech or high tech entrepreneurs.

(c) According to motivation

(i) Pure entrepreneur

(ii) Induced entrepreneur

(iii) Motivated entrepreneur

(iv) Spontaneous entrepreneur

(d) According to the growth

(i) Growth entrepreneur

(ii) Super growth entrepreneur

(e) According to the stages of development

(i) First generation entrepreneurs

(ii) Modern entrepreneurs

(iii) Classical entrepreneurs

(f) According to the area

(i) Urban entrepreneur

(ii) Rural entrepreneur

(g) According to age and gender

(i) Young entrepreneur

(ii) Old entrepreneur

(iii) Male entrepreneur

(iv) Female entrepreneur

(h) According to the scale of operation

(i) Small scale entrepreneur

(ii) Medium scale entrepreneur

(iii) Large scale entrepreneur

(i) Other type

(i) Professional and non professional entrepreneur

(ii) Modern entrepreneur

(iii) Traditional entrepreneur

(iv) Skilled and non-skilled entrepreneur

(v) Forced entrepreneur

(vi) Inherited entrepreneur

(vii) National or International entrepreneur etc.

(a) Entrepreneurs according to the type of business.

(i) Business entrepreneurs:

Business entrepreneurs are individuals who conceive an idea for a new product or service leading to new business. He deals with product development, marketing and sales.

(ii) Trading entrepreneurs:

Trading entrepreneur is one who undertakes trading activities and is not concerned with the manufacturing work. He is engaged in only trading.

(iii) Industrial entrepreneurs:

Industrial entrepreneur is generally a manufacturer who identifies the potential needs of customers and tailors a product or service to meet the marketing needs.

(iv) Corporate entrepreneurs:

Corporate entrepreneur demonstrates his innovative skill in organizing and managing corporate undertaking.

(v) Agricultural entrepreneur:

Agricultural entrepreneurs undertake agricultural activities such as raising and marketing of crops, fertilizers and other inputs of agriculture. They cover a broad spectrum of the agricultural sector and includes its related areas.

(b) Entrepreneurs according to technology

(i) Technical entrepreneur:

Technical entrepreneur also called as "craftsman", develops improved quality goods. His concentration is oriented towards manufacture than marketing and selling. His aim is to develop quality goods using his innovative ideas and craftsmanship.

(ii) Non-technical entrepreneur:

Non-technical entrepreneur is not concerned with technical aspects of a product. They are mainly concerned with development of alternative marketing and distribution strategies to promote their business.

(iii) Professional entrepreneurs:

Professional entrepreneur is a person whose interest is to establish a business but does not deal with its management and organizing it. Generally speaking a professional entrepreneur sells out the established business and starts another venture. He is very dynamic who keeps on conceiving and venturing new ideas.

(c) Entrepreneurs according to motivation:

(i) Pure entrepreneur:

A pure entrepreneur is a person who gets motivated by psychological and not by economic rewards. He works for his own satisfaction or for his own status.

(ii) Induced entrepreneur:

An induced entrepreneur is one who is induced to take up a task due to policy measures that provide assistance, incentives, and concessions etc., to start an enterprise. Many small scale industries are started by people because government and institutions are giving support and lots of concessions.

(iii) Motivated entrepreneur:

New entrepreneurs are motivated by the desire for self-fulfillment. They come into existence because of the possibility of making and marketing some new product.

(iv) Spontaneous entrepreneurs:

This type of entrepreneur start their business by natural talents inherent in them. They possess traits like initiative, boldness and self confidence which motivate them to take up entrepreneurship.

(d) According to growth:

Growth of an enterprise may be termed as low, medium, high or super high growth. The development of a new venture leads to a chance of growth. Growth entrepreneurs are those who take up an industry with substantial growth prospects. On the other hand, super growth entrepreneurs show enormous growth performance in any venture they take up.

(e) According to stages of development:

(i) First generation entrepreneur:

A first generation entrepreneur is one who starts an industrial unit by his own innovative ideas and skills.

(ii) Modern entrepreneur:

A modern entrepreneur is one who undertakes those projects that are well needed and suited for changing demands.

(iii) Classical entrepreneur:

A classical entrepreneur is one who is concerned with the customers and marketing needs while developing a new venture.

(f) Others

(i) Innovative entrepreneur:

Innovative entrepreneur is one who sees the opportunity for introducing a new technique of production process or a new product or a new market or a new service using his innovative ideas.

(ii) Initiative entrepreneur:

Initiative entrepreneur are revolutionary and take lot of initiative in any work. He can set in motion the chain reaction which leads to cumulative progress. He is more an organiser of factors of production than a creator.

12.5 INTRAPRENEUR:

Intrapreneurship is the entrepreneurship with in an existing business structure. It is used to bridge the gap between science and market place. Existing business will have the financial resources, necessary skills to carry out business, the marketing and distribution systems to commercialise the innovation. But many times, in bureaucratic structure, due to the focus on short-term profits and a highly structured organization, prevent creativity and development of new products. As a result the organizations who have recognized these innovative factors and need for creativity, have attempted to establish an intrapreneurial spirit in their organisations. In the present era of competition, the need for new products and the intrapreneurial spirit have become so great that more and more companies are developing an intrapreneurial environment.

The differences in the entrepreneurial and managerial domains have contributed towards an increased need for intrapreneurship. This need is growing due to variety of events occurring on social, cultural and business levels. In social level, there is an increasing interest in 'doing your own thing' and doing it on one's own terms. Some individuals having self confidence, self motivation and belief in their own talents, often desire to innovate new things on their own. They want to own responsibilities, and to work in their own way. They become frustrated if this freedom is not given to them and get demotivated. Intrapreneurship is one such method of providing freedom, stimulating and capitalizing on individuals in an organization who think that things can be done in different and better way.

The resistance against flexibility, growth and diversification can be overcome by developing a spirit of entrepreneurship within the organization which is called as intrapreneurship. An increase in intrapreneurship reflects a proportionate increase in social, cultural and business pressures. Intrapreneurship is reflected more strongly in entrepreneurial activities and also in top management.

Elements of intrapreneurship:

The intrapreneurship has four important elements.

(i) New business venturing:

This is the corporate venturing, the creation of new business with in the organization. This includes redefining the company's products or services, development of new market segment or formation of new corporate ventures.

(ii) Innovations:

Innovation is the development of new products, improvement of existing products, development of improved and simplified production methods and procedures.

(iii) Self-renewal:

This is the transformation of an organization through the renewal of main ideas. This includes a redefinition of a business concept, reorganization or modifications in the system with an aim to initiate innovating.

(iv) Proactiveness:

Proactiveness includes initiative and risk taking, competitiveness and dashing to take new challenges. Organisations with this type of pro activeness spirit will lead the market than follow the competitors.

Brief comparison of intrapreneurs, entrepreneurs and managers is given below:

Point	Intrapreneur	Entrepreneur	Manager
1. Goal management	Independent, innovates new ideas	Independent, starts new venture and leads direct involvement.	Delegates and supervises more than direct involvement
2. Status	Not concerned about traditional status, but wants recognition.	Not concerned about status	Concerned about status symbol
3. Risk	Owns moderate risk	Bears all the risk and uncertainty	Does not bear any risk.
4. Rewards	Gets fixed reward for his work. Many get extra for	Since there is risk, he may get profit or loss depending	Works for salary for his service which is fixed and

	his innovations	on outcome.	definite.
5. Innovation	Innovative	Very innovative	Need not be innovative. He manages the ideas of top management
6. Decision making	Moderate, limited to his work.	Very much involved in decision making	Delegates the decisions of top management

12.6 ENTREPRENEURSHIP

12.6.1 Concept of entrepreneurship:

Entrepreneurship is a process undertaken by an entrepreneur to augment his business interests. Some authors define it as "Entrepreneurship is the indivisible process flourishes, when the interlinked dimensions of individual psychological entrepreneurship, entrepreneur traits, social encouragement, business opportunities, Government policies, availability of resources and opportunities coverage towards the common good, development of the society and economy".

Entrepreneurship lies more in the ability to minimize the use of resources and to put them to maximum advantage. Above all, entrepreneurship in today's context is the product of teamwork and the ability to create, build and work as a team.

Entrepreneurship is the process of identifying opportunities in the market place, arranging the resources required to pursue these opportunities and inverting the resources to exploit the opportunities for better gains.

Higgins defined entrepreneurship as "the function of foreseeing investment and production opportunities, organizing an enterprise to undertake a new production process, raising capital, hiring labour, arranging the supply of raw materials, finding site, introducing new technique, discovering new source of raw materials and selecting top managers for day-to-day operation.

Cole's definition for entrepreneurship is "the purposeful activity of an individual or a group of associated individuals undertaken to initiate, maintain or organize profit by production or distributing of economic goods and services".

All the above definitions highlight the risk bearing, innovating and resource organizing, achieving goal through production of goods or services.

12.6.2 Characteristics of entrepreneurship:

The process of entrepreneurship is a complex one having multidimensional characteristics. The following are some of the commonly accepted characteristics suggested by experts.

(i) Innovation

Entrepreneurship involves innovation of new things to effect dynamic changes and good success in economy. It should create conditions for growth of the economy.

(ii) Risk-taking

Risk is a inbuilt element of any business. Entrepreneurship should be risk bearing to cater uncertainty of future.

(iii) Skillful management

Entrepreneurship brings together various functions of the management – planning, organizing, staffing, directing, controlling and leading.

(iv) Organisation

It brings together various facilities of production for an efficient and economical use.

(v) Decision making

Decision-making is a very vital characteristic of an entrepreneurship. Taking decisions at all levels and stages of an entrepreneurship is a routine task.

(vi) Making the enterprise a success

Entrepreneurship is mainly an economic activity as it deals with creating and operating an enterprise. It involves in satisfying the needs of customers with the help of production and distribution of goods and services. This makes the enterprise a success.

12.7 EVOLUTION OF ENTREPRENEURSHIP

Entrepreneurship existed even in very early stages in different kinds. Its evolution is discussed below.

(i) Early period:

An early example of entrepreneurship is known to be the example of Marco Polo who tried to trade routes to the Far East. He used to sign a contract with a venture capitalist to sell his goods. The capitalist was the risk bearer, the merchant-adventurer took the role of trading, bearing all physical and other risks. After his successful selling of goods and completing his trip, the profits were shared by the capitalist and merchant.

(ii) Middle ages:

In the middle ages, the term entrepreneur was referred to a person who was managing large projects. He was not taking any risk but was managing the projects using the resources provided. Some examples are the cleric who used to be incharge of big architectural works like castles, cathedrals etc.

(iii) 17th Century:

During 17th century, an amalgamation of risk with entrepreneurship had evolved. A person (entrepreneur) used to enter into a contractual agreement with government to perform a service or to supply some goods. This involved some risk since the contract price was fixed and the profit or loss was borne by the entrepreneur.

Cantillon, a noted author developed one of the early theories of he entrepreneurship during 17th Century. He viewed the entrepreneur as the risk taker, observing that merchants, formers, craftsmen, buy at a certain price and sell at an uncertain price, hence operating at risk.

(iv) 18th and 19th Century

As a result of industrialization during 18th century the person with capital (capitalist) is differentiated from the person who needs capital (entrepreneur). Many of the technical inventors did not have money to turn their inventions into products. Hence some capitalists had to finance them.

(v) 20th Century:

During this, the entrepreneurs were not distinguished from managers and were viewed mostly from the view of economy. The entrepreneur organises and operates an enterprise for personal gains. He takes risk, contributes his own initiative, skills, he plans, organizes and leads his enterprise. He owns and bears the loss or gain. In the middle or 20th century, the notion of an entrepreneur as an innovator was established.

The ability to innovate could be seen throughout history from the Egyptians who had designed, planned and erected pyramids with very heavy stone blocks, to the space launching technology, to a cell phones to an artificial pace maker in human heart. Although the tools have changed with advances in science and technology, the ability to innovate and risk taking has been present in all generations.

12.8 DEVELOPMENT OF ENTREPRENEURSHIP

The development of entrepreneurship started in the olden days. Ancient people invented wheel, fire by robbing stores, spears to hunt animals, new ways and means of cultivation etc. Then came the era of boats and ships opening the doors of trade at far places. The invention of steam engine revolutionized sea and land transportation. Eventually the industrial resolution during 19th century led to better and modern techniques of entrepreneurship.

The noteworthy pioneers of this era are Colt who invented fire power for weapons, Whitney who invented 'gin' which revolutionized spinning of cotton and Morse's telegraph that changed the life of communication. During 20th century foundation of modern industry was laid. America became leading industrial country. American steel industry was founded by Andrew Corregie, Henry Ford started automobiles in a very big way. Though Henry Ford was not an inventor, he was a great entrepreneur.

The contemporary period of entrepreneurship began with innovators such as Mc Cormic, who revolutionized mechanical reaper in agriculture, Alexander Graham Bell who invented telephone, Thomas Alva Edison who invented Electric bulb, Gillet who invested safety razor etc.

In the Indian context, pioneers like Jamshedji Tata, Birla etc., though not inventors, were great entrepreneurs who contributed to the technical and economic growth of India.

All these entrepreneurs have been responsible for noteworthy innovators that charged the human life for better. IBM converted the mechanical type writer to a electrically operated one. Apple developed Personal Computers.

Today, we consider some companies as giants in innovations and entrepreneurial ventures. To name some, Microsoft for office software, Sony for electric goods, Ford for cars, Intel for Micro electronics and I.Cs, Sun Micro systems for Electronic workstations etc.

In all above examples, starting from early period to today's entrepreneurs, there have been enthusiastic individuals who went out and extended their hands to create new ventures which created new avenues and satisfied needs of people.

12.9 STAGES IN ENTREPRENEURIAL PROCESS:

The process of starting a new venture is the main theme of entrepreneurial process which involves more than just problem solving in any typical management position. An entrepreneur must find, evaluate and develop an opportunity by overcoming the problem that arise in developing something new. This process has five important stages:

(i) Identification of an opportunity

(ii) Evaluation of the opportunity

(iii) Preparation of the business plan

(iv) Determination and organizing the resources

(v) Management of the enterprise.

(i) Identification of opportunity:

The first step in the entrepreneurial process is the identification of opportunity. This may be from his own idea or from external sources like consumers and business associates, members of distribution system, independent technical organizations, consultants, etc. Consumers are the best source of ideas for a new venture who spells out the need of a product or service. The business associates also can give ideas of a product or service.

Due to the close contact with the end user, member of distribution system also see product needs one can identify new business opportunities through a discussion with a retailer, wholesalers or a trade representative.

Some individuals are highly technical oriented and are not interested in any entrepreneurship. Such people conceptualise new business opportunities that can be given to the interested. Some government organizations and R & D centers also provide new ideas.

(ii) Evaluation of the opportunity

The opportunity identified by using either input from consumers, business associates, channel members or technical people, must be carefully screened and evaluated. This evaluation is perhaps the most critical element of the entrepreneurial process as it allows the entrepreneur to assess whether the specific product or service provides sufficient return on investment. The evaluation process involves looking at the length of opportunity, its real and perceived valve, its risks and returns, its fit with personal skills and goals of the entrepreneur and its uniqueness or differential advantage in its competitive environment.

The length of opportunity and the market size and share are two main aspects for deciding the risk and gains or profits. SWOT (strengths, weaknesses, opportunities and threats) analysis is one of the useful analysis tools. Strength and weakness are internal factors and related to the organization and opportunities and threats are external and related to the environment and competition. The risks reflect the market, competition, technology and amount of capital involved. The capital invested forms the basis for returns and profits. The opportunity must finally fit the personal skills and goals of the entrepreneur. It is very important that the entrepreneur must be able to put forth the necessary time and effort needed to see the venture succeed. An over all opportunity assessment plan is prepared to evaluate the opportunity. Unlike a business plan, this is a short one, focuses only on the opportunity with risks and rewards and makes it clear whether or not to go with it.

This plan includes:

- description of product or service
- agreement of opportunity
- assessment of the entrepreneur and his team
- resources needed
- amount and source of capital needed
- rewards and profit expected.

(iii) Development of a business plan:

To achieve the proposed business opportunity, a well defined business plan need to be developed. This is a tedious and time consuming activity of the entrepreneurial process. The business plan should contain the following in order.

- Title of project, table of contents and executive summary.
- Description of business and industry.
- Technology plan.
- Financial plan.
- Organization plan.
- Production and operation plan.
- Marketing and distribution plan.
- Summery of plan.

A good business plan is very essential to develop the opportunity and determine the resources received, pooling up the resources for successful managing of the proposed venture.

(iv) Determination and organizing the resources

This process begins with the assessment of present resources. Enough care must be taken not to underestimate the amount and nature of resources required. The risk involved with insufficient or incorrect resources should be calculated. organising the required resources at the appropriate time is another important aspect of entrepreneurial process. Alternative sources of supply, process of manufacture etc., are to be planned.

(v) Management of Enterprise

After resources are acquired, the entrepreneur must use them to implement the business plan. The operational problems of the growing enterprise must also be examined. This calls for a management with all functions like planning, organizing, staffing, directing and controlling.

12.10 ROLE OF ENTREPRENEUR IN ECONOMIC DEVELOPMENT

The role of entrepreneurs in economic development involves more than just increasing the output and income; it involves in initiating and effecting the change in the structure of business or society. This change gives way to growth and higher output that leads to higher profits. Innovation plays very important role in economic growth both in developing new products or services and stimulating idea of investment in new ventures. This new investment works on both the demand and supply sides of growth. The new capital created expands the capacity for growth on supply side and the resultant new spending brings new capacity and increased output on demand side.

In spite of the importance of investment and innovation in the economic development of an area, there is little awareness of the product evolution process. This is the process through which innovation develops and commercialises through the entrepreneur's activity which in turn results in economic growth.

Entrepreneur bridges the gap between science and the market place, creating new enterprises and brings new products and services into the market. Those activities of an entrepreneur significantly effect the economy of an area by building economic base and providing jobs. In some areas entrepreneur creates new products and new employment. Thus entrepreneur thrusts impact and plays vital role both in overall economic development and creating employment to people.

12.11 ENTREPRENEURSHIP IN INDIA

The evolution of entrepreneurship in India is the efforts of great people as well as professionals. It started as family business known to be around 1850s with the starting of cotton mill in Bombay (Mumbai). From then on, entrepreneurship had grown in all directions from cotton mill to manufacture, to services, electronic goods, health care, exports and imports, information technology, education, transport, space technology etc.

Past: In the past "business community" was involved in trade and commerce. This community is presently known to be "Vaisyas" or "Banias". The following points are noteworthy with respect to the entrepreneurship in the past:

(i) Manufacture and supply of a product was based on demand. The traders used to book orders from the required people and get them from the producer.

(ii) All the members of the family were involved in the business from planning to manufacture stage and finally selling them.

(iii) The industrial activity was controlled by the cast system. For example, weavers used to weave cloths, gold smiths used to make ornaments, formers used to produce food products etc.

(iv) The skill of any enterprise was inherited from ancestors.

(v) The trade activity was dependant on caste system.

The family based industries and trade were badly affected during British rule. Indian entrepreneurship was mainly in the areas of textiles, Iron and steel and hydroelectric projects etc.

Present:

There is tremendous growth of industries and services over last 50-60 years. Banking, automobiles, software development, petrochemicals, cement, steel, communication etc., are some of the major modern entrepreneurship areas, where lot of innovations had taken place.

Some of the noteworthy highly talented entrepreneurs of India are : G.D. Birla, J.R.D. Tata, Aditya Birla, Godrej, Jamnalal Bajaj, Wadia, Hindujas, Azim Premji of Wipro, Narayana Murthy of Infosys, Satyanarayana Raju of Satyam Computers, Dhirubai Ambani of Reliance, Karsanbhai Patel of Nirma etc.

Before 1940's the Indian business was almost dominated by British companies except for some well established companies like Tata Steel, Birla group, Wadias etc. It was very difficult to compete with British goods. After second world war (1945) more business opportunities were projected like cement, steel and other infrastructures. Indian industry began to expand in the core sector only after independence (1947).

12.12 BARRIERS OF ENTREPRENEURSHIP

The Entrepreneurship could not be taken up due to several reasons. The following are some of the barriers of entrepreneurship.

(i) Lack of capital.

(ii) Lack of technical knowledge.

(iii) Economic business cycles.

(iv) Non availability of raw materials and resources.

(v) Government regulations.

(vi) Obsolescence of technology or idea.

(vii) Unstable and unpredictable markets.

(viii) Globalisation and entry of foreign goods.

(ix) Risk.

12.13 WOMEN ENTREPRENEURS

Women constitute about 50% of the world population. In traditional societies, they are confined to house performing household activities and hence woman is generally called as "house wife" on "homemaker". But today in modern society, they have moved out of four walls of the house and are taking part in all areas of life. Nowadays women are seen in academic, teaching, politics, administration, software development, managing business enterprises, banking sector, hospitals, etc. The involvement of women in these activities generate good income to support them and their families.

12.13.1 Concept of women entrepreneurs

Women entrepreneurs may be defined as "a woman or group of women who initiate, organize and run a business enterprise". Government of India has defined woman entrepreneur as "An enterprise owned and controlled by a woman having minimum financial participation of 51% of the capital and giving at least 51% of employment generated in the enterprise to women". This definition is based on women participation in equity and employment of business enterprise. In brief, women entrepreneurs are those women who think of a business enterprise, initiate it, organize and combine the factors of production, run the enterprise and undertake the risk and economic uncertainty involved in running the business. As an entrepreneur, a woman has to perform all the functions involved in establishing an enterprise. These include idea generation and screening, determination of objectives, project preparation, product analysis, completion of promotional formalities, raising funds, procuring man power and other resources and operation of business.

12.13.2 Functions of women entrepreneur

As an entrepreneur, a woman has to perform all the functions involved in establishing an enterprise. Some of them are listed below.

(i) Exploration of the prospects of starting a new business

Women entrepreneur has to explore all the prospects of starting a new business. It involves in searching for new ideas, products, technology, market etc. She should be innovative and creative.

(ii) Pool up the resources

To start an enterprise, she needs the factors of production viz., land, labour, capital and technology.

(iii) Establish the industrial enterprise

Entrepreneurs main function is to establish and promote the enterprise. She has to select the location of enterprise and implement the idea into action.

(iv) Manage the business

She has to manage the business. In order to manage the business, she has to perform all functions of management – planning, organizing, staffing, coordinating, directing and controlling. She has to organize workers, material and other resources.

(v) Development of strategies

After starting the enterprise, a number of challenges, risks, difficulties, problems tend to begin. To face them, she has to develop strategies, play tactics and will to overcome them.

(vi) To assume risk and uncertainty

She has to bear risk and uncertainties that emerge in the enterprise. She should have good decision making capacity to take right decision at right time to suit a situation.

(vii) To develop business and business decision

She has to pay attention to business decisions. She has to take important decisions about business for its development. For the business development, she has to increase volume of production, market share, wealth etc.

(viii) Motivation

She should motivate employees to achieve the targets by putting their full effort.

(ix) Supervision and leadership:

She should supervise and lead the people towards goals.

12.13.3 Problems of women entrepreneurs

In addition to the general problems faced by any entrepreneur, women face other problems like gender problems. Some of the problems faced by women entrepreneur are presented here.

(i) Problem of finance:

Women entrepreneurs suffer from shortage of finance in two ways. First one is, women generally do not have property on their names to use as collateral security for getting loans from external sources like banks and other financial institutions. The second one is, some banks may feel women not so credit worthy and discourage women borrowers. The general belief is that they may leave the business at any time. Under such circumstances, women entrepreneurs have to depend on their own funds or funds from relatives and close friends.

(ii) Lack of education:

As per census, about 60% of women are still illiterate in India. In the absence of qualitative education, women are not exposed to business tactics, technology, management skills and functions, market knowledge, financial management etc., which are very essential for any enterprise.

(iii) Limited mobility:

In India, mobility of women is limited compared to men, due to various reasons. Women working in night shifts, staying alone in a room or return late in the night are still problems in India. With the advent of software technology this situation is slowly easing.

(iv) Family ties:

As per Indian tradition, it is mainly the women who take care of family, children, other elder people in the family and kitchen. This problem is more so with married women. The total involvement of family leaves a little or no time and energy to devote to business. Support of family members, specially husband is very essential for women to enter into business.

(v) Scarcity of raw materials:

Most of the enterprises managed by women suffer because of scarcity of raw materials and necessary inputs.

(vi) Stiff competition:

Due to limited facilities and funds, enterprises managed by women face stiff competition with man managed enterprises. Such a competition sometimes leads to loss and closure of women enterprises.

(vii) Low-risk bearing capacity:

Women in India are generally not well educated and economically not self-dependent. This leads them to low-risk bearing capacity while running an enterprise. They are not very strong minded to bear risk.

(viii) Social problems:

Women in India lead a protected life. They face social problems to come out and start an enterprise. They face problems in the society.

(ix) Male domination:

Male domination still prevails in Indian social culture. Though government says equal rights for male and female, in practice, women are given secondary treatment compared to men. In the male dominated Indian society, women are not treated equal to men, women are treated as weaker section in many sections of life.

12.13.4 Steps to be taken to develop women entrepreneurship

Though government is giving lot of support through institutions like National Bank for Agriculture and Rural Development (NABARD), Non-Government Organisations (NGOs), Nationalised banks, the issue of women entrepreneurship is not improved. There is still a wide gap between efforts and actual needs. In this situation, the following steps may be taken to develop/improve women entrepreneurship.

(i) Provide basic education and establish special institutions to train women entrepreneurs.

(ii) Conduct special workshops to women for better awareness.

(iii) Liberal financial support to motivate women entrepreneurs.

(iv) Favourable credit policies to women.

(v) Provide better marketing help to women entrepreneurs.

(vi) Provide need-based training for development of skills and entrepreneurship.

(vii) Establish Self-Help Groups (SHGs), voluntary agencies and social welfare organizations for women entrepreneurs.

(viii) Provide concessions to women entrepreneurs.

(ix) Provide a common platform to all the concerned agencies and R & D organizations to achieve an integrated approach for promoting women entrepreneurs.

12.13.5 Industries promoted by the women entrepreneurs are given below:

- Agarbathi manufacturing
- Papad making
- Embroidery
- Handicrafts for export
- Apparels manufacture/Readymade garments
- Catering service, running restaurants, hotels etc.
- Travel agency, Xerox, Photo studios, Telephone booths
- Printing presses and DTP
- Florists and Beauty Parlours, working women hostels
- Running schools and tutorial colleges etc.

12.14 ENTREPRENEURSHIP DEVELOPMENT PROGRAMME (EDP)

Entrepreneurship has become a matter of great concern in India. In India rapid growth of small-scale industries is mainly due to the entrepreneurship development. Entrepreneurship Development Programme (EDP) focuses on identifying entrepreneurship qualities of an individual, providing required training, preparing related project reports, preparing the entrepreneurs to manage finance, production, technology, marketing and infrastructure facilities. EDP also provides knowledge to solve problems and difficulties of entrepreneurs by showing remedial measures.

12.14.1 Need for EDPs

Past experience has shown that industrial promotion by provision of facilities, technical assistance, management training, consultancy, industrial information and other services alone will not be sufficient to develop entrepreneurs. Over the years, the EDPs have become a vital strategy for bringing out the untapped human skills, to channelise them into accelerating industrialization and growth of the small-scale sectors.

Nowadays, entrepreneurship development has become very important in achieving the all round development of our country. Many opportunities in the fields of electronics, chemicals, medicine, agriculture, communication, and food technology are made available for the entrepreneurs. It was need to motivate people to take up such opportunities for the development of enterprises. EDPs build confidence in the people and provide necessary training and guidelines to the young and prospective entrepreneurs. Hence there is a need for the EDPs in India.

12.14.2 Objectives of EDPs

The important objectives of EDP are:

(i) To develop and strengthen their entrepreneurial quality.

(ii) To analyse environmental set up relating to small industry and small business.

(iii) To select product.

(iv) To formulate project report for a product.

(v) To know the good and bad in becoming entrepreneur.

(vi) To appreciate the need of entrepreneurship.

(vii) To understand the process and procedures and formalities involved in setting up enterprise.

(viii) To give the knowledge of sources of help, concessions and help available for starting a small-scale industry.

(ix) To acquire the basic skills.

(x) To let the entrepreneur to set or reset the objectives of his business or service.

(xi) To prepare him to accept risk and uncertainty involved in running a business.

(xii) To enable him to take decisions.

(xiii) Enable him to communicate clearly and effectively.

(xiv) Develop broad vision of business, passion for integrity and honesty.

(xv) Make him understand and cope up with statutory obligations.

REVIEW QUESTIONS

1. What is entrepreneurship? Explain its model.
2. Explain the evolution of concept of entrepreneurship.
3. What are the characteristics of entrepreneur?
4. What are the qualities of entrepreneur?
5. Explain the functions of entrepreneur.
6. What are the types of entrepreneur?
7. Explain meaning and role of intrapreneur.

8. What are the elements of entrepreneurship?
9. Differentiate between entrepreneur and manager.
10. Differentiate between entrepreneur, intrapreneur and manager.
11. Differentiate between entrepreneur and intrapreneur.
12. Explain the concept of entrepreneurship.
13. Explain the characteristics of entrepreneurship.
14. Write about evolution of entrepreneurship.
15. Explain the development of entrepreneurship.
16. What are the various stages of entrepreneurship processes? Explain.
17. Explain the role of entrepreneur in economic development.
18. Write about entrepreneurship in India.
19. What are the barriers of entrepreneurship?
20. Explain concept of women entrepreneurs.
21. What are the functions of women entrepreneur? Explain.
22. What are the problems faced by women entrepreneurs?
23. What are the steps taken to develop women entrepreneurship?
24. Write about entrepreneurship development programmes.

CHAPTER – 13

SMALL SCALE INDUSTRY

Small-scale industries (SSI) play a key role in the industrialization of any developing country. Development of modern small-scale industries has been one of the most important factures of industrial development. After the independence, the government has been formulating various policies to develop or revive cottage and small-scale industries.

13.1 DEFINITION

The definition of small-scale industry is important. The first official idea was in terms of gross investment in land, building, plant and machinery and number of workers engaged. From time to time, there have been many changes in the limit of investment in plant and machinery. In the beginning, during 1955, for a small-scale industry, the ceiling limit for investment was 5 lakhs with less than 50 employees when using power or less than 100 employees when power is not used.

Further the term SSI has been defined in three ways.

(i) Conventional definition

Conventional definition includes cottage and handicraft industries that employ conventional labour-oriented methods to produce conventional products, mainly in the rural areas. Some examples are handloom and handicrafts.

(ii) Operational definition

The operational definition for the policy purpose includes "all the undertakings having an investment in fixed assets in plant and machinery, whether held on ownership terms or by lease or hire-purchase, not exceeding Rs. 60 lakhs". Ancillary units and Tiny units also come under the scope of SSIs.

(iii) National income accounting

National income accounting includes all manufacturing and processing activities, including maintenance and repair services, undertaken by both household and non-house-hold small-scale manufacturing units not registered under Factories Act.

A small-scale industry is defined as "A unit engaged in manufacturing, servicing, processing, servicing and preservation of goods having investment in plant and machinery, at an original cost not exceeding Rs. 60 lakhs". (Rs. 75 lakhs for Ancillary undertaking and Rs. 5 lakhs for Tiny sector).

With effect from 1997, the government has raised the investment ceiling in plant and machinery for the small-scale sector to Rs. 3 crore from the existing Rs. 60 lakhs. For ancillary units it is increased to Rs. 3 crore and for tiny sector, it is raised to 25 lakhs. Presently, the Government had reduced the ceiling on investment in fixed assets and machinery for SSIs and ancillary to Rs. 1 crore.

The details of ceiling limit of investment in SSIs over the time period are shown below:

Sl.No.	Year	Ceiling limit for SSIs
1.	1950	Capital assets upto Rs. 5 lakhs
2.	1958	Capital investment upto Rs. 5 lakhs
3.	1960	Gross value of fixed assets upto Rs. 5 lakhs
4.	1966	Value of plant and machinery upto Rs. 7.5 lakhs
5.	1975	Plant and machinery Rs. 10 lakhs
6.	1980	Upto Rs. 20 lakhs on plant and machinery
7.	1985	Upto Rs. 35 lakhs on plant and machinery
8.	1991	Upto Rs. 60 lakhs on plant and machinery
9.	1997	Upto Rs. 3 crore on plant and machinery

The new definition of SSI as per the Union Ministry of Commerce and Industries (1960) was "Small-scale Industry will include all industrial limits with a capital investment not more than Rs. 5 lakhs, irrespective of the number of persons employed".

13.2 CHARACTERISTICS OF SSIs

The following are some of the important characteristics of a small-scale industry:

(i) Capital investment is small and most of them have small number of workers.

(ii) Generally owned by a single or at the most two persons and engaged in production of small goods.

(iii) Most of them are family owned industries.

(iv) Workers are not well recognized and they may do different types of works as need arises.

(v) Funded by owner's savings or short-term loans.

(vi) Small-scale industrial activity is mainly dependent on owner's entrepreneurship.

(vii) Exploitation of natural resources and human resources.

(viii) Generally management and organization are very poor or nonexistent in SSIs.

(ix) Incidents of early closure are of highest order.

(x) Profit margins are less due to competition.

(xi) Innovation and risk bearing are high in SSIs.

(xii) Faces cut throat competition.

(xiii) Few of them many grow as medium scale industries.

(xiv) Technology may become obsolete, resulting in closure of SSIs.

(xv) Generally found in urban or semi urban areas.

13.3 NEED AND RATIONALE OF SSIs

In countries like India where plenty of labour is available and not enough capital, small-scale industries have a vital role to play in the industrialization and economy. Generally small-scale industries have a very high potential of employment with low capital investment. SSIs help encouraging entrepreneurship, providing jobs and improving economy particularly in semi-urban and rural areas. SSIs have high potential for local employment, promote entrepreneurship and promote earnings and improve economy of the country. The following are some of the important points that stress the need and rationale of SSIs.

(i) Innovative:

Small units are generally highly innovative. In SSIs, there will not be enough facilities, machines or resources. To get the jobs done with the limited available facilities, innovation arises.

(ii) Self satisfaction:

It gives lot of self-satisfaction to workers for having done a good job with limited facilities.

(iii) Caters to individual taste and styles:

SSIs can change or alter the process and production according to the changes in taste and fashions of the customers.

(iv) Small in operation

SSIs utilize local labour, small in operation and leads to satisfaction of the entrepreneur.

(v) Strength of nation

Small-scale industries are generally locally owned and well controlled. This leads to strengthening of a family and other social systems and thus strengthening of nation.

(vi) Spread over wide areas

Unlike large-scale industries that are concentrated at one or two places, SSIs can spread over the entire nation leading to uniform development of country. Government is supporting to starts SSIs in backward areas with an aim to improve the nation.

Thus SSIs play a vital role in the industrialization of a developing country. SSIs need smaller investment, offer a means of equal distribution of national income, better utilization of local skills and resources. They create the growth of industrial entrepreneurship and promote a wide spread ownership location.

13.4 OBJECTIVES OF SSIs

The objectives of SSIs are listed blow:

(i) Creation of employment opportunities.

(ii) Improvement of output, income and better standard of living.

(iii) Elimination of economic backwardness of rural and underdeveloped areas.

(iv) To reduce regional imbalances.

(v) To provide employment and means of a regular source of income to the needy people living in rural and semi-urban areas.

(vi) To improve the quality of industrial products produced in cottage industries and increase production and profits.

(vii) To facilitate import substitution.

(viii) To encourage entrepreneurship and self-reliance.

(ix) To mobilize regional resources of capital.

Development of SSIs has gained a remarkable importance in Five Year Plans of India. Promotional plans like – development of entrepreneurship, supported by consultancy services, technology know how, institutional support, allocation of site in industrial estates, rebates etc., are provided by Government for setting up SSIs.

13.5 SCOPE OF SSIs

The scope for small-scale industries is quite vast, covering a wide range of activities requiring less sophisticated technology. The following are some of the areas of scope of SSIs.

- Manufacturing activities
- Servicing/repairing activities
- Construction activities
- Financial activities
- Retailing activities
- Wholesale business
- Transport activities
- Public utilities
- Communication etc.

In order to strengthen the scope for small industry development in the country, the Government of India has, along with its other assistance programmes, announced its reservation policy for small sector in the country in 1967 with 47 items reserved for SSIs. By 1983, the list of reserved items included 836 items. Presently there are 824 items reserved for exclusive production in small sector. Some of the industries reserved for exclusive development in the small sector are:

- Food and Allied Industries
- Clock and watches
- Stationary items
- Textile products
- Sports goods
- Leather and Lather products including Footwear
- Mathematical and survey instruments
- Rubber and plastic products
- Miscellaneous transport equipments
- Chemical and chemical products
- Bicycle parts, tricycles and perambulators
- Glass and Ceramics
- Natural essential oils
- Electrical appliances, Electronic components and equipment
- Organic chemicals and chemical products
- Metal cabinets

- Boats and truck body building
- Mechanical Engineering and Transport Equipment etc.

13.6 ROLE OF SSI IN ECONOMIC DEVELOPMENT

Economic development is defined as an increase in per-capita income of a person resulting in improvement in the levels of living. The development of SSIs contributes to the increase in per-capita income. SSIs generate immediate employment opportunities with relatively low capital investment, promote evenly spread of national income, make effective mobilization of untapped capital and human skills and lead to dispersal of manufacturing activities all over the country. This in turn results in the growth of villages, small towns and economically lagging regions. This creates balanced regional development. Increase in number, production, employment and exports of small scale industries over a period of time are some of the parameters that indicate the role played by SSIs in India. The production has improved from Rs. 7,200 crore during 1973-74 to about Rs. 700,000 crore during 1006-07, and much more by now. The employment has increased from about 40 lakhs in 1973-74 to about 200 lakhs during 2006-07. Exports also have gradually increased to about Rs. 75,000 lakhs.

The small-scale industries have registered phenomenal growth in their number from about 2.5 lakhs during 1973-74 to about 36 lakhs by 2006-07. Statistics reveal that SSIs account for about 35% of the gross value of the out-put in manufacturing sector, about 78 to 80% of total employment in industries and about 38% of the total exports of the country.

13.7 ADVANTAGES OF SSIs

SSIs have both economic and social advantages, some of them are listed below:

(i) SSIs don't require to a high level of technology.

(ii) They do not require large capital.

(iii) The source and capabilities of under employed and unemployed people can be used for productive purpose.

(iv) The projects related to SSIs can be completed in short period and hence can become productive in a short period.

(v) SSIs can be based on the processing of locally produced raw mate-rials like agricultural goods, forest and mineral resources etc.

(vi) Possibility of earning and saving foreign exchange by exporting goods produced from local resources.

(vii) Source of employment for local people, either full time or pat time.

(viii) SSIs act like training area for local entrepreneurs.

(ix) SSI can bring about more uniform distribution of income in the society.

(x) SSIs create immediate employment at a relatively small capital investment.

(xi) SSIs have small gestation period.

(xii) They offer a method of equitable distribution of national income.

(xiii) SSIs facilitate mobilization of capital and skills which often remain unutilized.

(xiv) They meet the increased demand of consumer goods and mass consumption goods.

(xv) They help in economic growth of the country.

(xvi) SSIs make it possible to shift manufacturing activities from busy towns to rural areas. This helps in geographical distribution of skills and technology in the country.

(xvii) SSIs help in creating jobs for unemployed.

(xviii) They help in developing rural areas.

13.8 STEPS TO START A SSI

The development of small scale industries has been one of the most significant feature of industrial growth in our country. The main features of small-scale industries are that they create great employment opportunities, assist in entrepreneurship, ensure better use of resources like finance, raw material and technology. They need small amount to start with. They help in balancing of country's economy and uniform development of industries all over the country unlike large-scale industries that tend to concentrate in few cities and in the hands of rich.

The motto underlying the development of small and medium scale industries are the increase in the supply of manufactured goods, the development of local entrepreneurial talents and skills, the promotion of capital formation, creation of broader employment opportunities and utilizing the untapped investment.

The various steps involved in starting a SSI are given below:

(i) Selection of industry

(ii) Arrange for know-how/technology

(iii) Study of resource requirement

(iv) Selection of land and premises

(v) Study of investment requirement

(vi) Study of requirement of plant and equipment

(vii) Study of requirement of raw material and sources of supply

(viii) Study of economic viability like marketing and pricing strategy, financing, staffing, SWOT analysis, break even analysis, return on investment etc.

(ix) Preparation of project report

(x) Application to financial institutions for loan for fixed assets and working capital.

(xi) Application to Directorate of Industries for No Objection Certificate, Registration as SSI, Power and Permission.

(xii) Get NOC and permission from local body (municipality/village panchayat/corporation)

(xiii) Apply for power connection

(xiv) Recruit staff and workers

(xv) Order for plant and machinery

(xvi) Order for raw materials

(xvii) Install the machinery

(xviii) Trial runs

(xix) Production and sales

(xx) Profits and pay creditors.

13.9 GOVERNMENT POLICY TOWARDS SSI

Small-scale industries have been given importance in five years plans by Government of India. Government of India has started various programmes for the development of small-scale industries in India. Government has announced several objectives and intentions towards SSI through Industrial Policy Resolutions (IPRs). Since independence Government has announced several IPRs.

13.10 DIFFERENT POLICIES OF SSI

IPR 1948:

Importance of SSIs in the overall industrial development of the country was accepted for first time in IPR 1948. It was well recognized that SSIs are particularly suited for using the local resources and to create employment for rural. Initially SSIs faced lot of problems like shortage of raw materials and capital, non availability of skilled labour, marketing etc. The main thrust of IPR-1948 was to provide protection to SSIs.

IPR 1956:

IPR 1956 provided continuing policy support to the small sector and aimed to ensure that decentralized sector gained enough self support. About 128 items were reserved for exclusive production in small sector. In addition, Small-Scale Industries Board (SSIB) constituted a working group in 1959 for the purpose of examining and formulating a development plan for SSIs. During Third Five Year Plan period (1961-66), specific developmental projects like "Rural Industries Projects" and "Industrial Estate Projects" were started to strengthen the SSIs. IPR–1956 for SSIs aimed at "Protection and Development" and initiated the modern SSI in India.

IPR 1977:

The main thrust on of IPR 1977 was on effective promotion of cottage and small- scale industries widely spread in rural and urban areas. IPR 1977 classified small sector into three categories.

(i) Cottage and house hold industries:

This provides self-employment on a large-scale.

(ii) Tiny sector:

Tiny sector is one with investment in industrial units in plant and machinery upto Rs. 1 lakh and situated in towns with a population of less than 50,000 according to 1971 census.

(iii) Small Scale Industries:

SSIs comprising of industrial units with an investment of upto Rs. 10 lakhs and in case of ancillary units with an investment upto Rs. 15 lakhs.

The measures suggested for promoting SSIs are reservation of 504 items for exclusive production in Small Scale Industries and proposal to set up an agency called "District Industry Centre" (DIC) in each district to serve as a focal point for the development of SSIs.

IPR 1980:

Government of India adopted a new Industrial Policy Resolution (IPR) on July 23, 1980. The main objective of IPR 1980 was defined as facilitating an increase in industrial production through optimum utilization of installed capacity and expansion of industries. It helped the small sector by increasing the ceiling from Rs. 1 lakh to Rs. 2 lakhs for tiny industries, from Rs. 10 lakhs to

20 lakhs in case of small scale units and from Rs. 15 lakhs to Rs. 25 lakhs for ancillaries. District Industry Centres (DICs) are replaced with the concept of "Nucleus Plants" in each industrially backward district with an idea to promote the growth of small-scale industries in backward areas. It also emphasized the promotion of village and rural industries to generate economy in the villages. Similar to IPR 1956, IPR 1980 regenerated the spirit and encouragement of setting up SSIs.

IPR 1990:

It came into existence in June 1990. It also gave lot of scope and importance for SSIs to generate wage and self-employment based opportunities in the country. Some of the salient points to increase the development of SSI are:

(i) Investment ceiling in plant and machinery for tiny units is increased from Rs. 5 lakhs from Rs. 2 lakhs, provided the unit is located in an area having population of less than 50,000 as per 1981 Census.

(ii) Investment ceiling in plant and machinery for SSIs is raised to Rs. 60 lakhs from Rs. 35 lakhs.

(iii) Investment ceiling in plant and machinery for ancillary units is raised to Rs. 75 lakhs from Rs. 45 lakhs.

(iv) Implemented a new scheme of central investment subsidy exclusively for SSIs in rural and backward areas that are generating employment at lower capital investment.

(v) To improve the competitiveness of the products manufactured in SSIs, technology upgradation programs are implemented under Technology Development Centre in Small Industries Development Organisation (SIDO).

(vi) Small Industries Development Bank of India (SIDBI) was established in 1990 with an idea to ensure timely and adequate flow of credit facilities to SSIs.

(vii) About 836 items have been reserved by Government for the exclusive manufacture in SSIs.

(viii) Implementation of delicensing 100% Export Oriented Units (EOUs) set up in Export Processing Zones (EPZs) upto an investment of Rs. 75 lakhs. Also delicensing of all new units with investment upto Rs. 25 lakhs in fixed assets in non-backward areas and Rs. 75 lakhs in notified backward areas.

(ix) Emphasis to establish special cell in SIDO for developing and training women entrepreneurs.

New Small Enterprise Policy 1991

During August 1991, the Government of India issued a new policy for small scale enterprises titled "Policy measures for promoting and strengthening and supplementing small, tiny and village enterprises". The main idea of this new policy is to improve the growth rate of sector which in turn contributes the growth of economy of country in terms of increased output, employment and exports. The salient features of this "New Small Enterprise Policy 1991" are:

(i) Increase in the investment to Rs. 5 lakhs from Rs. 2 lakhs in tiny enterprises, irrespective of the location of the enterprise.

(ii) To give priority to small and tiny sector in the allocation of indigenous raw material.

(iii) Introduction of services to help the problems of delayed payments to small sector.

(iv) Industry related services and business enterprises are included as SSIs irrespective of their location.

(v) To widen the scope of the National Equity Fund (NEF) to enlarge the single window scheme and also to associate commercial banks with provision for corporate loans.

(vi) Introduction of limited partnership act.

(vii) To set up Technology Development Cell in the Small Industry Development Organization (SIDO).

(viii) Set up of Export Development Centre (EDC) in the SIDO.

(ix) To introduce the scheme of Integrated Infrastructural Development (IID) with technology backup services to SSIs.

(x) Market promotion of small-scale industries products through cooperate/public sector institutions other specialized professional/marketing agencies and the consortium approach.

Important observations of New Small Enterprise Policy 1991.

(i) The New Small Enterprise Policy 1991 is prepared on thorough understanding of the basic problems of SSI and proposed remedial measures to over come the problems faced.

(ii) Introduction of limited or restricted partnership to facilitate investment of equity capital by relations and friends who were otherwise hesitating to invest their capital.

(iii) Equity participation upto 24% by another undertaking in a small-scale unit. This allows big industries to start or invest in small-scale industries.

(iv) Removal of change of location of tiny industries and area with less than 50,000 populations has encouraged development of tiny industries in towns also. The raise of ceiling from Rs. 2 lakhs to Rs. 5 lakhs in tiny industries also help setting up of tiny industries.

(v) Made provisions for continuous support to the tiny sectors, like easy access the institutional finance, preference in Government purchase and relaxation of certain labour laws.

Industrial policy resolution 2000

Industrial policy 2000 was actually a comprehensive policy package for SSIs and tiny sectors. Main focus of this policy is as follows:

(i) The exemption for excise duty limit raised from 50 lakhs to Rs. 1 crore to improve the competitiveness.

(ii) Credit linked capital subsidy of 12% against loans for technology upgradation was provided in specified industries.

(iii) The third census of small scale industries by the ministry of SSI was conducted, which also covered sickness and its causes in SSIs.

(iv) The limit of investment was increased in industry related service and business enterprises from Rs 5 lakhs to Rs 10 lakhs.

(v) The scheme of granting Rs 75000 to each small scale enterprise for obtaining ISO 9000 certification was continued till the end of 10th plan.

(vi) SSI associations were motivated to develop and operate testing laboratories. One time capital grant of 50% was given on reimbursement basis to each association.

(vii) The limit of composite loan was increased from Rs. 10 lakhs to Rs 25 lakhs.

(viii) A group was constituted for streamlining of inspection and repeal of redundant laws and regulations.

(ix) The coverage of ongoing Integrated Infrastructure Development (IID) was enhanced to cover all areas in the country with 50% reservation for rural areas and 50% earmarking of plots for tiny sector.

(x) The family income eligibility limit of Rs. 24000 was enhanced to Rs 40000 per annum under the Prime Minister Rozgar Yozna (PMRY).

Industrial policy resolution 2001-02

This policy emphasizes the following:

(i) The investment limit was enhanced from Rs 1 crore to Rs 5 crore for units in hosiery and handloom sectors.

(ii) The corpus fund set up under the Credit Guarantee Fund Scheme was increased from 125 crore to 200 crore.

(iii) Credit Guarantee cover was provided against an aggregate· credit of Rs 23 crore till December 2001.

(iv) 14 items were de-reserved during June 2001 related to leather goods, shoes and toys.

(v) Market Development Assistance Scheme was launched exclusively for SSI sector.

Industrial policy resolution 2003-04

The following are the highlights of this policy:

(i) 73 items reserved for exclusive manufacture in the SSI sector were de-reserved in June 2003. These consist of chemical and chemical products, leather and leather products, laboratory reagents etc.

(ii) Selective enhancement of investment in plant and machinery was from Rs 1 crore to Rs 5 crore.

(iii) Banks were directed to provide credit to SSI sector within an interest rate band of 2 percent above and below their Prime Lending Rates (PLR).

(iv) The composite loan limit for SSI was raised from Rs 25 lakhs to Rs 50 lakhs.

(v) The limit of dispensation of collateral requirement was raised from Rs 15 lakhs to Rs 25 lakhs on the basis of good track record and financial position of the unit.

(vi) The lower limit of Rs 5 lakhs on loans covered under the Credit Guarantee Scheme was removed. All loans up to Rs 25 lakhs were made eligible for guarantee cover under the Credit Guarantee Scheme.

(vii) Specialized bank branches were made operational for SSIs.

(viii) Small and Medium Enterprise (SME) fund of Rs 10000 crore was set up under SIDBI to solve the problem of inadequate finance for SSIs.

(ix) Laghu Udyami Credit Card Scheme was liberalized. Under this scheme. the credit limit was increased to Rs 10 lakhs from Rs 2 lakhs. But it was only for borrowers with satisfactory track record.

Industrial policy resolution 2004-05 Main features of this policy are as follows:

(i) The National Commission on Enterprises in the unorganized/ informal Sector was set up in September 2004. It suggested measures considered necessary for improvement in the productivity of these enterprises, generation of large scale employment opportunities, linkage of the sector to institutional frame work in areas like credit, raw material supply, Infrastructure, technology upgradation, marketing facilities and skill development by training.

(ii) 85 items were de-reserved in October 2004.

(iii) The investment limit in plant and machinery was raised from Rs. one crore to Rs 5 crore in October 2004, in respect of seven items of sports goods to help to upgrade the technology and enhance competitiveness.

(iv) The Small and Medium Enterprise (SME) fund of Rs 10000 crore was started by SIDBI since April 2004 with 80% of the lending for SSI units. The interest rate was 2% below the prevailing Prime Lending Rate (PLR) of the SIDBI.

(v) The Reserve Bank of India raised the composite loan limit from Rs 50 lakhs to Rs one crore.

(vi) Promotional Package for small enterprises was initiated.

Industrial policy resolution 2005-06.

Industrial policy resolution 2005-06 offered following package for SSIs.

(i) The Ministry of Small Scale Industries has identified 180 items for dereservation.

(ii) Small and Medium Enterprises were recognized in the services sector and were treated on par with SSIs in the manufacturing sector.

Government is aware of the challenges faced by SSIs and has been trying to improve their competitiveness through various measures. These consist of the following:

(i) Tax concessions have been provided to SSIs to promote investment in this sector and also to grant relief to small entrepreneurs.

(ii) Technological facilities have been increased.

(iii) In order to facilitate adequate flow of credit, efforts have been made.

(iv) Measures have also been taken to improve infrastructure facilities and promote marketing of products.

(v) To improve access to latest information, automation of the Ministry of SSI Office of DC (SSI), Directorate of Industries and District Industries Centers have been set up.

(vi) Other initiatives, such as, Advisory and Monitoring Services, Technology Business Incubators, Suppliers Rating Accreditation Services have been taken up.

13.11 GOVERNMENT SUPPORT TO SSIs DURING 5 YEAR PLANS

Government has given a lot of importance to the development of SSIs in its five year plans. The expenditure on small sector has been continuously increasing. The details are given below.

(i) First Five Year Plant 1951-56

In the first five year plant, Rs. 48 crore was spent in SSIs (about 48% of total plan expenditure of industry) covering the entire field of small scale and cottage industries, six boards were formulated by the end of first five year plans. They are: All India Handloom Board, All India Handicrafts Board, All India and Village Industries Board, Small Scale Industries Board, Coir Board and Central Silk Board.

(ii) Second Five Year Plan (1956 – 61)

The second five-year plan focused on dispersal of industries with an out lay of Rs. 187 crore. As may as 60 industrial estates were established for providing basic facilities like power, water, transport etc., under one roof.

(iii) Third Five Year Plan (1961 – 66)

Third five year plan outlayed Rs. 264 crore for the development of SSI and cottage industries. It has put lot of stress on the extension of the coverage of SSIs. Establishment of SSI underwent a slight recession during this plan.

(iv) Fourth Five Year Plan (1969 – 73)

Fourth five-year plan also adopted and encouraged the development of SSIs like the earlier three plans. SSI has seen remarkable diversification and expansion owing to the various developments programming during fourth five-year plan period. The planned out layout for fourth five-year plan is Rs. 293 crore. During fourth five plans about 346 industrial estates were completed providing employment to about 80,000 people.

(v) Fifth Five Year Plan (1974 – 78)

The main thrust of fifth year-plan was to develop SSIs to help reducing poverty and in equating prevailing in society. Government had initiated wide development programmes leading to the development of SSIs. The planned out lay of fifth five-year plan was Rs. 611 crore.

(vi) Sixth Five Year Plan (1980 – 85)

The planned out lay of sixth five-year plan was Rs. 1945 crore. The sixth plan included many programs like: Reservation of 409 items for purchase from

SSIs and 836 items are reserved for exclusive production in small scale industries, established Council for Advancement of Rural Technology (CART) in 1982, with an idea to provide technical inputs to the rural industries and providing consultancy services in technical, managerial and marketing through SIDO.

(vii) Seventh Five Year Plan (1985 – 90)

The planned outlay of seventh five-year plan was Rs. 2752 crore. The main thrust of seventh plan was upgradation of technology to increase competitiveness of SSIs. Owing to various development programmes, the small sector witnessed significant development in all directions. The number of small-scale industries had gone up, the employment also increased considerably from 96 lakhs to about 120 lakh persons.

(viii) Eighth Five Year Plan (1992 – 97)

Eighth plan has a plan outlay of Rs. 6334 crore. It started with a main focus of employment generation. In order to upgrade the technology, the eighth plan proposed to establish appropriate tool rooms and training institutes. Similar to growth centers, the eighth plan proposed to set up integrated infrastructure development centers. The eighth plan ensured timely and adequate availability of credit by the establishment of SIDBI, introduced new initiatives like sanction of composite loans under single window concept and concessional loans to state corporations for infrastructure development.

13.12 IMPACT OF LIBERALIZATION, PRIVATIZATION AND GLOBALISATION ON SSIs

Liberalisation, Privatisation and Globalisation (LPG) process started in India in July 1991 that had changed the face of industry. It has attracted new areas of development, foreign direct investments and new business areas which were unheard before 80's. This made Indian economy to grow to new heights. Past 3 decades Indian economy is growing at an average steady rate of 5% of per-capita income. The exports have increased.

Liberalisation had made import of scarce and non-available raw materials easy. This had led to many new openings. New entrepreneurs have started many SSIs which otherwise was not possible due to non-availability of certain raw materials and resources, liberalization helped getting them from abroad and use them. The best example for effect of liberalization is electronic and computer industries that have seen tremendous growth in past-2 decades.

Privatisation also helped the growth of SSIs in a big way. Earlier, certain products/services were produced only by Government organizations and no competition existed. With privatization, it threw open to many challenging entrepreneurs to produce similar goods and service at much competitive price and of better quality. One example of privatization was the production of telephones. Hither to, Bangalore based Indian Telephone Industries (ITI) was producing the telephones. With the privatization, many players had entered the arena producing better, good looking phones with additional facilities. The other important development due to privatization is life insurance sector which was earlier monopolized by LIC. Now there are many private agencies offering Life insurance, health Insurance and others.

Globalisation has helped in setting many small scale industries. It made possible the export of goods produced in SSI. Industries and service providers are going global from India. Indian entrepreneurs in Pharma Sector, I.T. Sector, Steel Sector have gone to many countries to start new ventures. Indian entrepreneurs have used the globalisation for the growth of service sectors. Accordingly investments and quality levels in service sectors have increased. The spectacular growth is observed in Business Process Outsourcing (BPO), transport, repair services, entertainment and hospitality sectors.

There has been a big growth of entrepreneurial activities in rural India in the areas like food processing, ready-to-eat and parked food, export of food products like fish, meat, prawns etc., due to LPG.

13.13 GATT / WTO

13.13.1 GATT

General Agreement on Tariffs and Trade (GATT) was a treaty signed by a group of 123 nations agreeing in principle to promote trade among members in 1947. GATT was a multilateral global initiative. It was an important mile stone in global trade. After World War II the forward looking thinkers in trade and industry felt that political disputes and problems could be solved by coming together and singing agreements similar idea is extended to business, commerce and industry. With British and USA initiatives and discussions GATT was made possible.

In its existence of more than five decades GATT had many challenges. They are:

- E-commerce
- Agriculture commodities
- Narcotics, nuclear and dangerous materials
- Political and regional forces on trade and industry
- Development of backward regions

- Barter deals
- Counter trade
- Bilateral trade agreements and monopolies
- Regional trade blocks
- Services
- Trade information
- Trade disputes in international business
- High tariffs by some countries
- Trade restrictive practices
- Subsidies

GATT had no enforcement powers. The losing party could ignore the ruling given by GATT. The various causes like language, legal issues, distances, and communications delayed settlement of disputes for years. Even then GATT could handle hundred of large trade disputes and concluded to satisfaction of parties involved. It gave a new direction of settlement by discussions, mediation, taking opinions of experts and negotiations. It highlighted problems of different trade practices and contract issues. It advocated free trade and open trade policies for commerce in industry and stages across the globe.

13.13.2 World Trade Organisation (WTO)

World Trade Organisation was establish in January 1st, 1995 as a successor to the General Agreement on Tariffs and Trade (GATT), serves as the legal and institutional foundation of the multilateral trading system. The Uruguay Round Table Agreement that created WTO also eliminated tariffs for some manufactures' goods, reduced barriers to trade in agriculture, expanded protection for copyrights, patents and other intellectual property, provided some reduction in barriers to services and foreign investment. It also reformed the multilateral trade process and included a strong dispute settlement mechanism. WTO has 123 members, another 31 countries have applied for the membership.

Objectives of WTO:

Make Optimum utilization of world's resources for improving the incomes and standard of living, promoting employment and expanding production and trade activities among varies countries.

Encourage sustainable development and ensure that environment care and developmental activities together.

Efforts should be made that poor countries as well as developing countries get an opportunity to have a share in the growth in the world trade:

Functions of WTO

- It covers all the commodities that are internationally traded and have formulated rules and procedures for each category as a guideline to member countries.
- Though WTO does not interfere in economic and political issues of the member countries, it does involve in case of policies regarding international trade.
- WTO has various expert committees and subcommittees for different categories to review various subjects and also to work as consultants.
- It arranges visits of its expert committees to various countries for training and development activities.
- WTO acts as an arbitrator to sort out disputes between various countries in the international trade.
- It reviews and advises trade policies of various countries so that such policies are conducive for international trade.
- Implementation and monitoring of multilateral and bilateral trade agreements which are essence of the WTO.
- To keep a track of trade related activities, member countries will inform WTO about various trade activities they have been doing in the global market.
- Evaluation of international trade and seek explanation wherever abnormal variations in terms of over dominance or very poor performance are observed.

Indian Issues in WTO

India is a member of GATT and WTO since its inception. India is closely working on the progress and development of the activities in WTO on its own as a member for developing business from India. In addition, India is also representing the group of G-21 developing nations in WTO, who jointly look after the interests of the developing world. The developing world would like to have their fair share of the global markets without any influence or twisting tactics of the rich nations.

Advantages of WTO

- Safeguards from unilateral actions of the developed nations.
- Increased access to export markets.
- Increased R&D efforts in the country.

- Access to advanced technology to the existing and new industries.
- Increased opportunity to subcontracting and job work for SSI.
- Increased global competition resulting higher efficiency and improved quality.

Business boost will take place in specified fields:

- Textiles and clothing
- Agriculture and food products
- Chemicals
- Software industry
- Export subsidies not prohibited till a country's per capita income is plus 1000 US Dollars
- Services

Disadvantages of WTO

- Developed countries are becoming protectionists themselves. The global trading system has been unfair to 'third world' Asia, and Latin America for over 2 centuries.
- 8 years of bargaining developing countries gained little or nil.
- Developed countries raising political and social barriers.
- India may gain about only 2 billion per year more exports which is too small.
- Pharmaceutical intellectual property right issue. Multinationals use exclusive market rights and increase price of drugs.
- SSI will be hit due to competition.

13.14 SUPPORTING AGENCIES OF GOVERNMENT FOR SSI

Starting a new venture requires various resources and facilities. Small scale enterprises generally find it difficult to have these resources and facilities on their own. Adequate finance is life blood to start and run an enterprise as it facilitates an entrepreneur to have enough funds to procure land, labor, materials. plant and machinery and so on. Recognizing it, government has come forward to help small entrepreneurs by providing them funds and other needed facilities and supports. Government has recognized the important role of entrepreneurs in the industrial development of the country, especially through the small-scale industries (SSIs). The government of India and state governments provide a number of special facilities and incentives to small-scale industries. The incentives not only motivate entrepreneurs to set up industries in the small-scale sector, but also strengthen the entrepreneurial base in the economy. The government offers a package of services through its specialized institutions and motivates entrepreneurs to take advantage of the various facilities and establish enterprises and flourish. It is hoped that institutional incentives would play a key role in the promotion of small enterprises and ensure their self-sustained growth. The institutions providing assistance to small scale industries are broadly classified into three categories namely:

- All India Institutions
- State Level Institutions
- Fund-Based Institutions.

13.14.1 All India Institutions

All India institutions supporting entrepreneurs are as below:

(i) Small Scale Industries Board (SSIB)

(ii) National Small Industries Corporation (NSIC)

(iii) The Khadi and Village Industries Commission (KVIC)

(iv) Small Industry Development Organisation (SIDO)

(v) Training Institutes

SSI Board is the apex nonstatutory advisory body constituted by the Government of India to render advice on all issues pertaining to the SSI sector. It provides a forum to its members for interaction to facilitate cooperation and inter-institutional linkages and to render advice to the Government on various policy maters, for the development of the small-scale industries. The Board was first constituted in 1954. Its term is for two years. The Board was last constituted on 18th January 2003, with 101 members and held its 48th meeting on 17 January 2004. The Industrial Minister of the Government of India is the chairman of the SSIB. Its key members are state industry minister, some members of Parliament, secretaries of various departments of Government of India, financial institutions, public sector undertakings, industry associations, eminent experts in the field etc.

(ii) National Small Industries Corporation (NSIC) Limited

The National Small Industries Corporation Ltd (NSIC) was set up in 1955 with· a view to promoting, aiding and fostering the growth of small scale industries in the country with focus on commercial aspects of these functions. NSIC continues to implement its various programs and projects throughout the country to assist the SSI units. The Corporation has been assisting the sector through several schemes and activities.

(iii) The Khadi and Village Industries Commission (EVIC)

The Khadi and Village Industries Commission (KVIC) is a statutory body created by an Act of Parliament in April 1957. The KVIC is supposed to do the planning, promotion, organization and implementation of programs for the development of khadi and other village Industries in the rural areas in coordination with other agencies engaged In rural development wherever necessary.

(iv) Small Industry Development Organization (SIDO)

The Office of the Development Commissioner (Small Scale Industries) is also known as the Small Industry Development Organization (SIDO). It is an apex body, established in 1954, for assisting the Ministry in formulating, coordinating, implementing and monitoring policies and programs for the promotion and development of small-scale industries. It has over 60 offices and 21 autonomous bodies under its management, including Tool Rooms, Training Institutions and Project-cum-Process Development Centers etc.

(v) Training Institutes

There are three National Level Training Institutes. These are:

(a) National Institute of Small Industry Extension Training (NISIET), Hyderabad, which undertakes operations ranging from training, consultancy, research and education, to extension and information services.

(b) National Institute for Entrepreneurship and Small Business Development (NIESBUD), New Delhi, which conducts national and international level training programs in different fields and disciplines.

(c) Indian Institute of Entrepreneurship (IIE), Guwahati was established to act as a channel for entrepreneurship development with its focus on the SSIs.

13.14.2 State Level Institutions

State level institutions supporting entrepreneurs are as below:

(a) State Small Industrial Development Corporations (SSIDC)

(b) State Directorate of Industries (SDIs)

(c) District Industries Centers (DICs)

These are discussed in detail in chapter 14.

13.14.3 Fund-Based Institutions

Fund-Based Institution supporting entrepreneurs are as below:

(i) Small Industries Development Bank of India (SIDBI)
(ii) Commercial Banks
(iii) State Financial Corporations (SFCs)

(i) Small Industries Development Bank of India (SIDBI)

The SIDBI was established in 1990 as the apex refinance bank. The SIDBI is operating different programs and schemes through 5 Regional Offices and 33 Branch Offices. The financial assistance of SIDBI to the small-scale sector is channelized through the two routes – direct and indirect.

(ii) Commercial banks

Credit requirement of SSIs is basically of two types – long term loans and working capital. Commercial banks with their extensive network of branches operating nation wide are primary channel for working capital requirement. Banks are required to compulsory ensure that defined percentage (currently 40%) of their overall lending is made to priority sectors as classified by RBI. These sectors include agriculture, small industries, export etc. The inclusion of small industries in this list makes them eligible for this earmarked credit. With the liberalization of the Indian economy, greater emphasis was placed on meeting the credit needs of SSIs. This was manifest through the following initiatives taken by RBI.

(a) Credit for tiny sector has been earmarked within overall lending to small industries. In order to ensure that credit is available to all segments of SSI sector, RBI has issued instructions that out of the funds normally available to SSI sector, 40% be given to units with investment in plant and machinery up to Rs. 5 lakhs, 20% for units with investment between Rs. 5 lakhs to Rs. 25 lakhs and remaining 40% for other units.

(b) Public sector banks have been advised to operationalize more specialized SSI branches at centers where there is a potential for financing many SSI borrowers. As on March 2002, 391 specialized SSI branches are working in the country.

(c) Single window scheme was extended to all districts to meet the financial requirements (both term loan and working capital) of SSIs.

(d) Laghu Udyami Credit Card (LUCC) Scheme was launched by public sector banks for providing simplified and borrowed friendly credit facilities to SSI, tiny enterprises, retail traders and artisans.

(e) Composite loan limit was enhanced to Rs. 50 lakhs from Rs. 25 lakhs.

Limit on collateral free loans was increases to Rs. 25 lakhs in deserving cases.

(iii) State Financial Corporations (SFCs)

The Industrial Financial Corporation of India (IFCI) set up in 1948 used to provide financial assistance to only large-sized industrial undertakings. In order to cater the financial requirements of a large number of small-scale units, the State Financial Corporation Act was passed. State Financial Corporation Act 1951 was brought into force to enable all the state governments to set up State Financial Corporations as regional development banks. The first SFC was set up in Punjab in 1953. Today there are 18 SFCs in the country, which exist almost in every state. A SFC has a board of directors, a managing director and an executive committee. A SFC can open its office at different places within the state. Presently following assistance is provided to small scale and medium scale undertakings.

(a) Providing long-term finance to industrial enterprises having sole proprietary, partnership, company and cooperative society form of business organization.

(b) Subscribing equity and debentures of industrial enterprises.

(c) Providing financial assistance to small and medium enterprises engaged in service sector.

(d) Provide working capital loans and meeting various short-term needs of their clients.

All these are explained with more details in Chapter 14.

13.15 ANCILLARY INDUSTRY AND TINY INDUSTRY

13.15.1 Ancillary Industry

"Ancillary industries are small industries having investment in fixed assets, plant and machinery not exceeding Rs. 75 lakhs and engaged in (a) manufacturing of parts, components, sub assemblies, toolings or intermediates or (b) the rendering of services, supplying, rendering or proposing to supply or render 30% production of the total services, as the case may be, to other units for production of other articles: Provided that no such understanding shall be subsidiary of or owned or controlled by any other undertaking.

All the service-oriented enterprises are now eligible for registration as SSIs and are entitled for the same concessions and incentives that are offered for SSIs.

Several clarifications are issued on the above definition of ancillaries by Government from time to time. Some of them are:

(i) In calculation of plant and machinery, the original price paid by owner irrespective of new or old is to be considered for accounting.

(ii) The cost of equipment such as tools, jigs and fixtures, dies and moulds, maintenance spares, consumables, generator sets etc., are included in accounting for value of plant and machinery.

(iii) Units importing machinery, the important duty is excluded from the value of plant and machinery.

(iv) Units producing intermediates are considered as ancillaries.

(v) Units providing service facilities like machining, pressure cleaning, sand blasting etc., are recognized as ancillaries.

(vi) An ancillary unit should supply not less than 50% of its production to one or more parent units.

(vii) The concept of parent units will also include SSIs. This enables one SSI to work as ancillary to another.

Advantages of Ancillary Units:

The following are some of the advantages in setting up ancillary units:

(i) Indirect development of business activities in areas where ancillary industries have been set up.

(ii) Creating cadres of single disciplined experts.

(iii) Providing an effective solution to the marketing problems of SSIs.

(iv) Complementary with regard to output and enable reduction in the production cost.

(v) Employment generation and utilization of money in untapped hands.

(vi) Reduction in gestation period of production.

Objectives of ancillary industries:

(i) Development of employment opportunities.

(ii) Help the medium and large scale industries with, specialized functions.

(iii) Increase the production of SSIs.

(iv) Develop single or multi-discipline expertise in different fields.

(v) Provide an effective solution to the marketing problems of SSI during their initial stage.

(vi) Growth of low cost economy.

(vii) Dispersal of industrial activities in various regions resulting in equitable distribution of economy.

(viii) Tapping the funds from untapped sources.

13.15.2 Tiny Industry:

A unit is treated as Tiny Industry where investment in plant and machinery does not exceed Rs. 5 lakhs.

The growth in Tiny industries – facilitates self-employment, results in wider dispersal of industrial and economic activities and ensures maximum utilization of local resources.

Advantages:

- Utilization of local resources like men and materials.
- Limited capital to start the industry.
- Less risk involved
- Smaller gestation period
- Production of goods as per choice of consumers.
- Exports, there by earning foreign exchange.
- Employment generation to rural people.
- Regional development and
- Entrepreneurial development.

REVIEW QUESTIONS

1. Define Small-scale Industry, Ancillary Industry and Tiny Industries.
2. What are characteristics of SSIs?
3. Explain need and rationale of SSIs.
4. Explain the objectives of SSIs.
5. Explain the scope of SSIs.
6. Explain the role of SSI in economic development.
7. What are the advantages of SSIs?
8. What are the steps to start SSI? Explain.
9. Explain various Government policies towards SSIs.
10. Briefly explain Government support to SSIs during 5 year plans.
11. Explain the impact of Liberalization, Privatization and Globalization on SSIs.

12. Explain GATT.
13. Explain WTO and its impact on trade.
14. Explain the functions of WTO.
15. What are the advantages and disadvantages of WTO?
16. What are various supporting agencies of Government to SSIs?
17. Explain the role of
    (i) SSIB
    (ii) NSIC
    (iii) KVIC
    (iv) SIDO and
    (v) Training Institutions in the development of SSIs.
18. Explain the role of commercial banks and SFCs in the development of SSIs.

CHAPTER 14

INSTITUTIONAL SUPPORT

14.1 INTRODUCTION

Starting a business or industrial unit requires various resources and facilities. Finance has been an important resource to start and run an enterprise since it facilitates the entrepreneur to procure land, engage labour, procure plant and machinery, raw materials and others. Many small entrepreneurs, though have ideas and skills, are not able to start any enterprise for the want of money. Hence Government has set up institutions to help in financing the enthusiastic and skilled people to start an enterprise and run it. SIDBI was started mainly for financial assistance to SSIs. Other organization like SIDO, SSIB, SISI, SSIDC, NSIC etc., provide necessary assistance to SSI units.

Financial assistance and concessions could not over come the difficulties of infrastructure, in setting up an enterprise. Creation of infrastructure facilities like communication, transport, water, power, raw material etc., involve large amount of funds which are not available in the hands of small entrepreneurs. In view of this, various Central and State Government institutions have come forward to help small entrepreneur by providing various facilities. Institutional support helps make the economic environment more conducive to the business or enterprise.

Some of the support and facilities provided by various institutions to the entrepreneurs to help them to establish the industries are explained here.

14.2 INSTITUTIONS TO ASSIST SSI ARE TWO TYPES:

(i) State level institutions:

- State Directorate of Industries
- State Small Scale Industries Development Corporation (SSIDC)
- District Industries Centres (DICs)
- State Finance Corporations (SFCs)
- Technical Consultancy Organisation (TCOs)
- State Industrial Area Development Board (SIADB) etc.

(ii) Central Government Institutions

- Department of Small Scale Industries (DSSI)

- Small Scale Industries Board (SSIB)
- Small Industries Development Organisation (SIDO)
- National Small Industries Corporation (NSIC)
- Industrial Credit and Investment Corporation of India (ICICI)
- Industrial Finance Corporation of India (ICFI) etc.

14.3 STATE SMALL INDUSTRIES DEVELOPMENT CORPORATION (SSIDC)

Under the Companies Act, SSIDC were started in 1956 in all the states. These State Government undertakings take care of the growth and development needs of village industries, tiny industries and small industries. Different states give focus and importance to different industries based on the availability of raw-material and skill in their states. The main functions of SSIDC are as under:

(i) procurement and distribution of scarce raw materials,

(ii) supply of machinery on hire-purchase basis,

(iii) providing assistance for marketing of the products of small scale units

(iv) construction of industrial estates/sheds, providing allied infrastructure facilities and their maintenance,

(v) extending seed capital assistance on behalf of the State Governments

(vi) providing management assistance to production units.

A change in the role of SSIDCs has been prompted by the new Industrial Policy. SSIDCs are gearing up to change themselves from raw material distributors to organisations that will take care of various aspects of small industry development, especially marketing. SSIDCs would, thus, help the tiny and small industries increase their market share. The new policy calls for establishment of counseling and common testing facilities and provision of a mechanism to allow corporation of the latest technology in the small sector. SSIDCs are also planning to set-up centres for display of/and information dissemination on SSI products, and for providing small office spaces for SSIs in need.

At present there are 18 SSIDCs are in operation in India. In Karnataka it is called Karnataka State Small Industries Development Corporation (KSSIDC).

14.4 SMALL SCALE INDUSTRIES BOARD (SSIB)

SSIB was started in 1954 by the Central Government with the objective of developing small-scale industries throughout the country. The development work of small-scale industries involves various Ministries and Departments and other factors like land owners, financial institutions etc. In order to facilitate the coordination activities more effectively the SSIB has been created. The Director of the SSIB advises the Government about various development activities of small industries and the related matters. Since this has more involvement of Ministers, Secretaries and Government Departments, the committee governing SSIB consists of Industries Minister (as chairman) and various Secretaries. Member of Parliament and State Government Industry Ministers and the Committee. The apex body of these members takes decisions on all matters related to small industries.

14.5 DISTRICT INDUSTRIES CENTRES (DICs) / SINGLE WINDOW CONCEPT

The District Industries Centres (DICs) programme was started during 1978 with a view to provide integrated administrative framework at the district level for promotion of small-scale industries in rural areas. The DICs are envisaged as a single window interacting agency with the entrepreneur at the district level. Services and support to small entrepreneurs are provided under a single roof through the DICs. They are the implementing arm of the Central and State Governments of the various schemes and programmes. Registration of small industries is done at the District Industries Centres.

The organisational structure of DICs consists of one General Manager, four Functional Managers and three Project Managers to provide technical service in the area relevant to needs of district concerned. Management of the DICs is done by the State Governments. The scheme has now been transferred to the states and from the year 1993-94, funds will not be provided by the Central Government to the States for running the DICs.

Functions: The DICs role is mainly promotional and developmental. To attain this, they have to perform the following main functions:

- To conduct industrial potential surveys keeping in view the availability of resources in terms of material and human skill, infrastructure, demand for product etc., to prepare techno-economic surveys and identify product lines and then to provide investment advice to entrepreneurs.
- To prepare an action plan to effectively implement the schemes identified.
- To guide entrepreneurs in matters relating to selecting the most appropriate machinery and equipment, sources of its supply and procedure for procuring imported machinery, if needed, assessing requirements for raw materials etc.

- To appraise the worthiness of the various proposals received from entrepreneurs.
- To assist the entrepreneurs in marketing their products and assess the possibilities of ancillarisation and export promotion of their products.
- To undertake product development work appropriate to small industries.
- To conduct artisan training programmes.

About 430 District Industries Centres (DICs) have been set up covering major districts of the country leaving out the metropolitan cities and some new districts.

14.6 TECHNICAL CONSULTANCY ORGANISATIONS (TCOs)

- In various states TCOs were established to provide total consultancy services as a package under single roof. Overall 17 organisations were started in various states by the group of financial organisations like IDBI, IFCI and ICICI. The activities of TCOs are as follows:
- Identify potential industrial projects and prepare feasibility survey reports.
- Evaluation of various project proposals put up by the entrepreneurs .
- Provide turn key services in project reports preparations and project implementation.
- Undertake market surveys for various existing and new products.
- Carry out study on sick industries and advice for rehabilitation schemes.
- Undertake entrepreneurial development training programmes.
- Undertake consultancy for export oriented projects.

It has been observed that small and medium industries are not taking full advantages of TCOs due to disinterest or inability to pay the consultancy fees. Hence the consultancy and development programmes sponsored by the World Bank, Central Government or the State Government are mainly implemented for the benefit of various small and medium industries. Large industries however take the services of private consultants as per their needs.

14.7 SMALL INDUSTRIES SERVICE INSTITUTES (SISIs)

The Small Industries Services Institutes (SISIs) are set up to provide consultancy and training to small entrepreneurs-both existing and prospective. The activities of SISIs are coordinated by the Industrial Management Training Division of the DCSSI's office. There are 28 SISIs and 30 Branch SISIs set up in State capital and other places all over the country.

The main functions of SISIs include:

- To serve as interface between Central and State Governments.
- To render technical support services.
- To conduct Entrepreneurship Development Programmes.
- To initiate promotional programmes.
- Economic Consultancy /Information/EDP Consultancy.
- Trade and market informations.
- Project profiles.
- State industrial potential survey.
- District industrial potential surveys.
- Modernisation and in-plant studies.
- Workshop facilities.
- Training in various trade/activities.

14.8 INDUSTRIAL CREDIT AND INVESTMENT CORPORATION OF INDIA LTD. (ICICI)

The Industrial Credit and Investment Corporation of India Ltd. (ICICI) was set up in January 1955 under the Indian Companies Act with the primary objective of developing small and medium industries in the private sector. Its issue capital has been subscribed by the Indian banks, insurance companies and the individuals and corporations of the United States, the British Eastern Exchange Bank and other companies and general public in India.

The ICICI performs the following functions:

(i) It provides assistance by way of rupee and foreign currency loans, underwriting and direct subscriptions to shares/debentures and guarantees.

(ii) It offers variety of financial services such as deferred credit, leasing credit, installment sale, asset credit and venture capital.

(iii) It guarantees loans from other private investment sources.

The ICICI has recently set up a Merchant Banking Division which is working very creditably. It has also set up ICICI Asset Management Company Ltd., in June 1993 to operate the schemes of the ICICI Mutual Fund. Yet another subsidiary called ICICI Investors Services Ltd., (March 1994) and ICICI Banking Corporation Ltd., (January 1994) have started operations.

Assistance sanctioned by the ICICI during 1994-95 increased by 77% to Rs. 15,000 crore, while disbursements went up by 55.9% to Rs. 6,800 crore. Cumulatively, upto end March 1995, sanctions amounted to Rs. 53,300 crore and disbursements aggregated Rs. 30,000 crore. The ICICI assists all sectors, that is, the private sector, the joint sector, the public sector and the cooperative sector. It is worth mentioning that the private sector continued to claim the largest share (90 %) of ICICI sanctions during 1994-95, distantly followed by public sector (5 %), joint sector (4 %) and cooperative sector (1%). Thus, the major beneficiary of the ICICI's assistance is the private sector mainly comprising of small-scale units.

14.9 NATIONAL SMALL INDUSTRIES CORPORATION (NSIC)

NSIC was started by the Central Government in 1955 with the objective of promoting and developing SSI units throughout the country. It started with multiple objectives of helping SSI units for:

(a) providing machinery on hire purchase,

(b) assisting, marketing and exports,

(c) enlisting SSI units for tender participation in Government purchases,

(d) organising supply of raw materials,

(e) training of personnel and

(f) assistance in modernisation of the units.

The important functions of NSIC are as under:

- Financial assistance by way of hire purchase scheme for purchase of local and imported machinery.
- Provision of various equipments on lease basis.
- Assistance for marketing the products in the country and also to help in exporting the products of SSI units.
- Enlisting quality conscious good SSI units for sending enquiries of Government stores and purchase departments.
- Training of workers in various trades required for SSI units.
- Assistance in upgradation of technology, processes and modernisation of plant and machinery.
- To make bulk purchases of important raw materials and distribute to SSI units at reasonable rates. This avoids speculation and exploitation by the traders.
- To develop industrial estates and testing facilities in the industrial areas.

NSIC has got offices in various industrial cities and towns and is having socioeconomic approach in industrialisation of non-industry areas. It aims to create an industrial atmosphere with facilities and management support, so that small entrepreneurs take up new projects. As a nodal agency in playing supportive role to small industries, it has helped to reduce the control of private traders who were exploiting the small industries in many ways. Its other objective of developing backward areas is still to prove successful in view of the various problems of business activities and demoralisation set in due to failures of industries started in backward areas.

14.10 SMALL INDUSTRIES·DEVELOPMENT ORGANISATION(SIDO)

This organisation as the name suggest is mainly created for development of various small-scale units in different areas. SIDO is a nodal agency for identifying the needs of SSI units, coordinating and monitoring the policies and programmes for promotion of the small industries. It undertakes various programmes of training consultancy, evaluation for needs of SSI and development of industrial estates. All these functions are taken care with the Organisation Structure of 27 offices, 31 SISI (Small Industries Service Institutes), 31 Extension Centers of SISI and 7 Centers related to Production and Process Development. Its various activities can be explained under different headings as follows:

(a) Coordination activities of SIDO

(i) To coordinate various programmes and policies of various State Governments pertaining to small industries.

(ii) To maintain relation with the Central Industries Ministry, Planning Commission, State Level Industries Ministry and Financial institutions.

(iii) Implement and coordinate in the development of industrial estates.

(b) Industrial development activities of SIDO

(i) Develop import substitutions for components and products based on the data available for various volume-wise and value-wise imports.

(ii) To give essential support and guidance for the development of ancillary units.

(iii) To provide guidance to SSI units in terms of costing, market competition and to encourage them to participate in the Government Stores and Purchase Tenders.

(iv) To recommend the Central Government for reserving certain items to produce at SSI level only.

(c) Management activities of SIDO

(i) To provide training, development and consultancy services to SSI to develop their competitive strength.

(ii) To provide marketing assistance to various SSI units.

(iii) To assist SSI units in selection of plant and machinery, location, lay-out design and appropriate process.

(iv) To help them get updated with various informations related to the small-scale industries activities.

14.11 INDUSTRIAL DEVELOPMENT BANK OF INDIA (IDBI)

Prior to 1964, there was not any apex organisation to coordinate the functions of various financial institutions. Then it is identified that the country needed a central development banking institution for providing dynamic leadership in the task of promoting a widely diffused and diversified and yet viable process of industrialization. To fulfill this objective, the Government decided to establish the Industrial Development Bank of India (IDBI). The IDBI was established on July 1, 1964 under the Act of Parliament as the principal financial institution in the country. Initially, it was set up as wholly owned subsidiary of the Reserve Bank of India. In February 1976, the IDBI was made an autonomous institution and its ownership passed on from the Reserve Bank of India to the Government of India.

The IDBI provides assistance to the small-scale industries through its scheme of refinance and through its bills rediscounting scheme. As it is not feasible for the IDBI to reach a large number of small-scale industries scattered all over the country, the flow of its assistance to this vast number has, therefore, been indirect in the form of refinancing of loans granted by the banks and the State Financial Corporations (SFCs).

The IDBI has shown its particular interest in the development of small-scale industries. Of particular mention is the setting up of the Small Industries Development Fund (SIDF) in May 1986 to facilitate the development and extension of small-scale industries. In 1988, the IDBI also launched the National Equity Fund Scheme (NEFS) for providing support in the nature of equity to tiny and small-scale industries engaged in manufacturing not exceeding Rs. 5 lakhs. The scheme is administered by the IDBI through nationalised banks. The IDBI has also introduced the single window assistance scheme for grant of term loans and working capital assistance to new, tiny and small-scale enterprises. The IDBI has also set up a Voluntary Executive Corporation Cell (VECC) to utilize the services of experienced professionals for counseling small units, tiny and cottage units and for providing consultancy support in specific areas.

During 1987-88, the IDBI sanctioned assistance worth Rs. 1,500 crore to the small-scale industries out of total sanction of Rs. 4,580 crore. It means about one-third of total industrial assistance was given· to small-scale sector alone.

14.12 SMALL INDUSTRIES DEVELOPMENT BANK OF INDIA (SIDBI)

SIDBI was set up in 1989 as a wholly-owned subsidiary of the IDBI. The idea of starting SIDBI was in response to the demand from small-scale sector for an apex level institution for promotion, financing and development of small-scale industries. This should take care of both financial and non-financial assistance to the small-scale sectors. It does both direct and indirect financing to the small-scale sector. SIDBI does collaborative efforts to facilitate timely flow of credit for both term loans and working capital to small-scale industries in collaboration with commercial banks.

Earlier SIDBI was doing refinancing and discounting of bills. Now in addition to this it directly participates in the equity type of loan on soft terms, term loan, working capital both in rupee and foreign currencies, bill discounting, venture capital support and different forms of resource support to banks and other institutions.

Amongst support functions SIDBI finances for technology transfer and upgradation, quality improvement, exports, environmental care and industrialisation. For these activities SIDBI involves consultants and national and international level for improvements.

14.13 STATE FINANCIAL CORPORATIONS (SFCs)

SFCs are setup in 1948 to provide financial assistance to medium and large-scale industries. Later on in 1951 the role was extended for assistance to small-scale units also. There are 18 SFCs in different states with each having prefix of the state name. For example KSFC is Kamataka State Financial Corporation. Each SFC has its own Managing Director, Executive Director, Board of Directors and Management team to take care of the activities independently.

Term loans are provided to various small, medium and large industries in various categories like proprietary, partnership, cooperative, private and public limited companies. The loans are given based on securities like land, buildings, machineries and shares etc. SFC also subscribes to shares and debentures floated by the companies. Since the coverage of loans is spread to all sectors, even small transport owners and service centers take the assistance of SFC for starting of their units. They have different schemes for women, ex-service men, physically handicapped and SC/ST to give them opportunity to become entrepreneurs. Apart from industries, loan is given for Transport operators, Hotels, Hospitals, Nursing homes and Tourism facilities like lodges and guest houses etc.

Objectives of SFCs

- To provide term loans for purchase of land, buildings, machinery and other facilities.
- To promote self-employment for professionally qualified men and women entrepreneurs interested in starting their own projects.
- Financial assistance for expansion, modernisation and mechanisation in the existing setup.
- Financial assistance for rehabilitation of sick units.
- To give financial assistance for promotion of rural industries, cottage industries and urban service centers.
- To provide financial assistance for transport vehicles and tourism related activities.
- To arrange entrepreneurial development programmes and seminars for up coming young industrialists.
- To provide financial assistance for quality improvement and environmental control needs.

SFC caters to all categories of small and big industrialists, tourism operators, service centers like Hospitals and Hotels, service activities thus attending the various needs of a socioeconomically developing society.

Problems of SFCs

- Since SFCs are started by respective State Governments the usual problems of State bureaucracy of procedures, delays, castism and favouritism do occur.
- In the state offices problems of corruption and other malpractices continue to bother the applicants.
- In case of repayments very strict procedures are followed and units are sealed.

14.14 INDUSTRIAL FINANCE CORPORATION OF INDIA LTD (IFCI)

The Government of India set up the Industrial Finance Corporation of India (IFCI) under IFCI Act in July 1948. Since July I, 1993, it has been brought under Companies Act, 1956.

The IFCI extends financial assistance to the industrial sector through rupee and foreign currency loans, underwriting/ direct subscriptions to shares/ debentures and guarantees and also offers financial services through its facilities of equipment procurement, equipment finance, buyers and suppliers credit, equipment leasing and finance to leasing and hire purchase companies. It also provides merchant banking with its Head Office in Delhi and a branch in Bombay.

The financial resources of the IFCI are constituted of the following three components: (i) Share capital, (ii) Bonds and Debentures; and (iii) Other Borrowings. Its paid-up capital as on March 31, 1995 stood at Rs. 350 crore from an initial of Rs. 5 crore in 1948. The Industrial Development Bank of India, scheduled banks, insurance companies, investment trusts and the cooperative banks are the shareholders of the IFCI. Apart from paid-up capital and reserves, the major sources of the IFCI are issue of bonds and debentures, borrowings from the Government, the Reserve Bank of India, Industrial Development Bank of India and foreign loans.

The IFCI started its lending operations on a modest scale in 1948. The operations of the IFCI have grown over the years.

In recent years, the IFCI has started new promotional schemes, such as interest subsidy scheme for women entrepreneurs; consultancy fee subsidy schemes for providing marketing assistance to small-scale industries encouraging the modernisation of tiny, small-scale ancillary units; and control of pollution in the small and medium-scale industries. The IFCI has shown its growing concern in the development of backward districts.

The IFCI has shown impressive performance over the years. But there are certain flaws in its functioning which have invited criticism from different quarters. To quote, the important ones are: (i) The IFCI's lending operations have encouraged concentration of wealth and capital. It still pursues a discriminatory policy to the disadvantage of medium and small-scale units. (ii) There are great delays in sanctioning loans and, then, making the amount of the loan available. (iii) The. IFCI has failed to exercise necessary control over the defaulting borrowers. Further, in many cases, the assistance has not been used for the specific purpose for which they are given. Here also, the IFCI has failed to take any action against such practices.

REVIEW OF QUESTIONS

1. Discuss the necessity of institutional support to the SSIs.
2. Narrate the function of SIDO for growth of SSIs.

3. Explain the role of SSIDC in developing the small-scale industries.
4. Explain the role of DICs.
5. Explain the roles of IDBI/SIDBI.
6. Write notes on ICICI.
7. Write about NSIC.
8. Explain the need for support to SSIs.
9. Explain the role and help extended by SISIs in developing SSIs.

CHAPTER 15

PREPARATION OF PROJECT

The basic necessity of an entrepreneur is to decide upon a project. Success of any enterprise depends on the selection of right project. Thus project is the foundation for any venture. Establishing oneself as a good entrepreneur depends mainly upon choosing a good idea for project. Entrepreneur cannot succeed in this venture without a good project. Innovation and vision form an integral aspect of a project programme.

15.1 MEANING OF PROJECT

The project is a 'scientifically evolved work plan' devised to achieve a specific objective within a specified period of time. The dictionary meaning of a project is that 'it is a scheme, design, a proposal of something intended or devised to be achieved'. Each project differs in size, nature, objectives and complexity. Project management scholars emphasize that a project is an unique and non-repetitive activity which aims at systematically coordinating inputs in the direction of intended outputs. General economists and bankers have defined a project in different ways. Some of them are presented below.

"Project is an approval for a capital investment to develop facilities to provide goods and services" – The World Bank.

"Project is a non-routine, non-repetitive, one-off undertaking normally with discrete time, financial and technical performance goals" – Harrison.

"A project typically has a distinct mission that it is designed to achieve and a clear termination point, the achievement of the mission" – Newman, Summer and Warren.

"A Project is any scheme or a part of scheme for investing resources which can be reasonably analysed and evaluated as an independent unit. It may be item of investment activity which can be separately evaluated". – Little and Mirless.

"A project is the whole complex of activities involved in using resources to gain benefits". – Gillinger.

"A project is a scientifically evolved work plan devised to achieve a specific objective within a specified period of time". – Vasanth Desai.

The projects may differ in size, nature, aims, time and complexity, but they have three basic attributes common viz.,

- A course of action
- Specific objectives
- Definite time duration

Classification of project:

Different authors have classified projects in different ways. Following are the major classification of projects:

(i) Quantifiable and non-quantifiable projects:

Projects for which a right quantitative assessment of benefits can be made are termed as quantifiable projects. Projects related to power generation, mineral development, industrial development etc., are examples of quantifiable projects. Projects for which quantitative assessment cannot be made are termed as non-quantifiable projects. Projects involving health, education and defence are some examples of non-quantifiable projects.

(ii) Sectoral projects:

Projects are classified based on different sectors. Some examples are:

- Automobile sector
- Agricultural sector
- Power sector
- Health sector
- Education sector
- Transport sector
- Manufacturing sector
- Food processing sector
- Mining sector
- Irrigation sector
- Miscellaneous sector, etc.

(iii) Techno-Economic projects:

Projects can be classified based on techno-economic characteristics. This classification has three groups.

(a) Factor Intensity–oriented classification:

Based on intensity of factors, projects may be classified as capital intensive or labour intensive. If a large investment is made in plant and machinery, then such projects are called capital intensive. On the other hand, if the projects involving large numbers of human resources are termed as labour intensive.

(b) Cause-oriented classification:

Under this, projects are classified as demand based or raw material based. The existence of demand for some goods or services makes the project demand-based and the availability of raw material, skill or other resources make the project raw material based.

(c) Magnitude oriented classification:

Projects are classified on the basis of magnitude of investment. Based on this, the projects may be classified as large scale, medium scale and small-scale projects, depending upon the level of investment in project.

Project classification based on techno-economic characteristics is found useful in facilitating the process of feasibility appraisal of the project.

15.2 PROJECT IDENTIFICATION

A project having good market is generally selected as a project by any entrepreneur. Hence identifying project is a crucial step in any business and plays a vital role. An entrepreneur will have a wide choice of projects.

Project identification is concerned with collection of economic data, compiling and analyzing it to identify the possibility of investment to produce the goods or service for making profit.

According to Peter F. Drucker, there are three types of opportunities: additive, complementary and break through. Utilizing of the existing resources and facilities without any change in the business are known as additive opportunities. There is no risk involved in this type of opportunities. The opportunities involving new ideas that cause some change in the existing structure are known as complementary opportunities. There is some amount of risk involved in this type. Break through opportunities involve fundamental changes in both character and structure of business. This type involves higher risk than the other two.

Project identification may come from one or other of the following ways.

(i) Observation: Observation is one of the very important sources of project idea. The scarcity of a particular product or service may lead to the development of that. The available of raw material or skill may lead to an idea of utilizing them to produce goods. Observations of existing processes/products also sometimes leads to new project ideas.

(ii) **Trade and professional magazines:** Trade and professional literature keeps a person in touch with latest developments and trends and also stimulate to develop new ideas.

(iii) **Bulletins of Research Institutions:** R & D bulletins of some institutions also provide some new ideas based on the findings which are published in the bulletin.

(iv) **Government sources:** Departmental publications of various departments of Government also provide useful information that can help in identification of new project ideas.

The project ideas can be discovered from various sources. They are given below.

(i) Knowledge of potential customer need.

(ii) Watching emerging trends in demands for certain products.

(iii) Knowledge about the Government policy, concessions and incentives, list of items reserved for manufacture in SSIs.

(iv) Ideas generated by concerned people.

(v) Scope for producing substitute product.

(vi) Visiting trade fairs, exhibitions of new products etc.

(vii) Observation of market and similar products.

(viii) Competitor's products.

(ix) Ideas given by friends and relatives based on their intuition and observation.

All of these sources put together may give a few ideas about the possible projects to be examined as the final project. This process is known as "opportunity scanning and identification".

15.3 PROJECT SELECTION

Project selection starts from where project identification ends. After identifying some projects, these are analyzed in the light of existing economic conditions, the government policies, target markets, profit, availability of raw materials and skills etc. One of the well-known tools for this analysis is SWOT or SCOT analysis. This is the analysis of strengths, weakness or constraints, opportunities and threats.

The entrepreneur analyses all the strengths of the enterprise like skills, manpower, capital, technology etc., with respect to this product. Then the weakness or constraints are listed down with an idea to find means to overcome them. The various opportunities that emerge with the development of the product are studied. This includes market share, profit, life of product, export possibilities etc. Finally the threats like competition, import of similar product into market, government policies, technological obsolescence etc, are analysed. SWOT analysis is a very useful tool in all situations.

The other points to be considered in selection of a project are listed below:

(i) Technology: The technology required to develop the project should be available within or preferably available indigenously. It makes life easier to start with. It may be difficult and costly to get technology through foreign collaboration.

(ii) Equipment: The availability of equipment should be studied. The entrepreneur should select the best equipment available for the project.

(iii) Investment size: The study of investment required is to be made rationally and accurately. Wrong estimation may lead to shortage of funds in the middle or towards the end of project.

(iv) Location: Suitable location of project is very important. The entrepreneur should locate the project where resources and raw material are available. He should also consider possibility of setting up the project at notified area by Government, to avail certain facilities, concessions and subsidies.

(v) Marketing: The product should be marketable. One should estimate the correct/reliable demand and market share for his product.

15.4 PROJECT REPORT- NEED AND SIGNIFICANCE

A project report is a written document pertaining to any investment proposal. It contains relevant data on which the project has been appraised and found relevant. It is a course of action what the entrepreneur wants to do in his business and the means to do it. Thus the preparation of project report is of great significance for the entrepreneur. The project report essentially serves two functions: It serves as a road map describing the direction of the enterprises it goals and how to achieve them. It also serves to attract investors and lenders. The preparation of project report is beneficial for those entrepreneurs seeking financial assistance from financial institutions and commercial banks. Financial institutions provide financial assistance based on project report. A project report is prepared by an expert after detailed study and analysis of the various aspects of a project. It gives the complete analysis of the inputs and outputs of the project. It enables the entrepreneur to understand, at the initial stages, whether the project is sound in technology, commercial aspects, financial and marketing aspects.

There is no substitute for a well-prepared project report. The more concrete and complete the project report, the more likely it is to gain quick acceptance by outsiders, investors, banks and other supporting and approving agencies. Hence the project report needs to be prepared with great care and consideration.

15.5 CONTENTS OF PROJECT REPORT

The following are the contents of a good project report.

(i) General information:

The report should contain general information regarding the company, product profile and product details and specifications.

(ii) Promoter:

The details of promoter, name, educational qualifications, work experience, project related experience etc., are to be provided.

(iii) Location:

Details like exact location of project lease or own, location advantages etc., are to be indicated.

(iv) Land and Building:

Details of area of land, built up area, type of construction, cost of construction, plant layout, detailed plan and estimate are to be included.

(v) Plant and Machinery:

Details of machinery required, their capacities, suppliers, cost, various alternatives etc, are to be included.

(vi) Capital requirement and cost:

Information about all items of costs should be carefully collected and presented.

(vii) Operational requirement and cost:

Information about operational costs should be presented. They include cost of raw materials, fuel, power, utilities, labour, repair and maintenance, overheads etc.

(viii) Production process:

Description of production process, process chart, technical know how, alternate technologies, production programmes etc., are to be provided.

(ix) Raw material:

List of raw material required, its quality and quantity, sources of supply, cost, tie-up arrangements if any, alternate raw material, alternate suppliers etc., are provided.

(x) Man power:

Details of manpower required, skilled, semi-skilled, sources of man power supply, cost of manpower, and cost of training if required, are provided.

(xi) Products:

Products produced, by-products, product mix, product quality and standard etc, are to be mentioned.

(xii) Market:

Target users, distribution channels, selling price, trade practices, sales promotion, and estimated sales are to be included.

(xiii) Economic analysis:

Profits, return on investment, breakeven, market share, exporting etc., are made and included.

(xiv) Working capital:

Requirement of working capital, source of working capital, nature and extent of credit facilities available, offered and required are to be provided.

(xv) Requirement of funds:

Break-up of project cost in terms of cost of land, buildings, machinery, miscellaneous assets, preliminary expenses and working capital are to be included.

15.6 PROJECT FORMULATION

Project formulation is the systematic development of a project idea for the eventual purpose of arriving at an investment decision. It involves a step-by-step investigation and development of a project. It is a process involving the joint efforts of a team of experts. Each member of the team must be fully familiar with the broad strategies, objectives and other aspects of the project.

Normally small scale industries do not include sophisticated techniques in preparing project reports.

A general set of information given in project reports is listed below:

(i) General information
(ii) Project description
(iii) Market potential
(iv) Capital costs and sources of finance
(v) Assessment of working capital requirement
(vi) Other financial aspects
(vii) Economic and social variables
(viii) Project implementation.

(i) General Information:

The general information to be included in the report are:

(a) Biodata of promotor: Name and address, qualifications, general experience and experience in proposed area of project of the entrepreneur and his partners if any.

(b) Industry profile: A reference of analysis of industry to which the project belongs, eg., past performance, present status, its organization, its problems etc.

(c) Constitution and organization: The constitution and organizational structure of the enterprise, in case of partnership firm, its registration with the Registrar of firms, application for getting registration certificate from the Directorate of Industries/District Industry Centre.

(ii) Project description:

A brief description of the project covering the following aspects is given in the project report.

(a) Site: Location of enterprise, owned or leasehold land, industrial area, no objection certificate from Municipal/Concerned Authorities etc.

(b) Physical infrastructure: Availability of infrastructures like raw materials (requirement, availability, source of supply, whether imported or indigenous) and skilled labour (required, availability, training needs etc).

(c) Utilities: The details of utilities like: power required, requirement of fuel and water should be clearly stated in the project report.

(d) Pollution control: The points like nature and scope of dumps, sewage system, emissions if any are to be mentioned.

(e) Communication system: Details of availability of communication facilities like telephones, telefax etc.

(f) Transport facilities: Requirement of transport, mode and need of transport are to be included.

(g) **Machinery and Equipment:** A complete list of machinery and equipments required indicting the specifications and features, sources of supply, cost of machinery and equipment are to be furnished in the report.

(h) **Capacity of the plant:** The installed and licensed capacity of the plant along with details of shifts requirements should be mentioned.

(i) **Technology selected and R & D activity:** The technology selected, source of technology and know-how, any Research and Development activity proposed in future are to be included.

(iii) Market Potential:

Details like the projected market potential, demand and supply situation, projected price, marketing strategy, distribution channels, after-sales-service, mode of distribution, requirement of logistics etc., are to be provided in the report.

(iv) Capital costs and Sources of Finance

Detailed estimates of various capital items like land and buildings, plant, machinery, cost of installation, source of finance like owners stake, details of loan if any, name of bank/Financial institutions etc., are to be mentioned in the report.

(v) Assessment of working capital requirement

The requirement of working capital with sources of supply should be clearly stated in the report.

(vi) Other Financial Aspects

Other financial aspects like cost of production, projected profit, expected sales, revenue, projected profit and loss account, cash flow statement should be presented in the report. Break Even Analysis should be prepared and presented. Break-Even is the level of production/sales at which no profit/no loss situation exists.

(vii) Economic and Social variables

As a part of social responsibility, any damage to the society and the cost to control such damages, abatement costs, requirement of pollution control, effluent treatment and costs involved for the same etc., are to be mentioned in the report.

In addition to this, other details like employment generation, utilization of local resources, development of the local area, development of ancillaries, import substitution, any export potential etc., are to be included in the report.

(viii) Project Implementation

At the end, details of schedule of implementation of the various tasks of the project are to be included.

15.7 SPECIMEN OF A PROJECT REPORT

Based on the above explanation, a sample of a project report is presented here:

Project Report for Manufacturing Unit ....

1. PRODUCT DESCRIPTION
2. PRODUCTION AND GENERAL EVALUATION OF PROSPECTS:
3. MARKET ASPECTS
   - (i) Target users:
   - (ii) Sales Channels & Methods of distribution:
   - (iii) Geographical Extent of Market:
   - (iv) Competitive Situation:
     - (a) Domestic Market
     - (b) Export Market if any
   - (v) Market needed for plant described:
4. PRODUCTION REQUIREMENTS
   - (i) Annual Capacity (One/Two/Three-Shift Operation)
   - (ii) Capital Requirements for Land & Buildings on rent

     Equipment, furniture and fittings

     Working capital
   - (iii) Total capital which the entrepreneur would need for the whole project:
     - (i) Own
     - (ii) Borrowings (amount and sources)
   - (iv) Expected net profit per annum
5. CAPITAL REQUIREMENTS
   - (i) Fixed assets and working capital

(a) Land (….sq. metres) and
Building(….sq. metres) (at Rs. ….. per annum)

(b) Equipments:

(i) Production Equipment.

(ii) Other Tools & Equipment

(iii) Furniture and Fittings

(c) Working Capital (Rs)

(ii) Raw Material & Allied Supplies (Annual)

Description	Qty.	Rate Rs.	Annual Requirements
1. Material – 1			
2. Material –2			
3. Material – 3 etc.,			
4. …….			
5. Power, Fuel & Water			
6. Maintenance & spares			
7. Other Supplies			
			Total

(iii) Manpower (Annual)

Description	No.	Rate per month (Rs.)	Annual Cost Rs.
Manager			
Foreman			
Supervisors			
Skilled Workers			
Semi-Skilled Workers			
Unskilled Workers			
Office Staff			
Others			
			Total

(iv) Other Costs (Annual)

(a) Depreciation on equipment, furniture & fittings / Annum

(b) Interest on capital (fixed and working) per annum

(c) Administrative Costs

(d) Sales cost (Including Sales Commission, Advertisement, etc)

(e) Provision for discount, bad debts and miscellaneous contingencies

(f) Training costs

6. Total Annual Costs, Sales Revenue and net profits

(a) Annual Costs

(i) Rent for Land & Buildings

(ii) Raw Materials and Allied Supplies

(iii) Manpower

(iv) Other Costs

(b) Annual Sales Revenue

(c) Expected Annual Net Profit (b – a)

(d) % Profit on Own Capital

(e) % Profit on Total Annual Sales Turnover

(f) % on Total Investment

7. Remarks:

Signature

Date:

15.8 GUIDELINES BY PLANNING COMMISSION FOR PROJECT REPORT

Planning Commission of India issued some guide lines for preparing / formulating realistic project reports. The project formulation stage involves the identification of investment options by the enterprise and in consultation with the Administrative Ministry the Planning Commission and other concerned authorities. The summery of the guidelines by Planning Commission are presented here:

(i) General Information:

The feasibility report must include the analysis of the industry to which it belongs. The report should deal with description of type of industry, its priority, past performance, increase in production, role of public sector, technology, allocation of funds and information about the enterprise.

(ii) Preliminary Analysis of Alternatives

The details like gap between demand and supply of proposed products, availability of capacity, list of all existing plants in industry, indicating their capacity, level of production attained, list of present projects and list of proposed projects. All technically feasible options are considered here. Location of plant/ project, requirement of any foreign exchange, profitability, Return on Investment, alternative cost calculations etc., are to be presented.

(iii) Project Description

The feasibility report should provide a brief description of the technology / process selected for the project, information pertaining to the selection of optimal location, population, water, land, environment, pollution and other environmental problems etc., are to be provided.

The report should contain details of operational requirements of the plant, requirement of water, power, personnel, land, transport, construction details for plant and offices etc.

(iv) Marketing plan:

The details like marketing plan, demand, target price of product, distribution methods etc., are to be presented.

(v) Capital Requirements and Costs

Information with regard to capital requirement and costs with breakup are to be provided. The estimates should be realistic and based on logical information.

(v) Operating Requirements and costs

The costs incurred after the commencement of commercial production are called operating costs. Cost of raw material, fuel, power, salaries, repair and maintenance, rent, selling and marketing expenses, transport, interest burden if any etc., are some examples of operating costs. All these are to be provided in detail.

(vi) Financial Analysis

Financial analysis is essential to assess the financial viability of the project.

A proforma balance-sheet, details of depreciation, clearance for foreign exchange, details of any income tax rebate, incentives for back word areas are to be included.

(viii) Economic Analysis

Social profitability analysis is to be made. Impact of the operations on foreign trade, direct costs and benefits are to be included in the report.

(ix) Miscellaneous aspects

Depending upon the nature and size of operation of a particular project, any other relevant information may be included in the project report.

15.9 NETWORK ANALYSIS:

Network is a set of symbols connected with each other with a sequential relationship with each step making the completion of a project/event. A business plan or any project contains various activities. Any delay in any activity will effect the other activities, project is delayed, costs will go up leading to reduced profit. A number of networking techniques have been developed for project scheduling. They are:

(i) Programme Evaluation and Review techniques (PERT)

(ii) Critical Path Method (CPM)

(iii) Line of Balance (LOB)

(iv) Graphical Evaluation and Review Techniques (GERT)

(v) Work shop Analysis and Scheduling Programme (WASP)

Among these, PERT and CPM are the most widely used network analysis techniques in project management.

15.9.1 Importance of Network Analysis

The network analysis helps in identifying the hidden stages involved in project estimates. By identifying them the management can improve on the on-going project estimates and learn for future use. The following are some of the points that speak about the importance of network analysis.

(i) The whole project has to be considered with reference to the sequence of activities and events. Sequence means activities that are to follow one after another leading to an event.

(ii) The events should be considered as different branches of operations.

(iii) The different segments of the project are treated as separate network which are finally integrated to the overall network. Then the entire project may be put on one network.

(iv) The time estimates may be done based on either previous experience of similar types of operations or may be based on probabilities for the ones where previous experience does not exist.

(v) Cost estimates would depend on the project time estimates and the charge of prices of different factors of production.

(vi) The physical progress of the project, nature of events, jobs formed and snags in different areas of project work would call for corrective action at appropriate time. The concept of crashing would be helpful to reduce penalties.

15.9.2 Programme Evaluation and Review Techniques (PERT):

PERT was first developed as a management aid for completing Polaris Ballistic missile project in USA during 1958. It worked well in completing this project well in advance. From then on PERT became a widely used project management technique. PERT schedules the sequence of activities to be completed in order to accomplish the project with in a short period of time. It helps to reduce both cost and time of the project.

Steps involved in PERT:

(i) The various activities involved in the project are drawn up in a sequential relationships to show which activity follows what.

(ii) The time required for completing each activity of the project is estimated and noted on network.

(iii) The critical activities of the project are determined.

(iv) The variability of the project duration and probability of the project completion in a given time period are calculated.

Advantages of PERT:

(i) It determines the expected time required for completing each activity.

(ii) It helps completion of project with in an expected time period.

(iii) It helps the management in handling uncertainties involved in the project there by reducing the element of risk.

(iv) If enables detailed planning of activities.

(v) It stresses for correct action at a given time period there by helping the project to be completed on time.

Limitations of PERT:

(i) Difficult to provide realistic/correct time estimates for new activities in the absence of past data.

(ii) There is no provision in this techniques about requirement of resources at various activities.

(iii) For the effective control of a project using PERT, it calls for frequent updates and revision of calculations which is a costly affair.

15.9.3 Critical Path Method (CPM)

CPM was first developed by Dupont of USA in 1956 for doing periodic overhauling and maintenance of a chemical plant. CPM differentiates between planning and scheduling of the project. Planning refers to determination of activities to be accomplished, scheduling refers to the introduction of time schedules for each activity of the project. The duration of different activities in CPM are deterministic. There is a precise known time for each activity in a project.

Advantages of CPM:

(i) It helps in ascertaining the time schedule of activities having sequential relationship.

(ii) It makes control easy for the management.

(iii) It defines the most critical elements in the project. Thus, the management is kept alert and prepared to focus their attention on the critical activities.

(iv) It makes room for detailed and better planning.

Limitations of CPM:

(i) CPM operates on the assumption that there is a precise known time that each activity in the project will take. But this may not be true in real practice.

(ii) CPM estimates are not based on any statistical analysis.

(iii) CPM cannot be used as a controlling device for the simple reason that any change introduced will change the entire structure of network. It is not a dynamic controlling device.

15.9.4 Difference between PERT and CPM

Though PERT and CPM look same, they differ in certain aspects. The differences between PERT and CPM are listed below:

PERT	CPM
1. Its origin is military	1. Its origin is industry
2. Event oriented approach.	2. Activity oriented approach.
3. Allows uncertainty.	3. Does not allow uncertainty.
4. It has three time estimates	4. Only single time estimate
5. Time-based	5. Cost-based
6. Probabilistic model	6. Deterministic model
7. There is no demarcation between critical and non-critical activities.	7. Marks critical activities.
8. It averages time.	8. Does not average time.
9. It is suitable where high precision is required in time estimates.	9. Suitable where requirement of precision is reasonable.

15.10 ERRORS OF PROJECT REPORT

Project report formulation is very important and not an easy task. The entrepreneurs often make errors while preparing project report. The following are some of the widely noticed errors in project report:

(i) Product Selection:

It is noticed that some entrepreneurs commit mistakes by selecting a wrong product for their enterprise. They select the product without giving due attention to product related and other aspects such as demand for that product, market need, competition, life cycle, availability of resources like raw materials, skilled labour, technology etc.

(ii) Capacity utilization estimates:

The entrepreneurs many times make over optimistic estimates of capacity utilization. Their estimates are based on completely false premises and are made in complete disregard of present performance of the enterprise, prevailing market conditions, competitive atmosphere, the technical snags etc.

(iii) Market Study

Production of goods is ultimately meant for sale. Hence market study plays vital role and is very important. Market study is a difficult task. Some entrepreneurs assume that there will be good market for their product without conducting effective market study, leading to failure.

(iv) Technology selection

The technology varies from product to product. Selection of wrong technology leads to wrong product or product with inferior quality. Selection of right technology is very important.

(v) Location Selection

There are two types of errors made by some entrepreneurs in selecting the location of enterprise. First, they are attracted by the concessions and government offers, financial incentives to establish industries at a particular location. This may lead to problems like marketing, non availability of resources like raw materials, skilled labour etc. Secondly the entrepreneur selects a location merely because it is nearer to his place of living, or own land available, that may not be an appropriate location for the plant.

(vi) Selection of Ownership Form

Many enterprises fail merely due to the ownership form of enterprises is not suitable.

15.11 PROJECT APPRAISAL

Project appraisal means the assessment of a project in terms of its economic, social and financial liability. This makes it necessary to recognize the interrelationship of various aspects of a project. This exercise is critical as it calls for a multidimensional analysis of the project. Financial institutions carry out project appraisal to asses its creditworthiness before giving finance to a project.

Methods of project appraisal

Any project is appraised under the following contexts:

- Economic analysis
- Financial analysis
- Technical feasibility
- Managerial competence and
- Market analysis.

(i) Economic analysis

Economic analysis of appraisal is fundamental one. Economic analysis includes requirements for raw materials level of capacity utilization, expected sales, expected expenses and expected profits. Business should have a volume of profit that decides sales to be achieved. The amount of sales has to be calculated to achieve the target profits. Demand for the product is to be identified carefully as it is the deciding factor of project feasibility points considered for the location of the enterprise are to be maintained. The Government policies in this regard should be considered. The government offers specific incentives and concessions for selling up industries in notified backward areas.

(ii) Financial Analysis

Finance is one of the most important prerequisites to establish an enterprise. It is the finance that facilitates an entrepreneur to bring together the labour, raw materials and other facilities to produce goods. Financial analysis includes assessment of financial requirements like fixed capital and working capital, land and building, plants and machinery are some of the examples of fixed capital assets. While assessing the fixed capital requirements, all items related to the asset like cost of asset, architect or engineer's fee, electric connection, water sources, cost of plant and machinery, pre production expenses etc., are to be considered. The working capital is also analysed. Working capital is that amount of funds which is needed in day-to-day's business operation. Break-even analysis is made to assess at what level of production/sales will result is no loss/no gain situation.

(iii) Technical feasibility

While making project appraisal, the technical feasibility of project is made. Technical feasibility means the adequacy of the proposed plant and equipment to produce the product at proposed technology. It should be ensured that know-how is available within the entrepreneur or should be obtained from outside in the form of either collaboration or purchase or franchise.

(iv) Managerial Competence

Managerial competence plays an important role in making the enterprise a great success. In the absence of managerial competence a technically and financially viable project may fail. Also good managerial ability may bring a bad project to an efficient one. Hence while conducting project appraisal, study of managerial appraisal is also important. Studies have revealed that most of the enterprises fail due to lack of good managerial competence.

(v) Market Analysis

Before the actual start of production, there is a need to study the market with respect to demand, target customers, when and where the products are to be sold. Production has no valve unless the produced goods are sold. Hence, knowledge of anticipated market for a product becomes an important aspect in every business. Demand forecasting is one such method of knowing the anticipated market. The various methods of estimating the demand for a product are:

- Opinion pool.
- Market Survey.
- Life cycle analysis.
- Desk survey.
- Dealers opinion etc.

15.12 IDENTIFICATION OF BUSINESS OPPORTUNITIES

Business opportunities can be obtained from various magazines, trade journals, financial institutions, government, commercial organisations, friends, relatives, competitors etc. Choosing of best business opportunity from the information collected requires ingenuity, skill and foresight of entrepreneur. An entrepreneur has to identify and select the most rewarding opportunity from the available ones. For this one has to evaluate the following areas and understand the gap between demand and supply.

(i) Study of government rules and regulations regarding the different business opportunities.

(ii) Extensive and indepth study of promising investment opportunity.

(iii) SWOT analysis of the business opportunities.

(iv) Market Feasibility study.

(v) Technical feasibility study.

(vi) Financial feasibility study and

(vii) Social feasibility study.

An opportunity can be defined as an attractive and excellent project idea which an entrepreneur searches for and accepts such idea as a basis for his investment decision. A good business opportunity must be capable of being converted into feasible project. Two major characteristics of business opportunity are : good and wide market scope and an attractive, acceptable and reliable return on investment.

15.12.1 Sources of business ideas

(i) Unfulfilled demand: An Unfulfilled demand will open doors to new products.

(ii) Own idea: Once own creative idea can result in a business opportunity.

(iii) Social and economic trends: Social and economic trends necessitate demand for new products.

(iv) Magazines/Journals/Research publications: Magazines/Journals/Research publications form a major role of ideas.

(v) Government: Government also identifies and proposes ideas and give support for business opportunities.

(vi) Emerging new technology and scientific know how: Commercial exploitation of indigenous and imported technologies and know-how is another source of opportunities.

(vii) Charges in consumer needs: The needs of consumers charge giving rise to requirement of new business opportunities.

(viii) Trade fairs/Exhibitions: Trade fairs and technical exhibitions also offer wide scope for business opportunities.

(ix) Banks and Government agencies: Commercial banks and government agencies encourage entrepreneurs by providing business opportunities, ideas subsidies, loan etc.

15.13 MARKET FEASIBILITY STUDY

Feasibility study is a detailed work of collection of data analysis and conclude the feasibility of that operation. Market feasibility study involves the study and analysis of the following aspects.

Market feasibility study will assess whether the product has good market. This needs to study the following:

(i) Nature of the market:

The nature of market in terms of monopolistic or perfect competition is to be studied.

(ii) Cost of production:

It is essential to study and control cost of production. Cost of production decides the selling price.

(iii) Selling price and profit

Selling price plays a vital role in profit. In price sensitive goods like cosmetics, one should be careful in fixing the price.

(iv) Demand

Present demand and demand forecast are prepared and studied. This will decide the facility planning.

(v) Market share

Estimated market share is to be made. Comparison is made with share of similar products.

(vi) Target market:

Study is made with regard to the target market and market segmentation.

15.14 TECHNICAL FEASIBILITY STUDY

In technical feasibility study, the following points are studied.

(i) Location of the project

The data regarding the location of project is very important. It may be located in rural, urban or semi-urban areas.

(ii) Construction of factory, building and its size

The construction details, the nature/type of building and its size for the project are to be analysed.

(iii) Availability of raw materials

The study of availability of raw materials, sources of supply, alternate sources, its quality and specifications cost etc., are to be studied.

(iv) Selection of Machinery

The selection of machinery required to produced the intended product is to be carried out. The specifications are capacity, cost, sources of supply, technology evaluation of various makes of the machine, their good and bad etc., are studied.

(v) Utilities

The detailed about availability of utilities like water, gas, electricity, petrol, diesel etc. are to be studied.

(vi) Production Capacity

Establishment off production capacity and utilization of production capacity are analysed.

(vii) Staff requirement

Study and analysis of requirement of workers, technical staff and officers etc. is to be made.

(viii) Technical viability

The technical viability of the opportunity is to be studied.

15.15 FINANCIAL FEASIBILITY STUDY

Financial feasibility is the most important aspect of a business opportunity. Some of the aspects involved in financial feasibility study are:

(i) Total capital cost of project

It is very essential to study the total cost of project. This includes fixed capital, working capital and interest factor.

(ii) Sources of capital

The study of main sources of capital is to be made. If capital is borrowed, interest burden is to be studied in detail.

(iii) Subsidiary sources for additional finance

After study of main sources of capital, subsidiary sources of capital are to be identified and studied.

(iv) Financing for future development of business

Finance requirement for future development of business are to be studied. Working capital requirement for at least three months running of enterprise are to be estimated.

(v) Break Even Analysis (BEA)

BEA is to be carried out to see at what level of production/sales will make the organisation no loss/no profit situation. BEA is very useful to identify the level of production that makes profit.

(vi) Estimation of cash and fund flow

It is very essential to make a study of estimation of cash and fund flow in the business.

(vii) Return on investment (ROI)

ROI is to be calculated to see the amount of return on investment for the investors/share holders and how much they get.

(viii) Proposed balance sheet

Proposed balance sheet is made showing liabilities and assets, depreciation, interest burden, profits expected etc.

(ix) Cost of labour and Technology

The cost of employees (Salaries etc.) is to be estimated and studied. If technology is not available then it has to be purchased from any R & D institution or by way of foreign collaboration.

15.16 SOCIAL FEASIBILITY STUDY

Social feasibility study is important in the social environment.

(i) Location

The location is in such a place that it should not have objection from the neighbours.

(ii) Social problem

The enterprise should not create any nuisance to the public.

(iii) Pollution

There should not have any sort of noise or other pollution objectionable society. Suitable measures are to be taken for controlling pollution.

(iv) Other problem

Any other problems related to the society and people are to be studied.

REVIEW QUESTIONS

1. Define the project. What is its nature?
2. Give the classification of projects.
3. Explain the phase of project identification with its sources.
4. Write about selection of project.
5. Write about the need and significance of project report.
6. Write about project Formulation process.
7. What are the contacts of project report. Explain.
8. What are the guidelines of Planning Commission for project report?
9. Explain network analysis. What are various techniques used for Network analysis.
10. What is the importance of Network analysis.
11. Explain PERT. What are its advantages and disadvantages.
12. Explain CPM. What are its advantages and disadvantages.
13. Differentiate between PERT and CPM.
14. What are common errors in project report. Explain.
15. Explain the process of project appraisal.
16. Write about identification of business ideas.
17. Write about market feasibility, financial feasibility Technical feasibility and social feasibility studies.
18. Write the importance of feasibility studies.

CHAPTER – 16

INDUSTRIAL OWNERSHIP

TYPES OF INDUSTRIAL OWNERSHIP

16.1 SOLE PROPRIETORSHIP

A sale trading concern is a business concern which is owned and managed by a single person for his exclusive benefit. He uses his own skill in the management of his business and bears all the business risks himself.

16.1.1 Features of sole proprietorship

The main features of sale proprietorship are as follows:

- The sole proprietorship concern is the oldest and the simplest form of business organisation.
- No legal formalities are required for the formation and the closing of a sole trading concern.
- It is owned and managed by a single person.
- As it is owned by a single owner, the single owner invests all the capital himself. However, if his capital is insufficient for the business, he supplements it by borrowing form his relatives, friends or banks.
- The sole trader puts his own labour in conducting his business. If necessity arises, he makes use of the services of the members of his family. He may also employ a few paid assistants to help him in his business.
- The sole-trader assumes all the risks involved in the business. As he assumes all the business risks, he takes all the profits and bears all the losses of the business.
- The liability of the sole trader is unlimited. That means: if his business assets are not sufficient to payoff business liabilities or debts, the balance of his business liabilities has to be paid out of his private assets. Thus, for business debts, not only his business assets but also his private assets become liable.

16.1.2 Advantages of sole Proprietorship

The main advantages of sole trading concern are as follows:

- No legal formalities like registration are necessary for the formulation of a sole trading concern. It can be formed easily.
- As the business carried on by a sole trading concern is simple in nature, generally, no difficulties will arise sole trading concern can be run easily.
- The sole trader can enjoy all the profit of the business as he is the sole owner of the business.
- As the sole trader can get all the profits of the business, he is encouraged to work hard for the efficient running of the business.
- As the sole trader is always present in the business premises, he can maintain personal supervision over all the works done in the business. The personal supervision increases efficiency in the running of the business.
- A sole trader can establish and maintain personal contract with his customers. The personal contact with the customers contributes to more business.
- A sole trader can maintain close contract with his employees. The close and cordial relation between the employer and the employees leads to smooth and efficient running of the business.
- The sole trader is the master of his business. He need not consult any other person while taking decisions on business matters. Therefore, he can take quick decisions on all business matters.
- A sole trading concern need not publish its annual accounts. Further, its business policies (i.e., the plans for the improvement of the business) are determined by only one man. Therefore, there is greater scope for maintaining business secrets in this type of business organizations.
- There is no scope for disputes among owners in this form or business organization, because there is only one owner.
- As the liability of the sole trader is unlimited he carries on his business very carefully without undertaking great risks.
- The unlimited liability of the sole trader helps him to get credit from others for the business.

16.1.3 Disadvantages of Sole Proprietorship

- The capital of a sole trader is limited. Therefore, he cannot expand the size of his business.
- The managerial ability of the sole trade is also limited.
- As the scale of the sole trader's business is small, he cannot get the benefits of large scale operations.

- It is said that two heads are better than one for taking right decisions on business matters. As the sole trader has no one else to consult before taking decisions, his decisions may go wrong. If his decisions go wrong, he has to suffer heavy loses.
- As the sole trader is the sole owner of the business, he has to bear all the losses of the business.
- The liability of the sole-trader is unlimited. Therefore, if his business debts are not paid in full out of his business assets, the balance of his business debts has to be paid out of his private assets. Thus, his private assets are also in danger.
- As the liability of the sole trader is unlimited, generally he will not be bold enough to undertake large-scale business or new business.
- The life of this type of business is limited, i.e., short. It is likely to be closed due to the death or the insolvency of the proprietor.

16.1.4 Scope

Before the industrial revolution, this type of organisation was the most popular form of organisation for conducting business or industry. However, after the industrial revolution, it has lost its importance, as it could not provide the large capital and the high managerial ability required for the modern industry.

The circumstances under which it is still considered importance are as follows:

- It is most suitable in those cases where the business is simple. Example: retail trade and small-scale industries.
- It is specially suitable for those lines of business where there are considerable and sudden changes in demand and prices, and where quick decisions and prompt action are required. Example: trading the precious metals like the gold and silver and shares.
- It is suitable for those lines of activities where the customers require personal attention. Example: professions such as medical practice, legal practice etc.
- It is suitable for those business where special regard has to be shown to the fashions and tastes of the customers. Example: tailoring or dress making.

16.2 DEFINITION AND MEANING OF PARTNERSHIP

Partnership is defined as "the relation between persons who have agreed to share the profits of a business carried on by all or any of them acting for all".

So a partnership is an association of two or more person who are to carry on a business jointly and share the profits of such a business.

The persons who form the partnership are called "partners" individually, and a 'Firm' collectively. The name under which they carry on the business is called the "Firm Name".

16.2.1 Characteristics of partnership

- A partnership arises from a contract between persons who wish to form the partnership. It does not result from status, i.e., natural relation arising from birth.
- As the partnership is the result of a contract, the persons who wish to form the partnership must have the capacity to enter into contract. Persons who do not have the capacity to enter into contact, such as minors, insolvents and lunatics cannot become partners.
- The contract between the persons to from a partnership can be oral or written. But the usual practice is to have the contract in writing.
- Contract must be between two or more persons. There must be at least two persons to form a partnership. The maximum number of persons permitted in a partnership depends on the type of business.
- The persons who form the partnership must carry on a business in common or jointly. It is not enough if they merely own a property in common. Joint ownership of property alone cannot form a partnership between them.
- The term business includes every lawful trade, occupation or profession.
- The contract between the persons must be for making profits and sharing the profits among themselves. Therefore, a contract between the persons for a charitable or social cause cannot form a partnership.
- The profits (or losses) of a partnership business are shared by all the partners according to some agreed proportion.
- The partnership business may be carried on by all the partners or by any one of them acting for all. It is not necessary that the partnership business should be carried on by all the partners. This is because every partner is both an agent and a principal. As an agent, he can bind the other partners by his acts, and as a principal, he is bound by the acts of other partners.
- In the eye of law, the firm and the partners are considered as one and the same.
- In the case of a partnership, the financial resources and the

managerial abilities of the partners are pooled together for their mutual benefit.

- The liability of the partners is unlimited. Further, each of the partners is jointly and individually liable for the debts of the firm.

16.2.2 Kinds of Partners

There are many kinds of partners, which are as follows:

Active or Working partners

Those who bring capital and take an active part in the management of the partnership business are called active or working partners.

Sleeping or Financing Partners

Those who do not take an active part in the management of the partnership business, but merely contribute capital or finance to the business are called sleeping or financing partners, Their liability is the same as that of the active partners.

Nominal partners

Those who neither contribute capital for the business nor take active part in the management of the business, but merely lend their names and credit to the firm are called nominal partners or partners in name only. They are not entitled to the profits of the firm. But they are liable to third parties like the other partners to an unlimited extent.

Partners in profits only

Generally, a partner who is entitled to share the profits of a firm is also liable to share the losses of the firm. But sometimes, a person becomes a partner of a firm on a specific agreement with the other partners that he should be given his share of the profits of the firm without being held liable for losses. Such a partner is called partner in profits only. A partner in profits only is not entitled to take part in the management of the partnership business. But he is liable to third parties for all the debts of the firm.

Partners by Estoppel

If a person represents himself either by words or by conduct to be partner of a firm, though, is really not a partner, he is estoppel (i.e. prevented) from denying the role, which he has assumed and becomes a partner by Estoppel. He is not a true partner of the firm. So, he is not entitled to the profits of the firm. But he is liable to an unlimited extent to the third parties who grant credit to the firm on the strength of that representation.

Partners by holding out

If a person is held out or represented to the public as a partner of firm and if he does not deny the fact that he is a partner even after knowing that his name is used as a partner, he becomes a partner by holding out. He is not a true partner of the firm. So, he does not have the right to share the profits of the firm. But he will be liable to all outsiders who given credit to the firm in the belief that he is a partner.

16.2.3 Partnership agreement or partnership deed

A partnership is formed by an agreement. The partnership agreement may be either oral or written. Both are equally binding on the partners. But it is desirable to have the agreement in writing in order to avoid future disputes among the partners. When the partnership agreement is written, duly stamped and signed by all the partners, it is called the partnership deed or Articles of partnership.

The partnership deed contains all the particulars. The usual particulars found in a partnership deed are as a follows:

- The name or the firm.
- The names and addresses of partners.
- The duration of the firm (the period for which the firm is formed).
- The nature of the business which the firm proposes to undertake.
- The amount of capital to be contributed by each particular and, the manner of contribution.
- The amount of withdrawal that can be made by each partner and the manner of withdrawal.
- If any interest is to be allowed on partner's capital, the rate of interest payable on partners capital.
- If any interest is to be charged on partner drawings, the rate of interest chargeable on partners drawings.
- The rate of interest payable on partners loan.
- The amount of salary or any other remuneration payable to any partner for any extra work done for the firm.
- The manner in which additional capital is to be introduced by the partners.
- The ratio in which the profits or losses are to be shared among the partners.
- The manner in which the work is divided among the partners.
- Clauses starting the rights and duties of the partners.

- How the capital accounts of partners should be kept.
- The basis of valuation of goodwill at the time of admission or retirement or death of a partner.
- The ratio in which the loss arising out of the insolvency of partner is to be borne by the solving partners.
- The methods of settlement of account in case of dissolution of the firm.
- The mode of settlement of accounts, in case of dissolution of the firm.
- Arbitration clause, laying down the procedure to be followed to settle disputes which may arise among the partners.

16.2.4 Registration of Partnership Firm

The registration of a partnership firm can be effected at any time. For the registration of a firm, a statement in the prescribed form must be submitted to the Registrar of Firms along with the necessary registration fee. The statement should be signed by all the partners or by their duly authorized agents. The statement should contain the following particulars:

- Name of the firm.
- Principal place of business of the firm.
- Names of other places where the firm carries on business.
- Date on which each partner joined the firm.
- Names and addresses of all the partners.
- Duration of the firm.

After receiving the statement in the prescribed form and the registration fee, if the Registrar is satisfied that the provisions of the partnership act have been duly complied with, he will enter the particulars of the statement in a register called Register of Firms. The Register of Firms at the Registrar's office is open to the public for inspection.

Any change in the above particulars after the registration must be brought to the notice of the Register of Firms within 14 days of such change.

Effect of Non-Registration of Firms

The Indian Partnership Act of 1932 neither makes the registration of firm compulsory nor imposes any penalty for non-registration. However, as unregistered firm suffers from certain disabilities such as:

- It cannot file a suit in a court of law against the third parties for the recovery of its debts exceeding Rs. 100.

- It cannot file a suit against any of its partners for the recovery of its debts.
- A partner of an unregistered firm cannot file a suit in a court of law against the third parties or against the firm or against his copartners for the recovery of his claims.

However, non-registration of a firm will not prevent a partner from bringing a suit for the dissolution of the firm and for the settlement of accounts of the dissolved firm. Further, non-registration will not prevent the third parties for filing a suit in a court of law against an unregistered firm or against its partners for the recovery of their claims.

16.2.5 Rights, Duties and Liabilities of Partners

The rights, duties and liabilities of partners are generally provided for in the partnership agreement. If the partnership Agreement fails to provide for their right, duties and liabilities, the following provisions laid down in the Indian Partnership Act of 1932 are applicable.

(i) Right of partners

- Every partner has a right to take part in the management of the partnership business.
- Every partner has a right to express his opinion on all matters relating to the partnership business.
- Every partner has a right to inspect and copy any books of a accounts of the firm.
- Every partner is entitled to share the profits of the firm equally with the other partners.
- Every partner is entitled to interest at 6% per annum on any amount advanced by him over and above his capital contribution.
- In case of any emergency, every partner has a right to do all the necessary acts for the purpose of protecting the firm's loss.
- Every partner has an equal share in the partnership property.
- Every partner is entitled to the indemnified (i.e., compensated) by the firm in respect of payments made and liabilities incurred by him in the ordinary and proper conduct of the business of the firm.
- Every partner has a right to continue in the partnership. In other words, a partner cannot be expelled from the firm.
- Every partner has a right to retire from the firm with the consent of the partners or by giving notice to the other partners, if the partnership is at will.

- Every partner has a right to prevent the admission of a new partner into the firm without his consent.

(ii) Duties of partners

- Every partner should carry on the business of the firm to the greatest common advantage.
- Every partner should attend to his work honestly and diligently.
- Every partner should be just and faithful to the other partner. He should keep and submit true and correct accounts of the partnership.
- Every partner should compensate the firm for loss caused to it by his fraud or willful negligence in the management of the partnership business.
- Every partner should share the losses of the firm equally with the other partners.
- A partner should not carry on any business which is likely to compete with the business of the firm. If a partner carries on a competing business, he must hand over the profits of such business to the firm.
- Every partner should use the partnership property for the benefit of the firm. He should not use the partnership property for his private purposes. If he earns personal profits by using the partnership property, he should hand over such profits to the firm.
- Every partner should act within his authority. If he exceeds his authority, he should compensate the firm for any loss arising from his unauthorized act.
- A partner cannot transfer his interest or share in the firm to a third party without the consent of the other partners.

(iii) Liabilities of partners

Every partner is liable for the debts of the firm to an unlimited extent. Therefore, his private assets are also held liable for the payment of the firm's liabilities, in case the firm's assets are not sufficient to pay the firm's liabilities in full.

Further, every partner is jointly and severally (i.e., individually) liable for all the debts of the firm. Therefore, the creditors of the firm can recover the amount due to them either from all the partners or from any one of them. Of course, if the creditors of the firm recover the amount due to them from one of the partners, the partner who is forced to make such payment is entitled to contribution from his copartners. In the context of partner's liabilities, the following points should be noted:

- An incoming partner i.e., a new partner who is admitted into an existing partnership firm is liable only to the debts incurred by the firm after he was admitted into the partnership. He is not liable for the debts incurred by the firm before his admission, unless he agrees to be so liable with the consent of the creditors.
- A retiring partner is not liable for the debts incurred by the firm after his retirement. He is liable only for the debts incurred by the firm before his retirement.
- In the case of a deceased partner, his estate (i.e., his legal representatives) is liable only for the debts incurred by the firm before his death. His estate is not liable for the debts incurred by the firm after his death.
- In case of a minor admitted to the benefits of a partnership, he is not personally liable for the debts of the firm. Only his share in the profits and assets of the partnership is liable for the debts of the firm.

16.2.6 Advantages of partnership

- No legal formalities are required for the formation of a partnership firm. Even the registration of a partnership firm is not compulsory. It can be formed easily.
- A partnership firm can collect more capital than a sole trading concern, because, in the case of a partnership firm, capital is contributed by more than one person.
- A partnership is an association of two or more persons. Therefore, it can secure greater managerial ability than a sole trading concern.
- In a partnership, there is scope for combination of capital and ability. The rich partners can contribute capital, and the talented partners can contribute ability. The combination of capital and managerial ability contributes to the expansion of the business.
- As there are two or more persons in a partnership, there is a scope for the application of division of labour. In other words, in a partnership, the work and responsibility can be distributed among the partners according to their ability, experience and qualification. This distribution, of work leads to efficient management of the business.
- As there are two or more persons in a partnership, there is an opportunity for the discussion of business problems. This discussion results in better decisions for the improvement of the business.
- As the partners not only own the business, but also manage it, they take great care and keen interest in the management of the business.

This leads to efficient and economical management.

- The unlimited, joint and several liability of the partners increases the creditworthiness of the firm and enables changes according to the changing business conditions.
- The unlimited, joint and several liability of the partners make them carry on the business carefully.
- A partnership enjoys flexibility in operations. The operations of a partnership can be easily adjusted or changed according to the changing business conditions.
- A partnership can maintain personal touch and contact with the customers to a greater extent than a sole trading concern.
- Minority interest is adequately protected in a partnership. All the partners must agree on the important matters. Only ordinary or unimportant matters can be settled by majority decision.
- A partnership firm is not required to publish its accounts (profit and loss account and Balance Sheet). Therefore, its affairs can be kept secret from third parties.
- A partnership is not subjected to strict Government control. Therefore, it enjoys greater freedom in administration.

16.2.7 Disadvantages of partnership

- For the success of a partnership, unity among the partners is essential. But the unity among the partners cannot be secure when the number of partners increases. When the number of partner increases, difference of opinion and dispute will arise and disturb the smooth working of the business.
- As the number of partner is limited to ten in the case of the Banking, and to twenty in the case of any other business, the capital that can be collected by a partnership is limited.
- The liability of the partners of a firm is unlimited, joint and several. This discourages many people from becoming partners of a firm.
- Each partner is an agent of the firm. He can bind the copartners by his activities. On account of this authority of the partners, honest partners have to suffer for the foolish, reckless or dishonest actions of dishonest partners.
- A partnership firm lacks continuity of existence. The death, insolvency, insanity or retirement of a partner may put an end to the partnership business.
- A partner of a firm cannot transfer his share in the firm to an outsider

without the consent of the other partners. As a result, the money invested by a person in a partnership business is blocked or tied up. The discourages many investors from becoming partners of a firm.

- Owing to the absence of strict government control and lack of publicity of its accounts, a partnership concern cannot enjoy public confidence.

16.3 JOINT STOCK COMPANIES

The sole trading concerns and partnership firms could not supply adequate capital and managerial ability required for large-scale undertakings, such as iron and steel industry, ship building industry, railways etc. Further, these two forms of business organisation suffered from unlimited liability and absence of continuity of existence. In order to remove these drawbacks, a new form of business organisation known as "Joint Stock Company' has been developed.

Definition

Lord Justice Lindsey has defined a company as "A voluntary association or organisation of many persons who contribute money or money's worth to a common stock and employ it in some trade or business and share the profit or loss arising there from".

From the above definition, it is clear that a joint stock company is a voluntary association of many persons who contribute money to a joint stock common stock, employ it in some business and share the profit or losses of that business, under a certificate of incorporation granted by the Government. Legally, it is an artificial person created by law with a perpetual succession and a common seal. The persons who contribute money and form the company are called members or shareholders.

16.3.1 Features of joint stock company

(i) ***Voluntary Association:*** A joint stock company is a voluntary association of persons. No person can be compelled to become a member of a company or give up his membership of a company.

(ii) ***Incorporated association:*** A joint stock company is an incorporated or registered association. It is incorporated under Companies Act.

(iii) ***Separate legal entity or existence:*** A joint stock company is an artificial person created by law. Therefore, even though it has no nature or physical existence (i.e., it has no body and soul), it has a separate legal existence (i.e., existence in the eyes of law) quite different from that of its members. As it has got a separate legal existence, it can enter into contracts, own properties and use its own

name like any other person. But, as it has no physical existence, it has to act through its agents known as Directors.

(iv) ***Perpetual succession or continuous existence:*** A joint Stock Company has a perpetual succession. In other words, it has a continuous existence or life. Its life is not affected by the death, insanity or insolvency of its members. It is remarked that members may come and members may go, but the company goes on until it is would up according to law. The life of the company is not affected by the death, insanity or insolvency of its members, because the company has a separate legal existence quite distinct from that of its members.

(v) ***Common seal:*** A company, not being a natural person, cannot by itself put its signature. Therefore, the common seal of the company (i.e., the seal on which the name of the company is engraved) is affixed to all important matters which require the company's signature. Whenever the common seal of the company is affixed to any document, it has to be witnessed by the signatures of at least two directors. The common seal is kept under the custody of the secretary of the company, and is used in accordance with the instructions of the Board of Directors.

(vi) ***Large membership:*** A joint stock company is an association of many persons. So, it has a large number of members. Any number of persons can become the members of a public company as there is no limit to the maximum number of members. But, in the case of a private company, the maximum number of members is fifty, excluding these members who are the present or past employees of the company. The minimum number of members is seven in the case of a public company, and two in the case of a private company.

(vii) ***Limited liability:*** The liability of the members of a company is generally limited to the extent of the nominal or face value of the shares held by them (in the case of a company limited by shares) or to the extent of the amount guaranteed by them (in the case of a company limited by guarantee). However, in the case of an unlimited company, the members cannot be asked to pay more than what is due to unpaid on the shares held by them or the amount guaranteed by them.

Transferability of shares: The shares of a public company are freely transferable. Therefore, a member of a public company can transfer the shares held by him to anyone else without the consent of the other members. However, the shares of a private company are not freely transferable.

Separation of ownership from management : Generally, the members of a joint stock company are large in number. All of them cannot take part in the day-to-day management of the company. Therefore, the owners of the company, i.e., the shareholders of the company, entrust the day-to-day management of their company to their elected representatives called Board of Directors.

16.3.2 Formation of a Joint Stock Company

The formation of a joint stock company reads like an interesting story. The formation of a joint stock company can be described with reference to the following procedures :

Invention of a business proposition

Gokak, the promoter goes to Gokak with a few experts to examine if all the raw-materials are available there to prepared cement. To prepare cement black mud, sand, limestone and water are necessary. His experts examine the area and find out that all these raw materials are available at Gokak. Then the promoter decides to start a cement company at Gokak. Now it is said that the cement company at Gokak that is the business proposition is invented.

Preparing Memorandum of Association and Articles of Association

After inventing the business proposition, the promoter takes a few of his trusted friends to form a Joint-Stock Company. He then prepares two important documents known as the Memorandum of Association and the Articles of Association.

Memorandum of Association contains the name of the company, place of its Registered Office, the objectives of the company, the amount of capital, the division of shares, kinds of shares, liability of shareholders etc. This Memorandum of Association is a very important document, because it gives a complete and a real picture of the company to be started.

The Articles of Association contains the byelaws of the company. This document mentions in details as to how the company is to be managed, the number of directors to be elected, their qualifications, the 'election or the appointment of the Managing Director, rights of the shareholders, method of calling the meetings etc. In short, the Memorandum of Association contains all the rules connected with the day-to-day management of the company. Sometimes along with these documents the promoter may also give to the Registrar of Joint Stock Companies a document containing the preliminary contracts made between the company and some persons.

Certificate of Incorporation

The promoter submits both the Memorandum of Association and the

Articles of Association to the Registrar of Joint Stock-Companies and requests him to give him permission to start the new company. The Registrar of Joint-stock Companies then carefully studies both the Memorandum and the Articles of Association. If he is satisfied that the new company would be a good and a sound company, then he issues a certificate of Incorporation to the Company. When once the Certificate of Incorporation is issued by the Registrar, the Joint Stock Company is said to be born.

Issue of prospectus

After the joint stock company is incorporated, the promoters of the company start collecting capital from the public. Before collecting the capital from the public the company issues a prospectus and advertise the prospectus in the important news papers. The prospectus, in fact, in an invitation to the public to subscribe to the share-capital of the company.

The prospectus contains the name of the company, the objectives of company, the names of the directors, the amount of shares to be subscribed by the shareholders etc. Different kinds of shares are also mentioned in the prospectus. The place of the factory, the place of the registered office of the company, the future prospectus of the company etc., are also given in the prospectus.

Allotment of Shares

The general public reads the prospectus in the new papers. If famous companies are mentioned as directors of the company in the prospectus then the public will have a great confidence in them. So they rush to buy shares of the company. Thousands of applications for allotment of shares are received in the office of the company. Then a meeting of the Board of Directors of the company is held. In this meeting shares are allotted to the applicants. If too many applications are received for shares, then some applications are rejected and a letter of regret is written to the rejected applicants. Thus the share-capital of the company is fully collected. Now the company is ready to start business.

Certificate to commence business

After the shares are allotted and subscribed, the promoters of the joint stock company submit a detailed statement to the Registrar of Joint Stock Companies giving particulars of shares allotted to different shareholders; their address etc. The promoters should also satisfy the Registrar regarding the fulfillment all the legal formalities. There upon, the Registrar issues a Certificate to Commence business. Now the company goes ahead with construction of the factory and after the construction is completed, begins production.

The joint stock company is managed by a Board of Directors elected by the share holders. The managing Director may be elected or nominated. The company may appoint a Secretary to help the Managing Director to carry on the day-to-day administration of the company. At the end of the year when the accounts are prepared, excess income (profits) over the expenditure is distributed among the shareholders in the form of dividends.

16.3.3 Advantages of a Joint Stock Company

- The liability of the shareholders of a joint stock company is limited to the extent of the free value of the share held by them. The limited liability makes investment in a joint stock company less risky.
- In this form of business organization, the risk of loss is spread over a large number of investors.
- Unlike a sole trading concern or a partnership firm, a joint stock company has legal existence quite different from that of its members. So, its life is not affected by the death, insolvency, or insanity of the members. In other words, it has a perpetual or permanent existence.
- The shares of a public company are freely transferable. The free transferability of shares encourages the investing public to invest the funds in the shares of a company.
- A joint stock company can raise huge capital, as its capital is contributed by a large number of investors, both rich and poor.
- By collecting the savings of small investors joint stock company promotes the habit of saving and investment among the people.
- A joint stock company can satisfy the tastes of different investors by offering different types of shares and debentures.
- Company organisation has contributed to the growth of the exchange market where shares are bought and sold.
- Owing to legal regulation and publicity of its affairs, a joint stock company in enjoys public confidence.
- As a company possesses a large amount of financial resources it can secure the services of highly qualified and efficient persons to look after its day-to-day management.
- The Management of a company is entrusted to a Board of Directors, Generally, the Board of Directors consists of expert management executive. Therefore, the management of a company will be efficient.
- A joint stock-company contributes to the welfare of persons, such as managers, secretaries, accountants, auditors etc.

16.3.4 Disadvantages of a Joint Stock Company

- Company formation is difficult and expensive documents have to be drafted, printed and stamped for the purpose of registration of a company.
- As a joint stock company is subject to the many legal formalities and restrictions, its normal working is disturbed.
- In a joint stock company, the majority group of shareholders rules the company. Therefore, the interest of the minority group of shareholders is neglected.
- The company organisation lacks unity of management. The unity of management is absent, because the management is the hands of a Board of Directors which consists of different persons with different views.
- There is lack of continuity of policies in the company organisation. A change in the personnel of the Board of Directors may result in the change of policies.
- In this form of organisation, there is separation of management from ownership, the owners of the company, namely, the shareholders are not directly responsible for the management. Though the shareholders can control the company, in actual practice, they do not control, the company for lack of cooperation among them.
- As the shareholders delegate their authority and responsibility to the Board of Directors, which in turn delegates its authority and responsibility to the paid officers, inefficiency and waste may be present in the management of the company.
- Quick changes cannot be made in the constitution and management of a company.
- This form of organisation lacks initiative and enterprise. As the employees of a company are merely paid servants, they may not take the initiative in the administration of the company.
- This form of business organisation may promote frauds unsound or bogus companies may be formed by some dishonest promoters. Further, sound concerns may be wound up by dishonest persons.

Sometimes, the directors who are in charge of management manage the company for their own welfare. The welfare of the shareholders may be neglected by dishonest directors.

16.4 TYPES OF COMPANIES

16.4.1 Chartered Companies

Chartered companies are those which are incorporated under a special charter or proclamation issued by the king or queen. The activities of such companies are laid down in the charter under which they are established. Such companies were generally started in the 17th and 18th centuries. The East India Company, The Bank of England, the Chartered Bank, etc., are examples of chartered companies. In India chartered companies are not in existence because there is no monarchy. This method of incorporation is rarely used now.

16.4.2 Statutory companies

Statutory companies are those which are incorporated under a special act of parliament or legislature. The activities of statutory companies are governed by the special act under which they are established. The method of incorporation is used for companies of national importance and public benefit, such as railways, electricity supply companies, water works etc. The Reserve Bank of India, the State Bank of India, the Life Insurance Corporation of India, the Indian Airlines Corporation, the State Trading corporation of India, etc., are examples of statutory companies.

16.4.3 Registered Companies

Registered companies are companies incorporated under the Companies Act. The activities of registered companies are governed by the Companies Act. Registered companies are the most important type of Companies, Most of the trading companies belong to this type, Registered companies may be divided into three classes from the point of view of liability of the members. They are

- Companies limited by shares,
- Companies limited by guarantee and
- Unlimited companies.

(i) Companies Limited by shares

These are companies in which the liability of the members is 'limited to the nominal face value of the shares held by them in the case of these companies, if a member has already paid the full nominal value of his shares cannot be called upon to pay even a paisa, more, whatever may be the debts of the company. But if he has paid only a part of the nominal value of his shares, he can be called upon to pay only the unpaid amount on his shares in case of need. These companies are usually trilling companies. Most of the companies registered under the Companies Act are of this type.

(ii) Companies limited by Guarantee

These are companies in which the liability of the members is limited to a fixed amount which they have guaranteed or agreed to contribute to meet the liabilities of the company in the event of its liquidation. The amount guaranteed by the members is mentioned in the Memorandum of Association Of Articles of Association. The members are required to pay the amount guaranteed by them only if the company is wound up and if the assets of the company are insufficient to meet its debts, art, science, sports, culture, religion, etc, these companies may or may not have share capital. If such companies have share capital, the members are to pay the amount which are in paid on their shares and the amount guaranteed by them. Such companies are very few in number.

(iii) Unlimited Companies

These are companies in which the liability of the members is unlimited as in the case of partnerships or sole trading concerns, If such companies go into allegation, the members can be called upon to pay an 'unlimited amount even from their private assets to satisfy the debts of the company. Such companies are rarely formed.

Registered companies may be divided into three classes from the point of view of interest of the general public. They are:

- Private Companies
- Public Companies
- Government Companies

(iv) Private companies

- Which has at least two members.
- Which limits the number of its members to fifty, excluding those members who are its present or past employees.
- Which restricts the right of its members to transfer shares and
- Which does not invite the public to subscribe to its shares or debentures.

(v) Public companies

- Which has at least seven members.
- Which has no maximum limit to the number of members.
- Which generally invites the public to subscribe to its shares and debentures and
- Which generally does not restrict the right of its members to transfer shares or debentures.

(vi) Government companies

A Government Company IS a company in which not less than 51% of the share capital is held by the Central Government Of by one or more State Government and partly Central Government and partly by one or more State Governments.

16.5 HOLDING AND SUBSIDIARY COMPANIES

A public or a private company may be holding company or a subsidiary company,

A Holding Company is one which holds more than half of the nominal value of the equity share capital of another company or which controls the composition of the Board of Directors of another company the company, the company which is so controlled by the holding company is known company. For example X Company holds 51% of the nominal value of the equity share capital of Y company, then X company is said to be a holding company, and Y company is subsidiary company.

16.6 DOMESTIC AND FOREIGN COMPANIES

From the point of view of the country of incorporation, companies can be divided into two classes namely Domestic and Foreign companies.

A domestic company is one which is incorporated in our country i.e., India.

A Foreign company is one which is incorporated outside India, but has a place of business in India.

A private limited company enjoys certain privileges. They are:

- Only the members are enough to form a private limited company.
- It can commence business immediately after its incorporation.
- It need not get the certificate to commence business.
- It can allot shares even before the minimum subscription is reached.
- It need not file a' prospectus or statement in lieu of prospectus with the Registrar.
- It need, not hold a statutory meeting and need not send statutory report to its 'members.
- Two directors are sufficient for the private limited company.
- It need not file with the Registrar a list of Directors and the consent of the directors to act as such.

- It need not get the approval of the Central Government either to increase the number of directors or to increase their remuneration.
- Its directors need not retire by relation.
- It can issue any class of shares including referred shares.
- In case of further issue, it need not offer its new shares to the existing members.
- Two members are sufficient to form a quorum for its meeting unless it is provided otherwise in the articles.
- It can issue shares with disproportionate voting rights.
- The copies of the balance sheet and the profit loss account submitted by a private limited company to the Registrar of companies are not open to inspection by the public.
- A private limited company need not have a separate index of members.
- It is free from the legal restrictions on remuneration to Directors or manager.
- It can grant loans to its directors without the approval of the Central Government.
- It can appoint a firm or body corporate as its manager.

Registrations on a private limited company:

- It's name must end with two rewords Private Limited.
- It cannot issue prospectus inviting the public to subscribe to its shares or debentures.
- It must submit a separate set of Articles of Association at the time of incorporation.
- Free transferability of its shares is restricted by its articles.
- As the free transferability of its shares is restricted, it cannot issue shares, warrants.

16.7 DIFFERENCES BETWEEN A PUBLIC LIMITED COMPANY AND A PRIVATE LIMITED COMPANY

- In a public company the minimum number of members is seven and the maximum is unlimited. But in a private limited company, the minimum number of members is two and the maximum is fifty, exclusive of employee and ex-employee shareholders.
- A public limited company can offer its shares to the public, whereas the private limited company cannot offer its shares to the public.

- A public limited company must issued a prospectus or must file a statement in lieu of prospectus with the Register of Joint Stock Companies. But a private limited company need not issue a prospectus or file a statement in lieu of prospectus with the Registrar.
- In a public company, shares are freely transferable. But in a private limited company, free transfer of shares is restricted.
- A public limited company can issued share warrants. But a private limited company cannot issue share warrants.
- A public limited company cannot commerce its business immediately after incorporation. It can commence its business only after obtaining the Business Commencement Certificate. But a private limited company can commerce its business immediately after incorporation.
- A public limited company cannot allot shares until the minimum subscription is received. But a private limited company can allot shares even before the minimum subscription is received.
- A public limited company cannot issue deferred shares whereas a private limited company can issue deferred share,
- A public limited company cannot issue shares with disproportionate voting rights, but a private limited company/ can issue shares with disproportion to voting rights.
- A public limited company is required to hold a statutory meeting and file a statutory report with the Registrar. But a private limited company is not required to hold a statutory meeting and file is statutory report.
- In a public limited company, the minimum number of directors is three, whereas in a private limited company, the minimum number of directors is two.
- A public limited company is required to file a list of its directors and the consent of the directors to act as such with the Registrar at the time of incorporation. But a private limited company is not required to file a list of directors and the consent of the directors to act as such.
- The quorum for a general body meeting is five is the case of public limited company, but two in the case of a private limited company.
- A public limited company need not have its own Articles of Association. On the other hand, private limited company must have its own Articles of Association. .
- A private limited company need not have a separate index of mem-

bers, whereas a public limited company must have a separate index of members.

- A private limited company is free from the legal restrictions on remuneration to directors or manager, whereas the public limited company is subject to the legal restrictions on remuneration to directors or managers.
- A private limited company can grant loans to its 1 directors without the approval of the Central Government. On the other hand public limited company cannot grant loans to its directors without approval of the Central Government.
- A private limited company can appoint a firm or a body corporate as its manager, whereas a public limited company cannot appoint a firm or a body corporate as its manager.

16.8 COOPERATIVE SOCIETIES

16.8.1 Definition

Cooperative society is defined as "a form of organisation where in persons voluntarily associate together as human beings on the basis of equality for the promotion of the economic interests of themselves". It is an association of persons, and not an association of capital. In a cooperative society, the members have equality of opportunity and control. A cooperative society is formed for satisfying the common economic needs of the members.

Cooperative societies are one of the forms of business organisation. They are found all over the world. Generally, they are formed by the economically weaker sections of the society to protect themselves against the exploitation by the economically stronger sections. Thus poor farmers may form cooperative against the exploitation of the money lenders. Similarly, small producers may form cooperative marketing societies to sell their products at favourable prices and protect themselves against the exploitation of the traders. Consumers belonging to the middle and low income groups may form consumers cooperative societies so as to get essential commodities at fair prices and protest themselves against the exploitation by the retailers.

The idea behind a cooperative society is that an isolated and powerless man, in association with others, can lift himself as well as others out of weakness into strength. "Cooperate (i.e., work together) for solving economic problems" is the theory of cooperation.

16.8.2 Principles of Cooperative society

(i) Voluntary Association

A cooperative society is essentially voluntary association of individuals. A person is free to join or not to join cooperative society as its member. Similarly, he is free to leave the society any time by giving due notice to the society. Thus, there is no compulsion, either to become a member or to continue as a member.

(ii) Association of persons

A cooperative society is an association of persons, and not of capital. Individuals join a cooperative society as human beings, and not as capitalists.

(iii) Open Membership

Of a cooperative society is open to all adults irrespective of caste, class, religion, sex etc.

(iv) Unrestricted membership

There is no limitation on the membership of a cooperative society. The number of members of a cooperative society can be increased to an unlimited extent.

(v) Equal voting Rights

In a cooperative society, each member has only one vote, whatever may be the number of shares held by him. One member, one vote and not one share, one vote is the basic principle of a cooperative society. This principle enables the members to have equal voice in the management of the society.

(vi) Democratic management

Democratic management is the fundamental principle of a cooperative society. As a cooperative society operates on a local scale generally, all the members attend the meetings. Further, at the meetings, each member has only one vote. Again in all the meetings, only those policies which promote common interests are laid down. Thus the day-to-day affairs of a cooperative society are conducted on the democratic principle of "each for all, and all for each".

(vii) Service Motive

A cooperative society is formed primarily for the purpose of rendering maximum service to its members, and not for earning maximum profits. "Service, not profit", is the main aim of a cooperative society.

(viii) Equity of distribution of profits

The principle of equity is adopted in the distribution of the profits of a co-operative society. The entire profits of a cooperative society are not distributed as divided among the members. A low rate of dividend, generally, 61.4% is allowed on the capital contributed by the members. A portion of the profits is transferred to general reserve. A small portion of the profits is used for the general welfare of the locality in which the society is working. The rest of the profits of the society is distributed among the members in proportion to their business with the society.

(ix) Corporate status and state control

A cooperative society may be registered under the cooperative societies act, it becomes a body corporate like a joint stock company, and enjoys separate legal entity; perpetual succession and a common seal. Further, a registered cooperative society enjoys certain privileges such as exemption from the payment of income tax, stamp duty and registration fees. In return for all these privileges, a registered cooperative society is subject to stricter Government control and supervision than an unregistered cooperative society.

(x) Liability

The liability of the member of a cooperative society may be limited or unlimited. The liability of the members is limited in the case of a limited cooperative society, and unlimited in the case of an unlimited cooperative society.

16.8.3 Advantages of cooperative society

- The registration of a cooperative society is simple. So cooperative society enjoys the facility of easy formation.
- The life of a cooperative society is not affected by the death, insolvency, etc., of a member. So a cooperative society has continuity of existence.
- A cooperative society helps to pool together the resources of the weaker section of the society for constructive purposes.
- It teaches its members the technique of self-government and thus acts as a training ground in self-government.
- It prompts the spirit of cooperation among the members.
- It does not aim at profit. It tries to render maximum service to its members. For example, a cooperative credit society provides cheap credit facilities to its members. A consumers cooperative society supplies pure and unadulterated goods to its members at fair prices.

- A cooperative society runs economically. Some of the management exposes are saved by the voluntary and honorary services of the members. It need not spend money on advertisement for getting customers. It can depend mainly on the loyalty of its members for business.
- A cooperative society is a democratic organisation. The members of a cooperative society have equal voice in the management. The basic principle of a cooperative society viz., one member, one vote ensure equal voice to all members in the management.
- A registered cooperative society enjoys certain privileges, such as exemption from the payment of income-tax, stamp duty and registration fees.

16.8.4 Disadvantages of cooperative society

- For the success of a cooperative society, the members must cooperative with one another. But disputes among the members of a cooperative society are quite common. The disputes lead to the collapse of the cooperative society.
- The success of a cooperative society depends upon the loyalty of its members. But it is often found that the members do not remain loyal to their society.
- A cooperative society suffers from inadequate capital.
- Managerial ability and business knowledge are limited in a cooperative society. It cannot employ highly qualified, experienced and efficient persons for management because of its limited financial resources.
- A cooperative society cannot undertake large-scale operation because of its limited financial resources and managerial ability.
- A cooperative society suffers from insufficient motivation of inducement. The rate return to the numbers is limited by law. Further, the remuneration to the managerial personnel also is low. So, neither the members nor the managerial personnel take sufficient interest in the working of a cooperative society.
- Secrecy of business affairs which is very essential for the success of any business enterprise is lacking in a cooperative society.
- A cooperative society is not able to enjoy public confidence because of the failure of many cooperative societies.
- Cooperative societies are subject to excessive state interference. Excessive x state interference affects the successful working of the cooperative societies.

16.9 METHODS OF RAISING CAPITAL

A private limited company can commerce business immediately after its incorporation. But a public limited company cannot commence business immediately after incorporation. It should raise the required capital and obtain another certificate known as certificate to commence Business or Business Commencement. Certificate for commencing the business.

In order to raise the required capital, a public company, generally issued a prospectus to the members of the public inviting them to subscribe to its shares. After the issue of the prospectus and the receipt of applications for shares from the public, a public limited company can proceed with the allotment of shares, only if it has received the minimum subscription from the public. If the minimum subscription is not received from the public within 120 days from the date of the issue of the prospectus, then, the application money received from the subscribers or applicants should be returned to them immediately. If the application money is not returned to the applicants within 130 days from the date of issue of the prospectus, the directors of the company will be jointly and severally liable to repay the money together with interest at 6% per annum.

16.9.1 Types of Shares

Ordinary of Equity shares

The ordinary or equity shares are really ordinary shares. The shareholder of the ordinary shares does not enjoy and special advantage over the preference shareholders. The ordinary shareholders will get their dividend (profit share) only after the preference shareholders are given their fixed dividend. If the company makes large profits, then the dividends received by the ordinary shareholders may be higher than the dividends received by the preference shareholders, because the dividend of preference shareholders is always fixed and excess profits are distributed as dividends to ordinary shareholders.

Preference Shares

Preference shares are so called because the preference shareholders receive special treatment above the ordinary shareholders. Preference shareholders receive a fixed dividend every year and after distributing the fixed dividend among them, whatever profits which remain over and above this is distributed as dividend to the ordinary shareholders. Even when the Company is would up, the preference shareholders receive special treatment over the ordinary share holders.

Preference shares are four kinds

- Cumulative preference shares.

- Non-cumulative performance shares.
- Participating and Non-participating preference shares and
- Redeemable and Irredeemable preference shares.

Deferred Shares

Deferred shareholders share the profits of the company after the fixed dividend is paid to the preference shareholders and after the dividend is paid to the ordinary shareholders. So the deferred shareholders come last in sharing the profits. They share the balance of profits which remains over and above the payments made to the ordinary and preference shareholders as dividends. So, deferred shares enjoy higher profits than other shares.

16.9.2 Debentures

A debenture is an instrument issued by a company under its common seal acknowledging its debt to the holder and promising to repay the debt after a certain period. In the meantime to pay interest thereon at a fixed rate at regular intervals (normally, half yearly). The persons to whom the debentures are issued or the persons who lend to the company by purchasing the debentures are called debenture holders. Debentures are loans and not Shares. Hence, debenture holders are the creditors of the company and not the owners of the company like the shareholders.

Kinds of Debentures

Simple debentures: Simple debentures are unsecured debentures. The simple debenture-holders do not have any security given by the company for their money or interest, in case the company is liquidated, the simple debenture-holders may lost their money. So simple debentures are dangerous.

Mortgage debentures: This debentures are secured debentures. For the repayment of the amount of such debentures, the company's property is mortgaged. So, when and if the company goes into liquidation, the mortgage debenture-holders will first get their money by selling the property of the company. Such debentures are very safe.

Bearer Debentures: Debentures may be bearer-debentures also like the bearer notes. In such cases no need is necessary to transfer the bearer debentures. A simple transfer will do and the bearer of such debentures will get his interest or principal. Such debentures are dangerous, because if they are lost or stolen, it is as good as losing the rupee notes. In case of other debentures, they bear the name of the holders and a transfer is done only by a deed. Bearer debentures do not bear any name.

Redeemable and Irredeemable debentures: Redeemable debentures are issued for a fixed period during which period a fixed interest is paid by the company or them. After the fixed period (say 5 years), the debentures are repaid. Hence they are called redeemable debentures.

- Some debentures are irredeemable, that is, they are never repaid by the company. Such debentures are transferred from person to person. Only in case of liquidation of the company such debentures are repaid and not otherwise.

16.10 DIFFERENCES BETWEEN THE PRIVATE SECTOR AND PUBLIC SECTOR IS OWNED AND MANAGED BY THE STATE OR GOVERNMENT

- A private sector is organized for the benefit of a few private individuals. Whereas a public sector is organized for the benefit of the public at large.
- A private sector may be small or large in size. But a public sector at large.
- Profit is the main motto of a private sector, whereas service is the main motto of the public sector.
- A private sector may not come forward to undertake risky ventures. On the other hand, a state enterprise often undertakes risky ventures avoided by the private enterprises.
- In a private enterprise, there is greater personal incentive for the managerial personnel to work hard. But in a public sector there is not much incentive for the managerial personnel.
- A private enterprise enjoys more flexibility of operations than a public sector.
- A private sector is considered to be more efficient than a public sector.
- A private sector is free from political interference, whereas a public sector may not be completely free from political interference.
- A private sector is managed by the proprietors themselves or by their elected representatives. On the other hand, a public sector is managed by a Government department or by a Board of Directors nominated by the Government.

REVIEW QUESTIONS

1. Explain the features of sole proprietorship
2. Enumerate advantage and disadvantages of sole proprietorship.

3. Explain the characteristics of partnership.
4. What are various kinds of partnership. Explain.
5. Enumerate the particulars of partnership deed.
6. Explain rights and duties of partners.
7. What are the liabilities of partners.
8. List the advantages and disadvantages of partnership.
9. Write the various features of joint stock company.
10. Enumerate the advantages and disadvantages of joint stock company.
11. List and explain various types of companies.
12. What are the privileges of private limited company.
13. Differentiate between public limited company and a private limited company.
14. What are the principles of cooperative societies.
15. What are the advantages and disadvantages of cooperative societies.
16. Explain various methods of raising capital.

Sixth Semester B.E. Degree Examination, June-July 2009

Management and Entrepreneurship

Time: 3 hrs. Max. Marks: 100

Note: Answer any Five full questions selecting at least Two full questions from each part.

PART – A

1 a. Define Management. (02 Marks)
   b. With a neat sketch, explain the functions of Management. (12 Marks)
   c. Briefly explain the concept of Modern Management approaches. (06 Marks)

2 a. Give any Four concrete reasons for the paramount importance of the planning functions. (04 Marks)
   b. Briefly explain the steps involved in planning. (06 Marks)
   c. What are the different types of decisions? Explain briefly. (10 Marks)

3 a. Briefly explain the principles of organization. (10 Marks)
   b. Write any four advantages of proper and efficient staffing. (04 Marks)
   c. Write short notes on the following:
   i) MBO ii) MBE iii) Span of control. (06 Marks)

4 a. With a neat sketch briefly explain Maslow's theory of motivation. (06 Marks)
   b. Define and explain the purpose of communication. (08 Marks)
   c. Briefly explain the essential of a sound control system. (06 Marks)

PART – B

5 a. Who is an Entrepreneur? (02 Marks)
   b. Briefly explain the characteristics of an Entrepreneur. (06 Marks)
   c. Explain in detail various types and functions of an Entrepreneur. (08 Marks)
   d. Distinguish between Entrepreneur and Intrapreneur. (04 Marks)

6 a. What is a Small Scale Industry? (02 Marks)

b. Briefly explain the rationale of Small Scale Industry development in India. (08 Marks)

c. List out the various objectives of developing small enterprises in India. (06 Marks)

d. Explain briefly the Government support for SSI during 5 year plans. (04 Marks)

7 a. With a neat skech, explain the activities of NSIC. (08 Marks)

b. Write short notes on the following:
i) SISI ii) SIDBI iii) DIC iv) TECKSOK. (12 Marks)

8 a. What are the criteria for selecting a particular project, an Entrepreneur should consider? (06 Marks)

b. Briefly explain the importance of project identification. (06 Marks)

c. Give the meaning of project appraisal. (02 Marks)

d. What are the steps followed in project appraisal? (06 Marks)

Fifth Semester B.E. Degree Examination, Dec. 08/Jan. 09

Management and Entrepreneurship

Time: 3 hrs. Max. Marks: 100

Note: 1. Answer any Five full questions taking at least Two from each part.
2. All questions carry equal marks.

PART – A

a. Define "Management" and bring out its nature and characteristics. (05 Marks)
b. Briefly explain the functional areas of management. (10 Marks)
c. List out the levels of management and also list the roles of management. (05 Marks)

a. Define planning and discuss its importance. (04 Marks)
b. Briefly explain the steps in decision making. (08 Marks)
c. Discuss the various steps in planning. (08 Marks)

a. Define an organization and distinguish between formal and informal organization. (04 Marks)
b. Discuss any two types of organization structures with a chart highlighting their merits and demerits. (10 Marks)
c. Distinguish between:
i) Centralization and Decentralization
ii) Selection and Recruitment. (06 Marks)

a. Define "Directing" and list out the principles of Direction. (04 Marks)
b. What is motivation? Explain the characteristics. (10 Marks)
c. Discuss the essentials of a sound control system. (06 Marks)

PART – B

a. List out the characteristics and qualities of an entrepreneur. (04 Marks)
b. Bring out a broad classification of entrepreneur. (10 Marks)
c. Explain the stages in entrepreneur process. (06 Marks)

a. List out the characteristics of Small Scale Industries (SSIs). (06 Marks)

b. Discuss the impact of Liberalization, Privatization and Globalization of SSIs. (06 Marks)

c. List out the supporting agencies of government for SSIs and explain any two of them. (08 Marks)

a. Classify and List out the institutions that assist SSIs. (06 Marks)

b. Explain any two institutions that assist SSIs. (08 Marks)

c. Briefly list out the objectives of KSFC. (06 Marks)

a. Briefly out line the contents of a project report. (06 Marks)

b. Explain the process of project appraisal. (08 Marks)

c. What is social feasibility? Explain. (06 Marks)

INDEX